The Life to Come

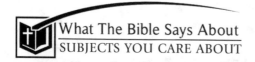

What The Bible Says About
SUBJECTS YOU CARE ABOUT

Other Topics in the Planning:
The Church, The Doctrine of God, Prayer

What The Bible Says About
THE AFTERLIFE

The
Life
to
Come

Kenny Boles

✝ **COLLEGE** PRESS
JOPLIN, MO • 1.800.289.3300
www.collegepress.com

To
Sydney, Simon, and Sarah

With whom heaven will be great fun!

Abbreviations Used in this Book and Others in the Series

AD.....................Anno Domini
ASV ....American Standard Version
BC.....................Before Christ
KJV....................King James Version
LXX ....Septuagint (Greek Translation of OT)
MT ....Masoretic Text (Standard Hebrew OT)
NASB ....New American Standard Bible
NIV ....New International Version
NRSV ....New Revised Standard Version
NT....................New Testament
OT....................Old Testament
RSV ....Revised Standard Version

ABOUT THE SERIES

W hat does the Bible say about that?" This is a question that should concern every Bible-believing Christian, whatever the particular subject being discussed. Granted, we know there are situations and activities that are not directly addressed by the Bible, because of changes in society, culture, and technology. However, if we truly believe that the Bible is to be our guide for living and especially for developing our relationship with God, then we need to look to it for information that will impact our everyday decisions. Even what may seem like abstract doctrinal matters will affect our religious practices, and if the Bible is indeterminate on a particular issue, then we need to know that too, so that we don't waste time on the kinds of controversies Paul warns about in 1 Timothy 1:4.

College Press Publishing Company is fully committed to equipping our customers as Bible students. In addition to commentary series and small study books on individual books of the Bible, this is not the first time we have done a series of books specifically dedicated to this question: "What DOES the Bible say?" Part of this stems from the background of CPPC as a publishing house of what has generally been known as the "Restoration Movement,"[1] a movement that gave rise to Churches of Christ and Christian Churches. The "restoration" of the movement's name refers to the desire to restore biblical teaching and emphases to our religious beliefs and activities.

---

[1] In order to be more specific and recognize that these churches are not necessarily unique in the plea to restore the church of the apostles, it is also known as the "Stone-Campbell Movement," after the names of some of the 19th-century leaders of the movement.

It is important to understand what this series can and cannot do. Every author in the series will be filtering the exact words of the biblical text through a filter of his or her own best understanding of the implications of those words. Nor will the Bible be the only source to be quoted. Various human authors will inevitably be referenced either in support of the conclusions reached or to contradict their teachings. Keeping this in mind, you should use them as tools to direct your own study of the Bible, and use the "Berean principle" of studying carefully every part of the Bible to see "whether these things [are] so" (Acts 17:11, ASV). We would not be true to our own purpose if we encouraged you to take any book that we publish as the "last word" on any subject. Our plea, our desire, is to make "every Christian a Bible Student."

A WORD ABOUT FORMAT

In order to emphasize the theme of "What the Bible Says," we have chosen to place Scripture quotations and Scripture references in distinct typestyles to make them stand out. Use of these typestyles within quotations of other works should not be taken as an indication that the original author similarly emphasized the highlighted text.

IN THIS BOOK

to the mind, the longings of the human heart for heaven become more predominant. God's ongoing revelation of the life to come takes more definite shape in His poetry, especially in Job, Ecclesiastes, and Psalms.

Part 2—Hell

In This Book

11

INTRODUCTION

No one but Jesus could write the final word about the afterlife. None of us has seen the splendor of heaven; none of us knows the horror of hell. It is with an extreme sense of inadequacy, therefore, that I have set out to explain what the Bible says about the life to come. How could anyone presume to be an expert on this subject?

Perhaps this is why we hear so few sermons and lessons on heaven and hell these days. Rather than say something incorrect about the afterlife, we prefer to say little or nothing at all. As I have spoken here and there on this topic, however, I have found a tremendous interest among the people in the pews. Believers want to know about their future: what does eternity hold in store for us?

Every time we attend a funeral, we ponder the possibilities of the future. Every time we sense the aging of our bodies, we wonder what lies ahead when death finally holds us in its grasp. And every time we consider, like the Teacher of Ecclesiastes, why life sometimes seems so meaningless, we are driven to question the purpose of it all. When our 70 or 80 years on earth are swallowed up into the infinite years of eternity, what will that greater life be like?

I do not presume to have all the answers. I do, however, have complete confidence that God's Word is completely true and that it has much to say about the afterlife. We may sometimes misunderstand what Scripture says, but even with our human limitations we can gain a vast amount of information by a careful study. It would be foolish to be dogmatic about our conclusions, but it would be even more foolish to abandon the search.

This book will be my attempt to trace what the Bible says about heaven and hell. It will not attempt to trace what everyone else has said on the subject. The total absence of footnotes through most of this study will, no doubt, make some readers frantic. But I have decided it is best to focus on what Scripture itself says, allowing the information to reach its cumulative climax. I pray that this heaven-focused journey through Scripture will be profitable.

Because Jesus has the final word on the subject of heaven, I have decided to begin this book with what He taught in *John 14:1-3*. Phrase by phrase, His words will set the tone for all that is to come in our study. Then we will make a thorough study of all Scripture, beginning with Genesis, to see how the truth about heaven beautifully unfolds. The pages of the OT introduce the joys of heaven slowly, as if moving from starlight to moonlight to dawn and finally to the full light of day. Likewise, the information about hell is somewhat scanty in the beginning, but is revealed in full horror in the NT. At each step along the way we want to follow the noble example of the Bereans, who *"examined the Scriptures every day to see if what Paul said was true"* (*Acts 17:11*).

This book is intended to be a guide to promote careful study of the Bible. It is not intended to give the reader a list of presumed truths about heaven so as to make Bible study unnecessary. Neither is it intended to be a systematic theology on eschatology. Here is our method: to locate texts about the afterlife, and to discuss the meaning of those texts in context. Here is our goal: to learn what the Bible says about the afterlife.

Heaven—our final home—will be a wonderful place. Hell—a destiny to be avoided at all costs—will be an eternal horror. If nothing else, this study of what the Bible says about the afterlife can serve as a strong encouragement to reach the one and escape the other. It is my prayer that these pages will make you *"all the more eager to make your calling and election sure"* (*2Pet 1:10*).

Part 1

Heaven

CHAPTER ONE

HEAVEN IN THE WORDS OF JESUS

John 14:1-3

Jesus reclined at the Passover table with His trusted disciples. Judas, the betrayer, had already gone. (But that was okay, since what Jesus was about to say did not apply to Judas anyway.) Jesus knew that His time had come. Tomorrow He would die on the cross for the sins of the world. Tonight He had to get His disciples ready.

Jesus had already shown the Twelve the lesson of servanthood by washing their feet (*Jn 13:1-17*). He had also told them that He would be betrayed—by one of them (*Jn 13:18-30*). Then He spoke these troubling words, *"My children, I will be with you only a little longer"* (*Jn 13:33*). Alarm and despair gripped their hearts. What they needed to hear in that crisis, indeed what we all need to hear in life's gravest moments, is what Jesus could tell them about heaven.

TRUST ME

"Do not let your hearts be troubled," Jesus said (*Jn 14:1*). It was not to rebuke them for being upset, for Jesus Himself knew what it was like to have a troubled heart. Just two chapters earlier Jesus had said, *"Now my heart is troubled"* (*Jn 12:27*). Just moments earlier at the table He was *"troubled in spirit"* as He testified that one of the disciples themselves would betray Him (*Jn 13:21*). So this command was not spoken as any kind of rebuke, but as a loving word of encouragement.

Then Jesus said what the disciples needed most. *"Trust in God,"* He said, *"trust also in me"* (*Jn*

I. Trust Me
II. My Father's House
III. Many Rooms
IV. If It Were Not So
V. I Will Prepare
VI. A Place
VII. For You
VIII. I Will Come Back
IX. Conclusion

17

14:1). Whatever the coming hours might bring, they needed to trust their Master. Whatever their fears for the future, whatever their uncertainty about what lay ahead, they must remember above all else these words of Jesus: "Trust me."

As we ourselves set out to explore what the Bible says about the afterlife, this must also be the attitude in which we search. Whenever we face the unknown, whenever we feel uncertain about the details, we just need to trust Jesus. Our future is not in doubt so long as we are in Jesus' hands. Therefore we will walk confidently toward our final destiny with the words of Jesus echoing in our ears: "Trust me."

MY FATHER'S HOUSE

Jesus was going to die. His disciples could not help but think of death as the final failure, the ultimate defeat. Everything they had hoped for was collapsing around them. They had followed Jesus for three years because He alone had the words of eternal life (*Jn 6:68*), but now the Teacher of life was going to be the victim of death.

But Jesus had good news for them, and for all mortals, about life beyond the grave. He spoke of that life as *"my Father's house"* (*Jn 14:2*). Other men might speak of the shadowy world of *sheol* or the vast uncertainty of the grave, but Jesus spoke of going home!

For believers, the world on the other side of death need not be frightening. It is a world that belongs to the Father. We will live there, and God will live there with us. Everything we know about God can be injected into our understanding of heaven. It will be God's great "Bed and Breakfast," where He is the welcoming Host. His holiness, His wisdom, His gracious love—all this and more defines what kind of heaven we can expect. As much as little children get excited about "going to Grandma's house," why shouldn't believers look forward to going to the Father's house?

At the Father's house God will be in charge. Just like in the garden of Eden, where everything God made was "very good," in heaven everything will be the way God wants it. Neither the failures of the fallen world nor the enticements of the devil will spoil our happiness. Finally, at our Father's house, everything will be right.

MANY ROOMS

When Jesus came into our world, there was no room in the inn. But His promise to His disciples was that they could expect a ready welcome. *"In my Father's house,"* He told them, there are *"many rooms"* (**Jn 14:2**). While this is not intended to say anything about the architecture of heaven, it certainly does say something about its roominess. No faithful child of God will ever be told, "Sorry, but there are just no more rooms."

The Greek word for "rooms" has also been translated as "mansions" (KJV) and "dwelling places" (NASB). Interestingly enough, this word is found only one other time in the NT—later in this same chapter. In **John 14:23** Jesus said, *"If anyone loves me, he will obey my teaching. My Father will love him, and we will come to him and make our 'home' with him."* The word is μονή *(mone)* in the singular **(v. 2)**, and μοναί *(monai)* in the plural form **(v. 23)**. It is derived from the verb μένω *(meno)*, which means "I abide, I stay." The point of emphasis in this word in both verses is the desired permanency of the dwelling. Just as believers want to know that they can expect to stay in heaven once they get there, so God and Jesus want to take up permanent residence in the believers' hearts.

There are many descriptions of heaven scattered throughout the Bible which will be included later in this book. Heaven has incredible wealth, abundant provisions, wonderful beauty, and dazzling variety. But none of that would do us any good without this additional truth: there will be plenty of room for all God's family.

IF IT WERE NOT SO

The distressed disciples must have looked uneasily at one another as Jesus spoke of His departure. Since none of them had ever seen the Father's house or the other side of death, how could they really believe these things? Rabbis and philosophers had many ideas about what happens after death, but how can anyone really know? Jesus told them what heaven would be, but what if it were not so?

Knowing their hearts, as always, Jesus emphasized the truth of His teaching. "If it were not so," He stated, "I would have told you." Jesus had never lied to them; neither would He do so now. He always told them the unvarnished truth, whether it was the tragic prediction of His approaching death or the good news of heaven.

The NRSV reads, *"If it were not so, would I have told you that I go to prepare a place for you?"* At issue is the word ὅτι (*hoti*), which means "that." This word is not found in some of the earliest copies of John, such as 𝔓₆₆. Therefore, the NIV and NASB do not include the word "that," and end the sentence as a statement. Either way, the emphasis of Jesus' words is on the opening premise, "If it were not so." These words are set up in the Greek as a condition contrary to fact, meaning that both the speaker and His hearers understand that this premise is false. They are to understand this as a double negative: it is *not* true that His teaching about heaven is not so.

A full appreciation of the blessing of heaven requires the consideration of this alternative: what if it were *not* so? What if there were nothing waiting for us on the other side? What if only in this life we had hope? What if the promised resurrection and the reception into Father's house were not going to happen? No heaven? No eternal life? Nothing beyond the grave? Paul's words to the Corinthian church would sum it up well: *"If only in this life we have hope in Christ, we are to be pitied more than all men"* (*1Cor 15:19*).

I WILL PREPARE

When the time for this Passover meal approached, Jesus had sent two of His disciples into Jerusalem to make preparations (*Mk 14:13-15*). But for the eternal banquet in heaven, Jesus Himself promised to go on ahead and make arrangements. *"I am going there,"* He said, *"to prepare a place for you"* (*Jn 14:2*) Just as the Master became Servant and washed the disciples' feet, soon the Master will be the One to prepare heaven.

In one sense, of course, heaven has always been completed. Through all eternity God has sat on its throne. But the Bible promises *"a new heaven and a new earth"* (*Isa 65:17; 66:22; 2 Pet 3:13; Rev 21:1*). In the original creation God prepared the seas and rivers for the fish, the dry land for the animals, and the open skies for the birds (*Gen 1:1-25*). Each creature was designed for its own environment, and each locale was exactly right for each creature. Everything was prepared; everything was just right. This is the divine precedent that demonstrates how Jesus *"will prepare a place"* for us.

The place will be prepared for the people, just as the people must be prepared for the place. Jesus takes care of both preparations. As Jesus prepares the place, He also prepares the access to that place. It is no accident that these verses about heaven lead directly to His statement, *"I am the way and the truth and the life. No one comes to the Father except through me"* (*Jn 14:6*). What Jesus did on the cross the next day forever opened the door to heaven.

A PLACE

As the disciples uneasily faced the impending future for Jesus and considered the ultimate future for themselves, many thoughts must have whirled through their minds. The Pharisees taught a belief in a general resurrection and a life after death, but the Sadducees denied both (*Acts 23:8*). Greek and Roman philosophers had filled the Mediterranean world with conflicting ideas of the afterlife, often denying that anything other than the spirit remained.

Jesus' words to the apostles were a welcome assurance of the reality of heaven. He promised to prepare "a place" for them, a word which regularly indicates a real place of real existence. Jesus did not describe His death as pouring His essence back into the great sea of life, nor as venturing into the great unknown, nor as simply ceasing to exist. He promised a future *place*, a prepared *place*.

In the coming pages of this study, as we explore the OT prophecies and the NT promises, we will notice a sustained emphasis on the reality of the place. It will be variously described as a new earth, a new Jerusalem, a new Eden that is cleansed and renewed—but always a place where real people live real lives. Heaven is not just a spiritual concept or a metaphysical state of existence. Heaven is a place.

FOR YOU

As Jesus spoke to His faithful followers gathered for the Passover meal, He did not speak in vague generalities or empty abstractions. He made promises specifically directed to the disciples. He promised that He Himself would go, *"And prepare a place **for you**"* (*Jn 14:2-3*).

Jesus knew each of His disciples personally and intimately. He knew their inner desires and their genuine needs. Therefore He knew how to prepare for their arrival. It was not for guests of little acquaintance that Jesus was preparing accommodations in the Father's house; it was not just for whoever might show up. Jesus was preparing a place for the arrival of His close friends.

As we extend this promise to ourselves, we realize that Jesus is preparing a place—a special place—for each of us as well. Jesus is the Good Shepherd who knows us as His sheep and calls each of us by name (*Jn 10:3,14*). Like the shepherd of David's psalm He knows what we need and leads us there (*Ps 23:2*).

I WILL COME BACK

"And if I go and prepare a place for you," Jesus continued, *"I will come back"* (*Jn 14:3*). Though the disciples did not yet realize it, this was a double promise. It was first of all a promise that they would not be left as orphans, because Jesus would return to their hearts in the form of the Holy Spirit (*Jn 14:16-18*). But the even greater promise was that He would return to them in clouds of glory at His second coming (*Acts 1:11; 1Th 4:16-17*). Jesus said He would come back and *"take you to be with me that you also may be where I am"* (*Jn 14:3*).

More than anything else Jesus said to the disciples, this dual promise would calm their troubled hearts. They would not be abandoned; Jesus would be with them in Spirit. They did not face an uncertain future; Jesus would welcome them into their eternal home. Some would meet Jesus soon, as did Stephen, the first Christian martyr, and James (*Acts 7:55-59; 12:2*). Others would live many years before they died. To the end of the days of the last apostle, the prayer that was constantly on their minds was, *"Come, Lord Jesus"* (*Rev 22:20*).

For believers today this continues to be one of the sweetest promises of all Scripture. Jesus is coming back for us! The Shepherd has not lost His sheep; the Father has not forgotten His children. Heaven is ready for all of us who have learned to trust.

CONCLUSION

It seemed appropriate to let Jesus have the first (and last) word in our study of what the Bible says about the afterlife. Later we will examine His other statements, regarding both heaven and hell. His teachings in this first chapter will serve as an introduction and backdrop for the rest of our search. We will begin with Genesis and proceed through both Testaments to glean the truths about heaven, and then the truths about hell.

WHAT DO YOU SAY?

1. Why should we even try to predict what heaven will be like?

2. Should the disciples have been more ready to understand what Jesus was saying about the life to come?

3. From what we know of Jesus, what kind of heaven can we "trust" Him to prepare for us?

4. How is going to heaven like going to your grandma's house?

5. Is "mansion" an appropriate word for where we will live in heaven? Why or why not?

6. Is heaven ready for us or not? What did Jesus mean by going to "prepare" it for us?

7. Besides being with God and Jesus, what is the best part of heaven going to be for you?

CHAPTER TWO

HEAVEN IN THE TORAH OF ISRAEL

PART ONE: *Genesis 1–3*

It is well known that the ancient Sadducees did not believe in the resurrection or the afterlife of the soul (*Mt 22:23; Acts 23:8*). They rejected all of the OT writings except the five books of the Torah, also known as the Pentateuch or the Books of Moses. They maintained that no doctrine of life beyond the grave could be found in those Scriptures. Because of the teachings of Jesus and the guidance of the rest of the Bible, we know that the Sadducees were wrong.

Even using only the Torah, however, there is much they could have learned about heaven. In these five books of the OT, especially *Genesis,* there is much that foreshadows our eternal home. With the advantage of hindsight we who have received the full revelation of God's Word can look back and see many clues about the afterlife that the Sadducees and others did not notice.

IN THE BEGINNING
GENESIS 1:1

In the beginning, God. All truth is based on this Truth; all reality is based on this Reality. There is a God, so there is a place where God exists. In other words, there is a heaven because there is a God, and heaven is His throne. Heaven draws its reality from the reality of God's own existence. Just as there has always been an eternal God, there has always been the place where He exists.

25

"In the beginning," at the earliest moment that the human mind can comprehend, *"God created the heavens and the earth"* (**Gen 1:1**). But even before the physical universe was created, God and heaven already existed. God, and perhaps His heaven as well, pervades our universe and is present in every part of it, but neither He nor heaven is part of the created universe.

When Genesis says that God created *"the heavens and the earth,"* it introduces a possible confusion concerning what is meant by "the heavens." From this verse onward, it is constantly necessary to distinguish between heaven as "sky" and heaven as "God's dwelling." The use of the same Hebrew word (*shamayim*) for both ideas is actually

> **It is constantly necessary to distinguish between heaven as "sky" and heaven as "God's dwelling."**

quite logical, since Scripture frequently pictures God as "looking down" on earth and its inhabitants. Therefore, the sky overhead suitably represents the dwelling of God, as both immediately near and unreachably distant.

The "earth," as well as the "heavens," is the creation of God. It also reflects and foreshadows the nature of what God has planned for the afterlife. The earth is not a timeless entity, independent of God; nor is it a shameful evil, unworthy of God. As the next few verses of Genesis will indicate, the good earth is created for the benefit and pleasure of mankind—just as heaven will be.

LET THERE BE . . .
GENESIS 1:2-25

In a primeval world of darkness and unformed chaos, the Spirit of God hovered like a hen hatching her chicks (**Gen 1:2**). Something was about to happen! Then came the voice of God, demanding, *"Let there be light"* (**Gen 1:3**). Just as God Himself dwells in unapproachable light (see **1Tm 6:16**), His first act of creation was to bring light into the darkness. Likewise, the final words about heaven in **Revelation** will focus repeatedly on God and Jesus as the eternal source of light (see **Rev 1:13-16; 4:5; 10:1; 21:11,23; 22:5**).

In each successive day the goodness of God was shown in His creation. Skillfully shaping and crafting each part, God created a universe in which there was a garden that was exactly suited for mankind. It is striking that most of the items mentioned in the six days of creation are found again in the book of *Revelation*, describing the wonders of God's final paradise—heaven.

On day two God made the "expanse" overhead (*Gen 1:6*) and called it "sky" (*Gen 1:8*) or "firmament" (KJV). It foreshadowed the overarching glory of heaven. Then on the third day God made the dry land. It was a place on which humans and all God's creatures could dwell (*Gen 1:9*), presaging a new earth (*Rev 21:1*) with mountain and city (*Rev 21:10*) and river and tree (*Rev 22:1-2*). On that day of creation God controlled the restless sea (*Gen 1:9*), saying, *"This far you may come and no farther; here is where your proud waves halt"* (*Job 38:11*). In heaven the peril of the sea will be forever taken away (*Rev 21:1*).

On day four God made two great lights, the sun and the moon, to illuminate the earth and to mark directions and seasons (*Gen 1:14-16*). Likewise in heaven, the darkness will be forever banished by the light of the Father and the Son (*Rev 21:23; 22:5*). Along with the two great lights, God placed stars in the sky (*Gen 1:16*). The constellations not only show the greatness of God's power (*Job 38:31-33*), they are also a foreshadowing of how the saints will arise to everlasting life and *"shine like the brightness of the heavens . . . like the stars for ever and ever"* (*Dan 12:2-3*). Even now God's children are to *"shine like stars in the universe"* in the midst of a crooked and depraved generation (*Php 2:15*).

On the fifth day God began creating the amazing variety of fish for the sea and birds for the air. When God surveyed the work of His hands, He saw that it was good (*Gen 1:20-21*). In the afterlife, Revelation does not say if there will be fish in the river of the great city (*Rev 22:1*) or birds in the sky. (The only mention of birds in *Revelation* is in connection with scenes of destruction prior to the end. See *Rev 8:13; 19:17-18*.) At least five things, however, would cause us to believe that such creatures will be there. First, there is God's obvious love for variety. Why should we think that heaven will be a barren desert or a trackless wasteland? Second, there is God's loving attention to care for these little creatures (see *Mt 6:26*). Third, there is God's own pronouncement that having fish and birds in His world was a good thing (*Gen 1:21*). Fourth, the animals are included in the rainbow covenant (*Gen 9:9-10*). Fifth, God describes the peaceful behavior of animals in the coming age (*Isa 11:6-8*).

On day six, the final day of active creation, God filled the land with another amazing variety of living creatures (*Gen 1:24*). He created some animals to be tame livestock, some animals to creep along the ground, and some animals to be wild in the forests and jungles. When God surveyed this spectacular array of creatures, as before, He *"saw that it was good"* (*Gen 1:25*). Elsewhere in Scripture, the paradise of the world to come is pictured with a variety of animals. The prophecy of *Isaiah 11:6-8*, for instance, lists wolf, lamb, leopard, goat,

> **We can only be astonished at the prolific imagination of God.**

calf, lion, yearling, bear, ox, cobra, and viper. (See also *Isa 65:25*.) And why shouldn't God fill heaven with the creatures He has designed, and perhaps even add to them?

We can only be astonished at the prolific imagination of God as we contemplate the variety and ingenuity of His creation. The perfection! The whole vast menagerie of fish, birds, and animals—with each one perfectly suited for its own environment and perfectly designed for its reproduction. The sounds! The song of the whale, the cry of the eagle, the roar of the lion, the amazing repertoire of the songbirds. The colors! The peacock, the cardinal, the canary; a dozen shades of kittens, a thousand designs of butterflies, ten thousand colors of wildflowers. The smells! The fragrance of a flower, the scent of falling rain, the alluring aroma of good food. The flavors! Every fruit on every tree (except one!) was there for the picking. None of this variety was really necessary—God just liked it that way. Projected onto the canvas of the life to come, the picture of the ultimate world is breathtaking! When we look back at the world when it was the way God wanted it to be, it tells us much about the loving wisdom of God and much about the way He will design the world to come.

LET US MAKE MAN
GENESIS 1:26-28

As the climax of the six days of creation, God said, *"Let us make man in our image, in our likeness, and let them rule"* (*Gen 1:26*). Preceding the Fall and the Curse, this is God's own statement of the original intent and purpose of the human race. It tells us who we are, why we are here—and more importantly—what God intends for our eternal destiny. Mankind was not just created to live briefly on this earth; mankind was created for eternity!

This mission statement for the existence of the human race teaches, first of all, that man is not just another animal. In days five and six of creation all the other creatures were more or less lumped together: fish for the seas, birds for the air, various animals for the dry land. Then God said something unprecedented: *"Let us make man in our image, after our likeness."* This was not said of any of the animals. Man is unique. While the fish/birds/animals display the power and ingenuity of God, only man reflects His image. This is even stated to Noah and his descendants as the reason for capital punishment: *"Whoever sheds the blood of man, by man shall his blood be shed; for in the image of God has God made man"* (**Gen 9:6**). It is clear that God created man with more in mind than just living like an animal. The immortal God of heaven has made man in His own image—to live forever there with Him.

God's purpose statement for the human race also teaches us that men and women have many of the traits of God Himself. We are made *"in his own image,"* a statement that includes both *"male and female"* (**Gen 1:27**). With eternity in view—not just the brief existence of the fallen world—God made us to be like Himself. In ways that cannot be matched in the animal kingdom, humans reflect the image of God. For instance, He is the Creator; we are inherently creative and inventive. Animals keep making the same nests and burrows as before, but humans are always trying to make something new. God is All-knowing; we have an unquenchable thirst for knowledge. Animals operate largely by instinct, but humans are always exploring, searching to learn more, adding to

> **In ways that cannot be matched in the animal kingdom, humans reflect the image of God.**

the storehouse of information. A mind is a terrible thing to waste, precisely because it is a special part of being made in God's likeness. God is Love; we know how to love because He first loved us (**1Jn 4:19**). Many other traits could be considered in contemplation of man's creation in the image of God, for He is holy, generous, wise, existing in eternal fellowship, etc. In each of these areas mankind has a built-in potential that cannot be found in any other creature.

The final part of God's statement deals specifically with the ultimate purpose of the human race. We are intended to rule! Even in that first week of creation God set mankind *"over the fish of the sea and the birds of the air and over every living creature that moves on the ground"* (**Gen 1:28; 2:19-20**). Man has been made caretaker and supervisor of all life on this planet. Man is superior to fish, birds, and animals; they exist for man's benefit. Man's assignment to rule over all other creatures is a stewardship, a delegated authority not to be abused. Just as God Himself is the ultimate Ruler, He has set the human race in a position to exercise authority over the animals. It should not be a surprise, therefore, to discover in the final chapter of Scripture that God's ultimate intention for us is that we *"will reign for ever and ever"* (**Rev 22:5**). In the world to come God will be pleased to delegate many of the responsibilities of heaven to humans. It is our destiny; it is the purpose of our creation.

As we contemplate the lessons of creation, we come to understand that design reveals the intention of the Designer. When God put gills and fins on fish and put them in the water, He intended them to swim. When God put wings on birds and put them in the air, He intended them to fly. Every creature is designed for its own environment, and flails around in frustration when not permitted to fulfill what God intended for it. When God made man in His own image and set him over all other creatures, He showed what He intended for the human race. Moreover, God's original design was not for a brief existence in a fallen world. God's intent was for man to live in a world that was the way God wanted the world to be. Thus, by seeing what God originally wanted and what God thought was "good," it is reasonable to make certain assumptions about what God will think to be good in heaven.

To be made *"in the image of God"* also provides much of the answer to a worrisome question: What will we do in heaven with all that time on our hands? Augustine imagined a heaven designed like a monastery. He said, "There we shall rest and see, see and love, love and praise. This is what shall be in the end without end." He said the only activity of heaven will be "to stand, to see, to love, to praise."

What will we do in heaven with all that time on our hands?

Christians are sometimes made to feel guilty if this does not appeal to them. But the underlying problem is that God did not create us to be like that. And if we are prevented from being and doing what God created us to be and do, it is no wonder that we feel an aversion to that kind of heaven. It should seem obvious that in heaven we will be doing what God created us to do. The Creator made us to be creative, so we will build and sculpt and paint and compose— all to the glory of God. The Omniscient One made us inquisitive, so we will learn and explore and study and teach. The Father in fellowship with the Son and the Spirit has made us to crave association with other people, so we will spend eternity getting to know the saints. Our loving God has taught us to love, so we will have unending ages to fulfill His great command: Love one another (*Jn 13:34*). And at the center of every activity as our Mentor and Guide will be the Father, watching with pride as we live out the lives He has intended.

AND IT WAS VERY GOOD
GENESIS 1:29-31

God was obviously pleased to present the bounty of Eden to the male and female He had made in His own image. *"I give you every seed-bearing plant on the face of the whole earth,"* He said, *"and every tree that has fruit with seed in it. They will be yours for food"* (*Gen 1:29*). The variety and quality of the garden's produce was God's loving gift. He had no obligation to create so many different kinds of plants and trees; a single spigot oozing gray paste could have sufficed to keep mankind alive.

It is significant that God created humans with an appetite and taste buds. In that sense, we still inhabit the same bodies as Adam and Eve in the beginning. Then God designed the appetite of hunger to be satisfied with the food He provided. The pleasure that comes from satisfying our appetites was God's idea! As He surveyed His finished product, with everything necessary for man's satisfaction, God *"saw all that he had made, and it was very good"* (*Gen 1:31*).

The abundance of the Garden of Eden is also a foreshadowing of heaven. Although some philosophers have not been able to imagine a future life that includes solid food, God's Word has always supported this view. Jesus described a day when *"many will come from the east and the west, and will take their places at the feast with Abraham, Isaac and Jacob in the kingdom of heaven"* (*Mt 8:11*). He said that those not allowed to participate *"will be thrown outside, into the darkness, where there will be weeping and gnashing of teeth"* (*Mt 8:12*). In the final Revelation, those who overcome are promised *"the right to eat from* the tree of life, which is in the paradise of God" (**Rev 2:7**) and they will be given "some of the hidden manna" (**Rev 2:17**). Later, the angel instructed John, "Write: 'Blessed are those who are invited to the wedding supper of the Lamb!" (**Rev 19:9**). Heaven is described as a joyful celebration (**Heb 12:22**) and a wedding feast—with food!

ON THE SEVENTH DAY
GOD RESTED
GENESIS 2:2

In six days God created everything, so on the seventh day He rested. It was not because He was tired; it was because He was finished (**Gen 2:2**). From that beginning point, God blessed the seventh day (**Gen 2:3**) and made it a special day—the Sabbath. This day of rest was formally commanded to Israel (**Ex 16:23**) and became the fourth of the Ten Commandments (**Ex 20:8-11**). Failure to observe the Sabbath rest was even punishable by death! (See **Num 15:32-36**.)

God's day of rest prefigures heaven, where He will share His rest with His people. Hebrews says, "There remains, then, a Sabbath-rest for the people of God; for anyone who enters God's rest also rests from his own work, just as God did from his" (**Heb 4:9-10**). The exhortation follows, "Let us, therefore, make every effort to enter that rest" (**Heb 4:11**). A final reward is promised to believers who thus persevere, as told by the angel to John: "Write: 'Blessed are the dead who die in the Lord from now on.' 'Yes,' says the Spirit, 'they will rest from their labor'" (**Rev 14:13**).

FROM THE DUST
OF THE GROUND
GENESIS 2:4-7

God created man with a physical body. He "formed the man from the dust of the ground and breathed into his nostrils the breath of life, and the man became a living being" (**Gen 2:7**). From the beginning, therefore, man has had a dual nature. The spirit part of man was made in the image of God; the physical part was made from the dust. Both parts are good, because God made them; both parts are necessary to complete the definition of "man." From the beginning, God wanted man to have a spirit and a body.

There will also be a body in the life to come. This fact will be developed throughout Scripture as a basic doctrinal truth (**Dan 12:2; Job**

19:25-27; Pss 16:10; 29:14; 1Cor 15:12-57; 2Cor 5:1-4; Php 3:20-21; 1Th 4:13-15). Nowhere does Scripture depict man without some sort of body. The body formed for Adam was a precursor to the resurrection body, although the body in the afterlife will certainly be different in some respects. It will be *"changed"* (*1Cor 15:51*) and *"transformed"* (*Php 3:21*) into something more glorious, but it will still be called a body.

The body that God made for Adam was a marvel of creation. It will be helpful to our study to consider the kind of body that God created and called "very good." The bodies that men and women have had from the beginning have five senses: taste, smell, hearing, touch, and sight. To be deprived of any of these by illness or accident is always considered a tragic loss. There is no reason to think that our bodies in heaven will suffer such a loss, or be diminished in any way. Our glorified bodies will be more—not less—than our earthly bodies.

The sense of taste and the consumption of food are not unholy. Jesus Himself drew criticism from people who did not really understand God, when they said, *"Here is a glutton and a drunkard"* (*Mt 11:19*). They disapproved of enjoying a good feast; Jesus did not. In a previous paragraph, discussing *Genesis 1:29-32*, we looked at the possibilities of food in the afterlife. Although it is often taught that there will be no need to eat in heaven (and therefore nothing available to eat there), Scripture paints a very different picture. In fact, rather than the body being diminished by losing its sense of taste, it may very well be that God has new and improved taste buds in store for us!

The sense of smell is closely tied to the sense of taste. Food that smells good, tastes good. In addition, there is the pleasure that is tied to the fragrance of flowers and other aromas. Adam and Eve came

> **It may be that God has new and improved taste buds in store for us.**

to life in the Garden of Eden in the midst of a virtual riot of wonderful smells. Why should we imagine that when we awake in heaven we will have something less? In fact, when we fail to envision heaven as a place of robust reality, with things to eat and fragrances to smell, heaven becomes pale and undesirable. Since God has not described heaven like that, why should we?

The sense of hearing was important for communication and fellowship in the Garden. God spoke to Adam (*Gen 2:16*); Adam spoke to God (*Gen 2:23; 3:8-12*); Adam and Eve spoke to one another. But hearing is a sense that often begins to fail people in their later years. It is reasonable to assume that this sense will be restored, and even improved, in heaven. There are certainly many sounds to hear in heaven. John heard a loud voice in *Revelation 1:10*, and twenty-six more times he writes, *"I heard."* We can expect to hear the voices of angels (*Rev 4:8; 5:11-12*), the rumblings and peals of thunder (*Rev 4:5*), the praise of the saints (*Rev 7:10*), new songs and the music of harps (*Rev 14:2-3; 15:2-3*), and most of all the voice of the Lamb (*Rev 22:16*) and communication with God the Father who will come to live with us (*Rev 21:3*).

The sense of touch is also an integral part of being human. Babies, for instance, do not thrive when they are deprived of being held and loved. For all of us an important part of connecting with each other comes through a handshake, a hug, a kiss, a pat on the back. Quite significantly, the Gospels frequently depict Jesus in the act of touching people. When He came to show us what God is like (*Jn 1:18*), He spent many moments in physical contact with people. In Matthew's Gospel alone Jesus reached out to touch a leper (*Mt 8:3*), a woman with a fever (*Mt 8:15*), a dead girl (*Mt 9:18,25*), a drowning disciple (*Mt 14:31*), little children (*Mt 19:13-15*), and two blind men (*Mt 20:34*). Those allowed to touch Him include an ailing woman (*Mt 9:21*), a woman (Mary) with expensive perfume (*Mt 26:7*), and a group of women after His resurrection (*Mt 28:9*). Mark adds the unusual healing (with spit) of a deaf and mute man (*Mk 7:33-35*) and in a similar fashion, a blind man (*Mk 8:22-25*). He also records that when Jesus set a little child before the disciples to teach them the nature of the Kingdom, He took the youngster *"in his arms"* (*Mk 9:36*). Luke describes in detail how a sinful woman wet His feet with her tears, wiped them with her hair, kissed them, and poured perfume on them (*Lk 7:38*). The Pharisees objected to all this; Jesus did not. Another woman, crippled for eighteen years, was healed when Jesus *"put his hands on her"* (*Lk 13:13*). John tells how Jesus put mud on the eyes of a man born blind (*Jn 9:6*) and washed dirt from the feet of His disciples (*Jn 13:4-12*). Finally, Jesus allowed Mary Magdalene to touch Him following His resurrection, although He insisted that she not keep holding on to Him (*Jn 20:17*). (The mistranslation of the KJV, "Touch me not," has falsely led some to think that the risen Lord could not be touched.) Only a few verses later Jesus insists that Thomas touch His hands and His side (*Jn 20:27*).

When we imagine a heaven filled with bodiless spirits, we create a place devoid of life and vitality. We subconsciously shrink back from such a place, with the unspoken realization that a heaven without touch is contrary to our basic natures. "Safe in the Arms of Jesus" should be more than an old, old song—it should be our confident expectation! In the glorified bodies of heaven we can fully expect to touch each other and to feel the embrace of God.

The sense of sight is a marvelous gift of God. Like Adam and Eve, we can recognize what seems to be a nearly infinite variety of colors and shapes. Our eyes focus the light wave/particles (photons) on the retina and interpret the sights in our brains. (This ability has always been one of the hardest for evolutionists to explain by saying, "It just happened.") Yet in spite of the phenomenal ability with which we have been blessed, scientists are now discovering that the human eye actually registers only a small fraction of electromagnetic wavelengths. We cannot see wavelengths smaller than ultraviolet or larger than infrared. In other words, there is a whole range of reality we cannot yet see. Like a color-blind man who is unable to see all the colors, we are vision-impaired people who cannot yet see all the glories of God. Perhaps we need another prophet Elisha to say, *"Lord, open his eyes so he may see"* (*2Kgs 6:17*).

The unlocking of a larger sense of sight may explain how we will be able to see God in heaven. Although He is presently "invisible," or at least "unseen," (*Col 1:15; 1Tm 1:17*), we will see Him in heaven. Jesus promised, *"Blessed are the pure in heart, for they will see God"* (*Mt 5:8*). Hebrews says, *"Without holiness no one will see the Lord"* (*Heb 12:14*). Revelation specifically promises, *"They will see his face"* (*Rev 22:4*). As surely as the disciples saw Jesus, we shall see God!

> **When we imagine a heaven filled with bodiless spirits, we create a place devoid of life and vitality.**

TWO TREES, FOUR RIVERS
GENESIS 2:8-17

Genesis proceeds with a further description of Eden that confirms the direction of the observations we have made. God made "all kinds" of trees grow in the garden, trees that were both *"pleasing to the eyes"* and *"good for food"* (*Gen 2:9*). God was pleased to provide pleasure for man. Contrary to a common philosophy of the Greeks and a common teaching of the monks, physical appetites are not "carnal" and "evil." Unless they are abused, both the appetites and the pleasures that satisfy them are the design of God. While it is true that *"man does not live on bread alone"* (*Mt 4:4*), it is also true that food is seen throughout Scripture as the gift of God, to be received with thanksgiving (*Mt 6:11,25-26; 1Tm 4:3*). And while God's children must not be ruled by the lust of the flesh and the lust of the eyes (*1Jn 2:16*), the Garden of Eden demonstrates that God intends for people to enjoy the beauty of what they see and the flavor of what they eat. This is how God sees things, and He is the God who made heaven.

In the middle of the garden, in addition to all the beautiful fruit trees, stood two more trees: the tree of life and the tree of the knowledge of good and evil (*Gen 2:9*). The tree of life, soon to be forbidden to Adam and Eve because of their sin (*Gen 3:22-24*), reappears in all its fruitful beauty in the pictures of heaven. Perhaps like a California redwood tree with a road cut through its trunk, the tree of life will have a river of crystal clear water flowing through it (*Rev 22:1-2*). Those who overcome will be given the right to eat from this tree (*Rev 2:7*), and new crops of fruit will appear every month. Eternity lost becomes eternity regained! The tree will give everlasting life, and its leaves will be for the healing of the nations.

Along with the tree of life in the middle of the garden stood the tree of the knowledge of good and evil. This tree will *not* have its counterpart in heaven, for this is the tree that caused all the trouble. Not content to be made in the image of God, Eve and Adam ate the forbidden fruit of this tree in a futile attempt to be just like God (*Gen 3:5*). The prohibition by God and the consequences of violating it tell us at least two things about heaven. First, man was never intended to be the equal of God. Contrary to Mormon doctrine, for instance, man will never become what God is. Throughout eternity we will praise God, serve God, and rule with God (*Rev 14:3; 22:3,5*), but nowhere does Scripture place us on the throne with God or on a throne like God. That place is reserved for the Lamb (*Rev 5:6,13; 22:1*). Second, God never wanted the earth to be full of disease and death. He said to stay away from the tree! He warned that if they ignored His warning and ate from the tree, they would bring death into the world (*Gen 2:17*). If the world had remained the way God wanted the world to be, it would have always been a perfect paradise. The good news is that one day the world will again be just the way God wants it. There will be no more pain and suffering, no more disease and death. In heaven both the tempter (*Rev 20:10*) and the tree of temptation will be gone.

A river flowed from Eden (*Gen 2:10*), actually dividing into four rivers (*Gen 2:11-14*). These rivers watered the garden and the antediluvian lands of Havilah, Cush, Tigris, and the area of the Euphrates. Just as these rivers flowed from Eden and brought life to those ancient lands, so the *"river of the water of life"* will flow from the throne of God with water that is crystal clear (*Rev 22:1*).

An interesting side note appears in *Genesis 2:11-12*. The first river flowed through the land of Havilah, *"where there is gold."* Not content to merely mention the gold, the text also says, *"The gold of that land is good."* Many philosophers, both ancient and modern, have belittled gold and jewels as unworthy carnal things, but God thought that the gold He had made was "good." With this in mind, we should take note of the fact that gold is repeatedly mentioned in the later descriptions of heaven. There are golden lampstands (*Rev 1:12*), a golden girdle (*Rev 1:13*), golden crowns (*Rev 4:4*), golden bowls (*Rev 15:7*), and a golden measuring rod (*Rev 21:15*). Even more dramatically, John describes an entire *"city of pure gold, as pure as glass"* (*Rev 21:18*), where even *"the great street of the city was of pure gold, like transparent glass"* (*Rev 21:21*).

The great street of gold creates an issue for many people. For some, their concept of heaven is too light and airy. How could a street of heavy gold bars keep from falling through the clouds? For others, gold represents greed and worldly wealth, which are not appropriate for heaven. For yet others, the "transparent as glass" description presents a stumbling block. The first two objections can be dismissed easily, since God's heaven is a real place and God's gold is good. But what about the transparency? A careful reading of *Revelation 21:18* indicates that the gold is not transparent, but that it is as pure as transparent glass. In other words, just as one can be sure there are no impurities in glass that is completely transparent, to that same extent one can be sure that the gold of God's heaven is totally pure. The emphasis in *Revelation 21:21* is the same—the purity of the gold matches the purity of transparent glass. Perhaps, therefore, we should

With all the gold in the first paradise of God, why not streets of gold in the final paradise? stop arguing about what we think is impossible or inappropriate and just accept John's description as accurate. Streets of gold? With all that gold in the first paradise of God, why not?

There is still one more parallel between these verses and heaven. When God put the man in the garden, the man's purpose was *"to work it and to take care of it"* (**Gen 2:15**; see also **Gen 2:5**). Mankind, made in the image of God, is never content to be completely idle. God is always working (**Jn 5:17**), and humans always feel the most satisfied when they are accomplishing something. Therefore, it is not surprising that in the life to come, God's children will be put to work. In a world that is no longer under the curse, however, this service will not be difficult and unrewarding toil. It will be a joy when *"his servants will serve him"* in the heavenly city (**Rev 22:3**), as they carry out His will and help govern heaven. In this sense they will reign with Him for ever and ever (**Rev 22:5**).

ADAM AND EVE
GENESIS 2:18-25

As God's designated ruler over all the animals and birds of the earth, Adam gave names to every creature (**Gen 2:19**). But as all the animals (and their mates) paraded past Adam, one thing became painfully clear. The animals already existed as both male and female; they were ready to reproduce and fill the earth. But Adam was alone. Therefore, as the climax of all God's creative activities, He made woman to be *"a helper suitable"* for man (**Gen 2:18**). The man and the woman accepted God's intention and design that they should become one flesh. They were naked in each other's presence, and they felt no shame (**Gen 2:24-25**).

Some of this is a picture that will be repeated in heaven, but some of it is not. God saw that it was *"not good for the man to be alone"* (**Gen 2:18**), so He provided Adam with ideal company. Just as Adam was then free to share intimacy with his wife in every respect, so shall we be free to love one another in heaven. Mutual love and affection among all the community of God has always been the Father's desire (**Lev 19:18; Mt 22:39; Jn 13:34; 1Th 4:9; 1Pet 1:22**). But Jesus specifically said, *"At the resurrection people will neither marry nor be given in marriage; they will be like the angels in heaven"* (*Mt 22:30*). It is important to see what Jesus said and what He did not say. He did not say a man would never see his wife again, or that a wife would never see her husband. He did not say they would be prevented from enjoying one another's company throughout eternity. What He said was that a man and a woman would not have an exclusive union in heaven, specifically in the context of sex and reproduction (see *Mt 22:23-28*). Since no one will ever die in heaven, neither will any more people be born. In the afterlife God will never have the need to say, *"Be fruitful and increase in number; fill heaven with people"* (compare *Gen 2:28*). The exclusive sanctity of the home, so necessary for producing and nurturing children, will no longer be necessary in heaven. The little family unit will be dissolved into the greater family of God, where all His children—both male and female—will be free to love one another as dear brothers and sisters.

GOD WALKING
IN THE GARDEN
GENESIS 3:8

Eve, followed shortly by Adam, tragically let the serpent deceive her and chose to eat from the forbidden tree. The age of innocence became the time of shame, as Adam and Eve made pathetic attempts to cover their nakedness (*Gen 3:1-7*). Soon they heard the *"sound of the LORD God walking in the garden in the cool of the day"* (*Gen 3:8*). In their shame they hid from God, shunning His call for fellowship. In heaven, however, paradise lost will become friendship regained. What God wanted in *Genesis* will be found in *Revelation*. *"Now the dwelling of God is with men,"* said the loud voice to John, *"and he will live with them"* (*Rev 21:3*). In addition, just as God provided garments for Adam and Eve (*Gen 3:21*), He will provide white robes for His children in heaven (*Rev 3:4-5; 7:9*).

THE CURSE
GENESIS 3:16-19

Because of their rebellion against God's will, the first couple fell under a curse. The penalty for Eve was painful childbearing; the penalty for Adam was painful, sweaty toil (*Gen 3:16-17*). They both would now live in a world of hardship and death, instead of the world God wanted for them. They would live out their days and then die; they would return to the dust from which God made them.

But none of this will be repeated in heaven! There will be *"no more death or mourning or crying or pain, for the old order of things has passed away"* (*Rev 21:4*). To put it more succinctly, *"No longer will there be any curse"* (*Rev 22:3*). Sin and death were ushered in by Adam, but righteousness and eternal life are freely given in the second Adam, Jesus Christ (see *Rom 5:12-21*).

HE MUST NOT BE ALLOWED . . . TO LIVE FOREVER GENESIS 3:22

Now Adam and Eve must be banished from the Garden. They must be denied access to the tree of life, lest they should eat its fruit *"and live forever"* (*Gen 3:22*). Actually, being banished from the tree of life was, in one sense, a good thing. Would it have been good for Adam and Eve to live forever in a world of pain and disease? To live forever in a state of rebellion and guilt? Therefore, as an act of wisdom and mercy, God did not allow these first humans to have access to what would keep them alive forever. Instead, He drove them from the Garden and began the long process of reclaiming fallen man through Christ.

Denial of access to the tree of life is a reminder that man is not by nature immortal. On their own, Adam and Eve did not have inherent immortality. Even before the Fall, they could live indefinitely only by having access to the tree of life. When the tree was taken away, their chance of living forever was also taken away. God alone is immortal (*1Tm 6:11*). The Father and the Son have life in themselves, and they give it to whomever they choose (*Jn 5:21,26*). Like Adam and Eve, all of us as human beings have life only because God sustains us (*Acts 17:28*).

But in heaven our access to the tree of life will be renewed! The fruit of this beautiful tree will be given freely to those who overcome (*Rev 2:7*). In the paradise of God, the water of life (*Rev 22:1*) and the tree of life (*Rev 22:2*) are the free gift of God (*Rev 22:19*). Intended to be immortal from the beginning, but cut off from immortality by his own sin, mankind will finally become what God had always meant for us to be.

SUMMARY

The Garden of Eden—the original paradise of God—has much to tell us about the heaven God has prepared for us. The parallels between the *first two chapters of Genesis* and the *last two chapters of Revelation* are remarkable. They show that God, who does not change like shifting shadows (*Jas 1:17*), has a consistent intention and goal for mankind. Although interrupted by the Fall, God's final purposes will not be thwarted. What God started in *Genesis* will be brought to completion in *Revelation*. Along the way, Scripture gives increasingly clear clues about the nature of the world to come. In the next chapter we will move from the Garden and follow salvation history as the story continues through Noah and the Patriarchs.

WHAT DO YOU SAY?

1. Why did God make a world at all, when He already had heaven?

2. What do the many similarities between *Genesis 1–2* and *Revelation 21–22* indicate?

3. Why do you think the ancient philosophers thought the physical world was bad?

4. What do you think about the notion that there will be animals in heaven?

5. In what ways is mankind made "in the image" of God? What does each tell us about the nature and activities of heaven?

6. Is the tree of life a real tree in heaven? Will we actually eat its fruit?

7. Is there any tragedy in life that is not a result from directly disobeying God's laws or from living in a fallen world that is under the curse?

8. Why didn't God prevent Adam and Eve from sinning, and just put them in heaven to start with?

CHAPTER THREE

HEAVEN IN THE TORAH OF ISRAEL

PART TWO: *Genesis 4—Deuteronomy*

As we leave the Garden of Eden with a sense of loss and regret, we enter a long period of human history. God will demonstrate the penalty of sin in Noah's time, and begin the solution for sin in Abraham. Along the way, as we make a more rapid perusal of Scripture, we will accumulate a growing body of clues that will tell us about the life to come.

THE GENERATIONS OF MEN
GENESIS 4:2,20-22

In obedience to God's original command (*Gen 1:28*), Adam and Eve were fruitful and increased in number. Their first son, Cain, became a dirt farmer; their second son, Abel, became a shepherd. It was not the curse of the fallen world that made them work; it was the intention of God from the beginning (*Gen 2:15*). Likewise, when new generations of men were born, they were also involved in creative, productive work. Jabel and his people made tents and raised livestock (*Gen 4:20*). Jubal and his people were musicians; they invented and mastered the harp and the flute (*Gen 4:21*). Tubal-Cain and his people learned how to make tools of bronze and iron (*Gen 4:22*). Made in the image of their

43

Creator, every man found ways to be creative. This was their nature; this was their inherent need. Because this is part of what it means to be made in the image of God, this was a foreshadowing of the activities of heaven.

AND THEN HE DIED
GENESIS 5:1-5

As if to remind us of a fact we should never forget, *Genesis 5* repeats the important truth, *"When God created man, he made him in the likeness of God"* (*Gen 5:1*). Then the generations of man begin to make their brief appearance on life's stage. Adam lived, had sons and daughters, *"and then he died"* (*Gen 5:5*). Short obituaries recount the lives of the leading sons of each new generation, ending in the inevitable conclusion: "and then he died." Men lived very long lives, of course, before God set limits on the human lifespan (*Gen 6:3; Ps 90:10*), but eventually every man died. The curse of the fallen world was universal; a place in heaven was man's ultimate necessity.

ENOCH WALKED WITH GOD
GENESIS 5:24

But there was an exception! One man had a strikingly different obituary. Enoch, the father of Methuselah, *"walked with God; then he was no more, because God took him away"* (*Gen 5:24*). We later learn why Enoch was an exception. He did not experience death and was taken directly to be with God because *"he was commended as one who pleased God"* (*Heb 11:5*). We cannot know what the ancients thought when they read about Enoch, but surely this gave them a foreshadowing of heaven. When this life is over, it is actually possible—and highly desirable—to go to be with God.

BRING TWO OF ALL
LIVING CREATURES
GENESIS 6:19-21

In the days of Noah man's wickedness became great upon the earth (*Gen 6:5,12*). God brought a great flood, demonstrating that He will take drastic measures to punish sin. In singling out Noah and his family for deliverance, God demonstrated that He will reward righteousness. Like Enoch of old, Noah was a righteous man who *"walked with God"* (**Gen 6:8-9**). His deliverance through water became a picture of how God would later save His people through the water of baptism (**1Pet 3:20-22**).

An interesting part of Noah's deliverance was God's instruction to save animals to reproduce on earth after the flood. God told Noah that a male and a female of every kind of bird, animal, and creeping creature would come to him *"to be kept alive"* (**Gen 6:20**). Noah was to take every kind of food that would be eaten by the various creatures during their year-long voyage on the ark. This is a reminder of two significant truths. First, God loves all His creatures. They were "good" when He created them, and He did not want an earth devoid of their presence. Second, God put man in charge of supervising the animal kingdom. In view of the impending flood, it was only natural that man should be put in charge of preserving animal life. Do not both of these facts—God's love for animals and man's ruling responsibility for them—show us a preview of heaven?

GOD'S RAINBOW COVENANT
GENESIS 9:1-16

After the great flood receded, God repeated His instructions for mankind to increase in number and fill the earth. Likewise, He repeated the fact of man's supremacy over the animals, saying, *"They are given into your hands"* (**Gen 9:2**). But now God would do something new. He told Noah that He would make a covenant *"with you and with your descendants after you and with every living creature that was with you—the birds, the livestock and all the wild animals, all those that came out of the ark with you—every living creature on earth"* (**Gen 9:9-10**). The rainbow in the sky would be *"the sign of the covenant I am making between me and you and every living creature with you"* (**Gen 9:11**). Repeatedly, Scripture puts emphasis on God's concern for the well-being of animals. This agrees nicely with the many prophetic declarations about the variety of animals living in peace in the age to come (see **Isa 11:6-8; 65:25**).

MANKIND AFTER THE FLOOD
GENESIS 10:5-11

As the generations grew into nations after the flood, Scripture describes men doing things in the likeness of their Father. They fathered their own sons and daughters, and spread out to rule maritime territories (*Gen 10:5*). One man became *"a mighty warrior"* and *"a mighty hunter,"* establishing a powerful kingdom (*Gen 10:8-11*). He and others built great cities: Babylon, Akkad, Nineveh. Fathers, adventurers, warriors, hunters, builders, rulers—these men were showing what man was meant to be. In far greater ways, we shall all serve God and reign with God in heaven, as we ourselves become all that being created "in His image" means.

THE TOWER OF BABEL
GENESIS 11:1-9

Just as Cain went out from the LORD's presence and dwelt in a land *"east of Eden"* (*Gen 4:16*), men again moved eastward in search of a place to call their home (*Gen 11:2*). They settled on a plain in the land of Shinar and came up with a terrible idea: *"Come, let us build ourselves a city, with a tower that reaches to the heavens, so that we may make a name for ourselves"* (*Gen 11:4*). Whether their attempt was to reach "heaven" (KJV, NASB) or "the heavens" (NIV, NRSV), they clearly were being insolent to God. (This can be compared with Isaiah's taunt against the King of Babylon: *"You said in your heart, 'I will ascend to heaven; I will raise my throne above the stars of God; . . . I will ascend above the tops of the clouds; I will make myself like the Most High"* (*Isa 14:13-14*).

The desire to get to heaven can be either noble or base. To reconnect with God, to restore the broken fellowship, to honor and adore His presence is a noble thing. It is an instinctive desire to fill the "God-shaped void" in our hearts. But mankind has often tried to force its way into heaven on its own terms, or to manufacture a heaven to its own liking. The early generation of men at the Tower of Babel was reenacting the original sin of Adam and Eve. They were trying to take matters into their own hands and make themselves equal to God. The LORD stepped in to frustrate their ambitions, scattering them to the eventual far corners of the earth.

THE CALL OF ABRAHAM
GENESIS 12:1-5

With Abraham, the man of faith, God began the long process of reclaiming the fallen race of man. God called him to leave his country, his people, and his father's household and go to the land that God would show him. Even though he did not know where God was taking him, Abraham set out for the unknown land of promise. Even after he arrived in the promised land, he lived in tents as a nomad all his life, *"For he was looking forward to the city with foundations, whose architect and builder is God"* (**Heb 11:10**). In sharp contrast to the arrogant self-assertiveness of the builders of Babel who tried to make their own way to heaven, Abraham put all his confidence in the leading of God. Admitting he was only an alien and stranger on this earth, he was *"longing for a better country—a heavenly one"* (**Heb 11:13,15**).

God made a covenant with Abraham that would potentially benefit all nations in all generations to come. *"You will be a blessing,"* God promised, *"and all peoples on earth will be blessed through you"* (**Gen 12:2-3**). Abraham himself would not be that blessing, however. As God specified to Abraham later, *"Through **your offspring** all nations of the earth will be blessed"* (**Gen 22:18**). The *offspring* did not mean all the descendants of Abraham, but one very special Descendant who would make salvation available to all men (**Gal 3:16**). From the time of Abraham through the rest of the OT, there is one all-important theme: God is making a way to heaven for the sinful race of men. Created in His image, but now fallen and guilty, mankind would yet become all that God intended.

POSSESSOR OF HEAVEN AND EARTH
GENESIS 14:14-24

Abraham had allowed his nephew Lot to choose which part of the promised land would be his. Lot chose the well-watered valley of the Jordan near Sodom (**Gen 13:1-11**). Some time later four kings from the east defeated the local kings, and Lot was taken with the others as a prisoner of war. When Abraham heard this distressing news, he took all his men and made a night attack on the forces of the four kings to rescue his nephew. As he returned with the spoils of this successful rescue mission, Abraham encountered Melchizedek.

As *"priest of God Most High,"* Melchizedek accepted a tithe payment from Abraham and blessed him. He pronounced the blessing in the name of *"God Most High, Creator of heaven and earth"* (**Gen 14:19**). These words are the first recorded human statement calling

God the *"Creator of heaven and earth."* The God of "heaven and earth" will become a familiar refrain through the rest of the Bible.

A VISIT BY THE ANGELS
GENESIS 18-19

The first clear mention of angels in Scripture comes in *Genesis 18 and 19*. Three visitors came to Abraham and one of them spoke as the LORD (*Gen 18:1-2,10*). As is usual in the rest of the Bible, when these angels appeared to humans they took on human form. What is significant about this incident is that it is a foreshadowing of what will take place in heaven. We shall enjoy the company of these marvelous beings as we join them in praise of God (*Rev 5:11-14*). Furthermore, as we take our designated places in heaven, reigning with God and the Lamb (*Rev 22:5*), we will even have superiority over the angels (see *1Cor 6:3* and *Heb 2:16*).

Two of the angels continued into the next chapter of Genesis, where they visited Lot in Sodom (*Gen 19:1*). The angels ate a supper with Lot (*Gen 19:3*) and later stepped in to protect Lot (*Gen 19:9-11*). Then they led Lot and his family to safety before the city was destroyed (*Gen 19:16*). Angels, who are *"ministering spirits sent to serve those who will inherit salvation"* (*Heb 1:14*), will frequently be found in Scripture as they rescue God's people from harm (*Gen 22:10-12; 48:16; Ex 14:19; 33:2; Num 20:15-16; 2Kgs 6:16-18; Ps 35:6; Dan 3:28; 6:22; Acts 12:11; Rev 12:7-9*). Even in their angelic glory, however, they are never to be worshiped (*Col 2:18; Rev 22:8-9*). Instead, they will join us in heaven as we worship God.

It should be noted that some have found an earlier mention of angels in *Genesis 6:2*, when *"the sons of God"* married the *"daughters of men."* While it is true that "sons of God" sometimes refers to angels *(Job 1:6; 2:1)*, God's "sons" also often refers to humans *(Deu 14:1; 32:5; Ps 73:15; Isa 43:6; Hos 1:10; 11:1; Lk 3:38; 1Jn 3:1-2)*. It is likely in *Genesis 6:2* that "sons of God" refers to the godly descendants of Seth and "daughters of men" refers to the less godly descendants of Cain.

A TEST OF FAITH
GENESIS 22:5

Following the birth of Isaac, Abraham was put to a terrible test. God told him to take his *"only son Isaac"* to the region of Moriah and sacrifice him there as a burnt offering. (According to **2 Chronicles 3:1** this mountain is the very place where Solomon would later build the Temple.) Abraham was immediately obedient, leaving early the next morning with two of his servants and Isaac. When they reached the mountain, Abraham told the servants to wait behind, saying, *"We will worship and then we will come back to you"* (**Gen 22:5**). On top of the mountain Abraham bound his son and placed him on the altar. With knife in hand, Abraham was ready to slay his own son, draining the blood just as he would with a sacrificial animal. How could Abraham do this? A later Scripture shows that Abraham already, in a sense, had faith in the afterlife: *"Abraham reasoned that God could raise the dead, and figuratively speaking, he did receive Isaac back from death"* (**Heb 11:19**). With perfect trust in a God who was stronger than death itself, Abraham named that place YHWH-jireh, *"The LORD will provide"* (**Gen 22:14**).

BURIAL OF SARAH
GENESIS 23:1-23

When Sarah died at the age of one hundred twenty-seven, Abraham sought to buy a site for her burial (**Gen 23:1-4**). Ironically, this was the only piece of the promised land that Abraham ever owned (see **Heb 11:9**). Abraham made no attempt to take the body of Sarah back to their original homeland where her ancestors were buried. Faithful to God's leading, Abraham now counted Canaan his home.

Through the entire story of Sarah's burial, nothing at all is said about a future life beyond the grave. While Abraham believed God could raise the dead, he had not been told about life in heaven. Likewise, when Abraham was buried with Sarah by his sons Isaac and Ishmael, nothing is stated about any expectation of heaven (**Gen 25:7-11**). While we may look back and find many clues about heaven in Genesis, the people of that time did not have God's full revelation.

SWEAR BY THE GOD OF
HEAVEN AND EARTH
GENESIS 24:3-4

In Abraham's old age God had given him Isaac, the son of the covenant blessing. But who would be the wife with whom Isaac would continue the family lineage? It would not be right for Isaac to take a Canaanite wife. Therefore Abraham sent his servant back to the town of Nahor, among Abraham's people, to find a bride for Isaac. As he sent the servant, Abraham made him take a significant oath. *"I want you to swear by the LORD, the God of heaven and earth,"* Abraham said, *"that you will go to my country and my own relatives and get a wife for my son Isaac"* (*Gen 24:3-4*). Echoing the words of Melchizedek in an earlier encounter (*Gen 14:19*), Abraham acknowledged that there is a heaven—and that it belongs to God.

JACOB'S LADDER
GENESIS 28:1-17

Isaac's son Jacob also needed to find a wife who was not a Canaanite woman, so he traveled back to Haran to take a wife from the daughters of Laban, his mother's brother (*Gen 28:1-2,10*). As he stopped one night on this journey, he had a dream in which he saw a stairway reaching to heaven (*Gen 28:12*). The angels of God were ascending and descending on this stairway—could it give men access to heaven as well?

At the top of the stairway stood the LORD. He who had made His covenant with Abraham and Isaac was now continuing the relationship with Jacob. *"All people on earth will be blessed through you and your offspring,"* said the LORD (*Gen 28:14*). The promise of the coming Messiah (*Gal 3:16*) was now connected with the stairway to heaven. *"How awesome is this place!"* exclaimed Jacob. *"This is none other than the house of God; this is the gate of heaven"* (*Gen 28:17*). Driven from the gate of the Garden so long ago, now mankind was learning to approach the gate of heaven.

DOWN TO THE GRAVE
GENESIS 37:31-35

Many years and twelve sons later, Jacob made another statement about the afterlife. This one was an utterance of despair. It came about after the other brothers were jealous of Joseph and sold him into slavery. They took Joseph's richly ornamented robe and smeared goat blood on it. When Jacob saw it, he assumed *"some ferocious animal has devoured him"* (**Gen 37:33**). In deep mourning, Jacob tore his clothes and put on sackcloth (a rough fabric made of goat hair). Refusing to be comforted by his sons and daughters, Jacob wept and said, *"No, in mourning will I go down to the grave to my son"* (**Gen 37:35**).

Two observations should be made about Jacob's words. First, his word for *the grave* was the Hebrew word *sheol*. This is the first instance of the sixty-six times *sheol* appears in the OT (translated in the NIV as "the grave," "death," "the depths," and "the realm of the dead"). *Sheol* was the general term for the place of the dead. It was sometimes described as a shadowy place where activity ceases (see **Job 3:13-19; 7:9**), but where individual identity was preserved. *Sheol* is almost always seen in negative ways, with death as the ultimate consequence of sin. A notable exception will be found in Hosea:

> I will ransom them from the power of **sheol**;
> I will redeem them from death.
> Where, O death, are your plagues?
> Where, **Sheol**, is your destruction? (**Hos 13:14**)

The second observation is that Jacob expected in some sense to go to his son when he went down to *sheol*. Like David in a later time (**2Sa 12:23**), he expected to rejoin his son, but without any anticipation of joyful reunion. He and his son would still have their own identities, but to what purpose?

Years later Jacob lay on his deathbed. He called for his son Joseph and said, *"Do not bury me in Egypt, but when I rest with my fathers, carry me out of Egypt and bury me where they are buried"* (**Gen 47:29-30**). In the family cemetery that Abraham purchased for Sarah, the bones of Jacob were laid to rest in a solemn ceremony of mourning (**Gen 50:1-11**). There seems to have been little awareness of life beyond the grave, but there was a strong dedication to be united with the fathers in the covenant with God.

THE GOD OF ABRAHAM, ISAAC, AND JACOB
EXODUS 3:1-6

Four centuries later the children of Israel had fallen from honored guests in Egypt to wretched slaves. Far away at Mount Horeb in Sinai,

God was summoning the man who would deliver them. As Moses led his father-in-law's sheep to the far side of the desert, he saw a strange sight: a burning bush that did not burn up. When Moses drew closer, God spoke to him from within the bush, *"Take off your sandals, for the place where you are standing is holy ground. I am the God of your father, the God of Abraham, the God of Isaac and the God of Jacob"* (*Ex 3:5-6*).

Jesus used this very passage to teach the Sadducees that there is, in fact, life after death (*Mt 22:29-32*). Jesus' point was that God did not say, "I *was* Abraham's God," He said, "I *am* Abraham's God"—indicating that Abraham was still alive. Abraham, Isaac, Jacob—the patriarchs of the covenant—were even then enjoying the blessing of their relationship with God. While Moses may not have appreciated this fine distinction of verb tenses, and it may not have been noted by many of his subsequent readers, Jesus knew exactly what this text implied.

THE BOOK OF LIFE
EXODUS 32:32-33

As Moses led the children of Israel to freedom, trouble arose. They cried out in fear of the pursuing army (*Ex 14:10-12*); they grumbled about the lack of good water (*Ex 15:24; 17:3*); and they whined about the food (*Ex 16:3*). Worst of all, when Moses was on Mount Sinai getting the stone tablets of God's law, they made a golden calf and gave it the credit for bringing them out of Egypt (*Ex 32:1-4*).

The wrath of the LORD burned hot against Israel and He threatened to destroy them. But Moses intervened with this remarkable plea: *"But now, please forgive their sin—but if not, then blot me out of the book you have written"* (*Ex 32:32*). Although it was not clear at this point in Scripture what it might mean to be blotted out from God's book, subsequent references to the "book of life" make it increasingly clear that it is a list of the people who will go to heaven (see *Ps 69:28; Dan 12:1; Php 4:3; Rev 3:5; 13:8; 17:8; 20:15; 21:27*).

God's Book of Life

1. God has a book *(Ex 32:32-33)*
2. Sinners are blotted out of that book *(Ps 69:28)*

3. People in the book are delivered from death *(Dan 12:1-3)*
4. Disciples should rejoice that their names are written in heaven *(Lk 10:20)*.
5. Faithful Christians are in that book *(Php 4:3)*
6. Those who overcome will never be blotted out *(Rev 3:5)*
7. The book also belongs to the Lamb *(Rev 13:8)*
8. Names in the book are written (or not) since creation *(Rev 17:8)*
9. This book overrules the ledgers of our wrongdoing *(Rev 20:15)*
10. Those in the Lamb's book of life will enter heaven *(Rev 21:27)*

YOU CANNOT SEE MY FACE
EXODUS 33:17-22

As God gave Moses instructions on Mount Sinai, He said, *"I am pleased with you and I know you by name"* (*Ex 33:17*). Emboldened by this word of approval, Moses made an audacious request: *"Now show me your glory"* (*Ex 33:18*). In response to this, God covered Moses in the cleft of a rock and allowed him to see only the trailing remnant of His glory after He had passed by. *"You cannot see my face,"* the LORD warned, *"for no one may see me and live"* (*Ex 33:20*). (This shows that when Moses and Aaron and the elders of Israel "saw the God of Israel" on an earlier occasion in *Exodus 24:10-11*, they did not actually see the full extent of His glory.)

Even though Moses spoke to God *"face to face"* (*Ex 34:10; Num 12:8*), he was never allowed to look at God directly. The same was true of the subsequent leaders of Israel. David longed to *"gaze upon the beauty of the LORD"* (*Ps 27:4*), but until he reached heaven it never happened. Isaiah *"saw the LORD,"* but only in a vision (*Isa 6:1-13*). Each of these incidents expresses the deep longing of the human heart—to see its Creator. Yet after all the OT leaders had come and gone, the Apostle John could still affirm, *"No one has ever seen God"* (*Jn 1:18*). Even so, as noted earlier in reference to the creation of man (*Gen 2:4-7*), there are specific promises that in heaven we will see God (*Mt 5:8; Heb 12:14; Rev 22:4*). No longer will we be held back and forbidden to see the previously unseen God.

GLORY FILLS THE TABERNACLE
EXODUS 40:34-35

The Tabernacle in the wilderness was complete. Aaron and his sons washed themselves, put on the sacred garments, and were anointed to serve as priests. All the furniture was placed in the proper position; all the necessary burnt offerings were made (see *Ex 40:1-33*). Now, only one thing remained: *"A cloud of glory covered the Tent of Meeting, and the glory of the LORD filled the tabernacle"* (*Ex 40:34*; see also *Ex 16:10; 24:15-17; Num 9:15-25; 20:6*). Just as God had promised, He came to dwell in the sanctuary (*Ex 25:8*), separated from human eyes by a shielding curtain (*Ex 39:34; 40:21*). Only the high priest could enter the sanctuary and stand before this representation of God's presence (*Lev 16:2,32-33*).

In later years the Jewish people came to call the presence of God the *Shekinah*. The word *Shekinah*, which came from a root word meaning "to dwell," referred to the radiant, glorious presence of God. It was thought to hover above the ark of the covenant as a glowing ball of light. *Shekinah*, however, is not a Bible word, and much of popular thought about this glowing manifestation of God is not really found anywhere in Scripture.

What Scripture does teach is that there will be no temple in the final, heavenly Jerusalem (*Rev 21:22*). No longer will there be curtains and fences to keep people away from God, restraining them to their respective positions: courtyard of the Gentiles, courtyard of the women, courtyard of the men, the Holy Place, the Holy of Holies. In heaven, *"the LORD God Almighty and the Lamb are its temple."* Where the glory and presence of God were carefully kept away from the people at the Tabernacle, and later at the Temple, we will enjoy immediate access to God in heaven (*Rev 21:3*).

MY DWELLING PLACE AMONG YOU
LEVITICUS 26:11-12

Through the next two books of Moses—Leviticus and Numbers— there is little additional information to create clear pictures of heaven. In fact, the word "heaven" or "heavens" is not used even once in these books. Perhaps it is not surprising that many of the ancient scholars who pored over the minute details of the laws in these books did not have any appreciation of the life to come.

One notable exception is found in *Leviticus 26*. There God promised Israel that if they kept His laws faithfully, they would enjoy peace and prosperity (*Lev 26:3-10*). Most importantly, God said, *"I will put my dwelling place among you, and I will not abhor you. I will walk among you and be your God, and you will be my people"* (*Lev 26:11-12*). In the immediate context of Leviticus, this was a promise that God would somehow be present among them at their Tabernacle. (*Verse eleven* reads literally, *"I will put my tabernacle among you."*) But the words are strikingly reminiscent of the words in *Revelation 21:3* (see also *Rev 3:20*). The same God who walked in the cool of the day in the first paradise promises that He will again one day walk among His people!

WHAT GOD IS THERE IN HEAVEN?
DEUTERONOMY 3:24

Israel had conquered Gilead, Bashan, and the kingdom of Og on the east side of the Jordan River. Now it was time for final marching orders to cross the Jordan and take the Promised Land. *"Do not be afraid of them,"* Moses told Joshua, *"the LORD your God himself will fight for you"* (*Deu 3:22*).

At that time Moses also made an appeal to God in his own behalf. He wanted to go over and see the good land beyond the Jordan with his own eyes. It is of interest in this study to note the words of his plea: *"For what god is there in heaven or earth who can do the deeds and mighty works you do?"* (*Deu 3:24*). Moses has become keenly aware that there is no god like the LORD God, either in heaven or on earth. It is also significant that in referring to places where God dwells, that Moses seems to have automatically thought first of "heaven."

MOSES CALLS HEAVEN AND EARTH TO WITNESS
DEUTERONOMY 4:26

As Moses continued to give instructions to the children of Israel in preparation for their invasion of Canaan, he emphasized the stipulations of their covenant with God. As was customary in ancient treaties, witnesses were summoned to make the arrangement legally binding. Warning the people what would happen if they fell into idolatry, Moses said, *"I call heaven and earth as witnesses against you this day that you will quickly perish"* (**Deu 4:26**). Very similar language is found later in these words of Moses: *"This day I call heaven and earth as witnesses against you that I have set before you life and death, blessings and curses. Now choose life, so that you and your children may live"* (**Deu 30:19**). Throughout the book of Deuteronomy there seems to be increasing attention to heaven as the throne of God. Twenty-six times in this final book of Moses there is reference to heaven, whether as the sky or as the dwelling place of God (or as a combination of both).

EVEN THE HIGHEST HEAVENS
DEUTERONOMY 10:14

Moses challenged the people to fear the LORD, to walk in His ways, and to love and serve Him with all their heart and soul, since all His commands were for their own good (**Deu 10:12-13**). Then he emphasized how the LORD has the right to make demands of the people, saying, *"To the LORD your God belong the heavens, even the highest heavens, the earth and everything in it"* (**Deu 10:14**). To speak of the heavens—*even the highest heavens*—shows that Moses realized that there was somehow a distinction from the mere sky above and the glorious dwelling of God. A similar distinction is reflected much later in the words of Paul in 2 Corinthians: *"I know a man in Christ who fourteen years ago was caught up to the third heaven . . . was caught up to paradise"* (**2Cor 12:2,4**). By that time it was common to consider the atmosphere as the first heaven, the starry sky as the second heaven, and the dwelling of God as the third heaven. It has always been difficult for mankind to define the location of God's heaven, but as the instances of revealed truth mount up, we have increasing surety that it is there.

HEAVEN, YOUR HOLY DWELLING PLACE
DEUTERONOMY 26:15

Moses taught the people of Israel to tithe. When they took possession of the land, they were to give God the firstfruits as they harvested their crops (*Deu 26:1-12*). When they presented their tithes they were to say a prayer of dedication, including these words: *"Look down from heaven, your holy dwelling place, and bless your people Israel and the land you have given us as you promised to our forefathers, a land flowing with milk and honey"* (*Deu 26:15*). In teaching this prayer, Moses was training the people to have a constant reminder of where God dwells—in heaven above.

The prayer also serves to teach us, thousands of years later. This is the lesson: God is pleased to provide His people a land of abundance. Just as the original Promised Land was "a land flowing with milk and honey," the future home in heaven promises an abundance of hidden manna, living water, and fruit from the tree of life. Eden's paradise, Moses' land of promise, the Christian's heaven—all express the loving generosity of God.

WHO WILL GO UP TO HEAVEN FOR US? DEUTERONOMY 30:12

One final passage from Deuteronomy will help focus our attention on heaven. As Moses neared the end of his summation of God's laws, he encouraged the people of Israel that what he was commanding them was not beyond their reach. God had placed the word in their mouth and in their heart. They could understand it, believe it, and obey it. *"It is not up in heaven,"* Moses said, *"so that you have to ask, 'Who will ascend into heaven to get it and proclaim it to us so we may obey it?'"* (*Deu 30:12*).

While the primary focus of this statement is on the accessibility of God's laws, it also had an additional teaching for Israel. It was a reminder to them that on their own they had no access to heaven. If they were ever to reach heaven, they were going to have to have help!

SUMMARY

Ejected from the Garden of Eden, mankind began the long pilgrimage back to paradise. Enoch showed that a man could go to be with God. With Noah the love of God for all His animals was revealed. At Babel, men learned they could not build their own way to heaven. In Abraham, Isaac, and Jacob, God began to reveal the great plan through which He would bless all the families of the earth.

Along the way, we encountered angels, burials, and a dream of a stairway to heaven. Moses led the children of Israel out of bondage and into the land of promise, a clear foreshadowing of what would be done in Christ.

WHAT DO YOU SAY?

1. How did the early generations of man exhibit the "image of God"?

2. God made a way to save the animals from the Flood, and then made a covenant that included them. What does this tell us about what God thinks of animals?

3. Abraham walked by faith and looked forward to a city built by God. In what specific ways are we like Abraham?

4. What is significant about the way God said, "I am the God of Abraham, the God of Isaac, the God of Jacob"?

5. At the Tabernacle God dwelt in the midst of His people. How do you envisage God living among us in heaven? Will we see His face?

6. Moses mentioned the "Book of Life." What do other passages tell us about this book?

7. In what ways is the Promised Land like heaven?

CHAPTER FOUR

HEAVEN IN
THE HISTORY OF ISRAEL

(Joshua–Esther)

As Israel settled in the Promised Land, they changed from a ragtag collection of freed slaves into an established nation. Through the conquests of Joshua, the ups and downs of Judges, and the messianic glimpse of Ruth, the nation settled into the rhythms of life in Canaan. In the history books of Samuel, the Kings, and the Chronicles we will encounter additional previews—although not in large number—of the afterlife.

THE WITCH OF ENDOR
1 SAMUEL 28:5-19

As King Saul pulled farther and farther away from God, he became fearful to the point of paranoia. He was fearful of David lest he should lose the kingdom into his hands (see *1Sa 18:8; 19:9-11; 20:33; 22:8; 23:8; 26:2*). He was especially fearful of the armies of Philistia (*1Sa 28:5*), since Samuel was dead, and Saul had no one to secure information from the Lord. In direct defiance of God's command (*Deu 18:11*) and as a reversal of his own decree (*1Sa 28:3*), Saul said, *"Find me a woman who is a medium, so I may go and inquire of her"* (*1Sa 28:7*).

Because of his earlier decree against mediums, Saul had to go to the woman in disguise. Asked to bring up Samuel, the woman reacted in apparent surprise when she saw *"a spirit coming up out of the ground"* (*1Sa 28:12-13*). While there are various interpretations of exactly what happened, the most straightforward explanation is that God allowed Samuel to return to speak to Saul in order to punish him. At any rate, *"Saul knew it was Samuel"* (*v. 14*), and Samuel spoke to him in behalf of the LORD (*vv. 16-19*). What Samuel told Saul turned out to be exactly correct: tomorrow the army of Israel would fall to the Philistines, and Saul and his sons would join Samuel among the dead (*v. 19*).

Although Samuel had died some time earlier (*1Sa 25:1*), here he was again—at least in the form of a spirit. He spoke as Samuel; he reacted as Samuel. He even expressed annoyance at having to return to speak with Saul (*1Sa 28:15*). While this incident does not give details about what it was like for Samuel in the afterlife, two things are clear. First, there is personally identifiable life that continues beyond the grave: Samuel was clearly Samuel. Second, that life is more desirable than the life on earth: Samuel did not want to come back. As to the differentiation between an afterlife of reward for Samuel and one of punishment for Saul, nothing is said.

THE GREATER SON OF DAVID
2 SAMUEL 7:12-16

After David had ascended to the throne of Israel, he was grieved to think that God would not allow David to be the one to build Him a stone Temple to replace the old portable Tabernacle. This task would be given to David's son. In a passage of beautiful double reference, God made a promise that would be true of both David's son Solomon and David's greater son Jesus. *"When your days are over and you rest with your fathers,"* God said, *"I will raise up your offspring to succeed you. . . . He is the one who will build a house for my Name, and I will establish the throne of his kingdom forever. I will be his father, and he will be my son"* (*2Sa 7:12-14*, see also **Heb 1:5**).

In examination of this text, it should be noted that David will "rest" with his fathers. Escape from endless toil and futile struggles will be one of the rewards of the afterlife (see **Rev 14:13**). More importantly, there is a clear messianic prophecy of an everlasting kingdom (*2Sa 7:13,16*), and it will be the kingdom of heaven (**Rev 5:13; 7:17**). He who reigns over this eternal kingdom is *"the Root and the Offspring of David"* (**Rev 22:16**).

CAN I BRING HIM
BACK AGAIN?
2 SAMUEL 12:23

David committed adultery with Bathsheba and arranged the death of her husband. A son was born from this illicit union, and to say the least, *"the thing David had done displeased the LORD"* (*2Sa 11:27*). Even after the child was born, David still had not come to grips with the enormity of his sin. Therefore, God sent Nathan the prophet to tell David the famous parable about a poor man and his little ewe lamb (*2Sa 12:1-4*). With David burning with anger against the rich man who had done the great wrong, Nathan said, *"You are the man!"* (*2Sa 12:7*). Among several penalties that David would suffer for his sins, the climax was that his infant son would die. Despite David's fervent pleas and desperate fasting, on the seventh day the child died.

The finality of death echoed in these words of David: *"While the child was still alive, I fasted and wept. . . . But now that he is dead, why should I fast? Can I bring him back again? I will go to him, but he will not return to me"* (*2Sa 12:23*). The passage from life to death was a one-way street, never to be reversed. In some rather vague sense David knew that he would join his son beyond the grave—with the son's identity still intact—but the son could not return to David.

ELIJAH RESURRECTS
A WIDOW'S SON
1 KINGS 17:17-23

Centuries pass. The kingdom divides, and unworthy kings sit on the throne—especially in the northern kingdom of Israel. In the days of Ahab and his wicked wife Jezebel, something happened that was unprecedented. The sorrowful passage of a widow's son from life to death was reversed! A son *did* come back from the dead!

In Zarephath lived a widow and her son, nearing starvation in days of famine. When she granted Elijah's request to give him food, the LORD graciously promised that she would not run out of flour and oil (*1Kgs 17:7-14*). But then, having been saved from starvation, some time later her son became ill and died. Elijah prayed to the LORD, *"O LORD my God, let this boy's life return to him!"* (*1Kgs 17:21*). God heard Elijah's desperate cry and gave life back to the boy. Carrying the child in his arms, Elijah proclaimed to the grieving mother, *"Look, your son is alive!"* (*1Kgs 17:23*).

Although Enoch had escaped death by going directly to heaven (*Gen 5:24*), no one in the history of the world had ever come back from the dead. In this monumental act God showed His power over death. This boy's resurrection was a preview of the fact that *"multitudes who sleep in the dust of the earth will awake,"* whether to everlasting life or everlasting contempt (*Dan 12:2*). It was also a preview of the resurrection of God's own Son, who would rise from the tomb as the firstfruits of all those who will rise from the dead (*1Cor 15:20*).

UP TO HEAVEN
IN A WHIRLWIND
2 KINGS 2:11

Elijah added another remarkable incident to the increasing body of knowledge about the afterlife. At the end of his prophetic career, when he was ready to hand over the leadership to his protégé Elisha, Elijah knew he was about to be taken from the earth. *"If you can see me when I am taken from you,"* said Elijah, then Elisha's request for a double portion of Elijah's spirit would be granted (*2Kgs 2:10*).

Suddenly, as they were talking, Elisha saw a chariot of fire and horses of fire appear. Apparently boarding this fiery conveyance, Elijah *"went up to heaven in a whirlwind"* (*2Kgs 2:11*). Other men went down to the grave at the end of their lives, but now Elijah had joined Enoch as another man who enjoyed a direct passage to heaven. In the final act of Elijah's life he proved that heaven is there, and it is accessible to mankind.

ELISHA RESURRECTS
A MOTHER'S SON
2 KINGS 4:20-37

In virtual repetition of the miracles of Elijah, Elisha provided an amazing quantity of oil for a woman in desperate straits (*2Kgs 4:1-7*) and brought the dead son of another woman back to life. The second woman was a well-to-do resident of Shunem who hosted Elisha from time to time in his travels. Elisha had prophesied the unlikely birth of her son (*2Kgs 4:11-17*) and later was summoned to the boy's unfortunate death (*2Kgs 4:18-22*). In a manner also reminiscent of his mentor, Elisha prayed to the LORD and stretched himself out upon the corpse. The body of the dead boy warmed; the boy sneezed and opened his eyes. Once again God had demonstrated that death is not final. He can and will give life to whomever He chooses (see *Jn 5:21*).

OPEN HIS EYES
SO HE MAY SEE
2 KINGS 6:17

When the king of Aram was at war with Israel, time and again Elisha alerted the king of Israel about the secret battle plans of the enemy. When the king of Aram was told that it was Elisha who kept revealing his secret plans, he sent an army with horses and chariots to surround the city where Elisha was and capture him (*2Kgs 6:8-14*). When the servant of Elisha went out early the next morning and saw the enemy forces, he cried out, *"Oh, my lord, what shall we do?"* Then Elisha prayed his famous prayer: *"O LORD, open his eyes so he may see"* (*2Kgs 6:17*). With eyes open to greater spiritual reality, the servant saw that the surrounding hills were full of horses and chariots of fire. The LORD of Hosts was ready to send His hosts to the defense of His prophet!

The lesson of this incident is that there is greater spiritual reality than meets the eye. There really are, as the song says, "angels all around." In a dimension of reality that normally goes unseen, there is an "invisible" God, a host of angels, and heaven—the place of God's eternal throne. In one sense, we already participate in this arena, since we have been raised with Christ and made to sit with Him in the heavenly realms (*Eph 2:6*; see also *Eph 1:3,20; 3:10; 6:12*).

THE MUSIC OF THE TEMPLE
1 CHRONICLES 25:6-7

God loves music. In the beginning the angelic chorus sang with joy (*Job 38:7*), and in the Temple trained musicians sang God's praise. Even before the Temple was built by his son Solomon, David already prepared men for using music in ministry in the house of God. These musicians accompanied the ministry of prophecy with harps, lyres, and cymbals (*1Chr 25:1-6*). In all there were 288 men who were *"trained and skilled in music for the LORD"* (*1Chr 25:7*). They were separated into 24 divisions, and cast lots to determine when each group would serve. (This arrangement of dividing Temple duties into 24 shifts was continued in the NT, as in the case of John the Baptist's father, who served in the priestly division of Abijah; see *Lk 1:5*.)

The music of the Temple was a clear foreshadowing of the music of heaven. John's Revelation repeatedly depicts the saints and angels in praise of God (*Rev 4:8; 5:9-13*). They sing a "new song" (*Rev 5:9; 14:3*) echoing the phrase of the OT that emphasizes how there will always be something more for which to praise God (see *Pss 33:3; 40:3; 96:1; 98:1; 144:9; 149:1; Isa 42:10*). Even the harps of the Temple era are mentioned repeatedly in the scenes of heaven (*Rev 4:8; 14:2; 15:2*).

God loves music. Mankind, created in the image of God, also loves music. In every generation and in every location where men have lived, there has always been some kind of music. Different societies may create different forms, but every society of the human race has music in its soul.

SUMMARY

Isolated incidents in the history of Israel give a foretaste of heaven. Samuel comes back from the dead as a spirit; David knows he will join his infant son in death. Elijah raises a dead boy and goes to heaven in a chariot of fire; Elisha raises a dead boy and opens dull eyes to the chariots of fire on God's hillsides. Trained musicians give a sampling of the music of heaven. Most important of all, God Himself promises an eternal kingdom to be ruled by David's greater Son. Even in the pages of simple history there are glimpses of heaven.

WHAT DO YOU SAY?

1. Why did God allow the witch of Endor to call up Samuel? Since he appeared as a spirit, does that mean that all God's people are spirits after death?

2. When God told David his son would build a Temple and rule a great kingdom, how do we know this refers to both Solomon and Jesus?

3. What do you think David imagined it would be like when he joined his baby in death?

4. Since God had Elijah and Elisha raise dead boys, why doesn't He do this more often?

5. Elisha prayed for his servant's eyes to be opened. What are the heavenly realities that we are presently unable to see?

6. What will the music of heaven be like?

7. Would it be a problem for you if heaven consisted only of singing praise to God?

CHAPTER FIVE

HEAVEN IN THE POETRY OF ISRAEL

PART ONE: *Job and Ecclesiastes*

I t is only natural that scenes of heaven should be found in the flights of biblical poetry. Where words are meant to speak to the soul even more than to the mind, the longings of the human heart for heaven become more predominant. God's ongoing revelation of the life to come takes more definite shape in His poetry, especially in *Job*, *Ecclesiastes*, and *Psalms*. The other three books of poetry, *Proverbs*, *Lamentations*, and *Song of Songs* have little to say about the afterlife. *Proverbs* is practical wisdom for the present life; *Lamentations* is a wailing lament for Jerusalem, which lay in ruins. *Song of Songs* is a description of romantic love, which may or may not have any role as a preview of Christ and His bride. Therefore, the current chapter will focus on *Job* and *Ecclesiastes* for their glimpses of heaven, and the following chapter will deal with the *Psalms*.

IN THE PRESENCE OF THE LORD
JOB 1:6-12; 2:1-7

The Book of *Job* is at least as old as Abraham, and probably older. It has no mention of the Law or the Tabernacle, no reference to Abraham or Moses. There was no priesthood through which Job approached God; he himself made burnt offerings in behalf of himself and his grown children (*Job 1:5*). Like the early patriarchs, he lived a long life, spanning a hundred and forty years (*Job 42:16*).

67

At some point very early in the history of mankind, therefore, a dramatic contest unfolded in heaven. One day the angels (literally, "the sons of God") came *"to present themselves before the* LORD, *and Satan also came with them"* (**Job 1:6-12**; see also **2:1-3**). At least six points about heaven can be made from this encounter. First, angels and Satan and God actually exist in a place that belongs to God. Second, heaven and earth exist simultaneously, for while Job lived his life on earth, a separate event took place in the presence of the LORD. Third, there is access between heaven and earth, because Satan reported that he had been *"roaming through the earth and going back and forth in it"* (**Job 1:7**). Fourth, there are real events that happen above and beyond the awareness of the human mind. Fifth, Satan opposes men; his very name is an everyday Hebrew word for "enemy" (as in **1Sa 29:4**, where "turn against us" is literally, "become a *satan* to us"). Sixth, God was pleased to bless Job with abundance—and even more at the end of the story.

In the life to come, we can anticipate with joy the fact that our great enemy will no longer be a threat. The devil will be thrown into a lake of burning sulfur, where he will be *"tormented day and night for ever and ever"* (**Rev 20:10**). And just as God rewarded Job for his patient faithfulness, so shall we be rewarded with many blessings. Job's riches do not begin to compare with our riches in heaven!

ASLEEP AND AT REST
JOB 3:13

Satan was permitted to do his worst, with one limitation: he could not kill Job. After Job lost his wealth, his children, his health, and the loving support of his wife, he was ready to die. *"Why did I not perish at birth,"* he lamented, *"and die as I came from the womb?"* (**Job 3:11**). If he were dead, he reasoned, he would be *"lying down in peace"*; he would be *"asleep and at rest"* (**Job 3:13**). Buried in the ground, he would be *"where the wicked cease from turmoil, and there the weary are at rest"* (**Job 3:17**).

Job's understanding of what happens in death did not show the truths revealed by God to later generations. Abraham, Moses, David, Elijah, Elisha—all showed greater knowledge of the life to come. But in his misery, Job could only think one thing: he wished he were dead. As far as he knew, death was simply a place where everything stopped. Kings would no longer have their palaces; captives and slaves would no longer have their masters. Death would be the great equalizer; but in their equality everyone would have nothing (*Job 3:14-19*).

With the life of Job, so early in the history of God's dealings with men, we take a step backward in the understanding of the afterlife. Even so, Job had it right on certain things: (1) you can't take it with you, and (2) after this life is over there will be rest. In regard to the first, we now understand that we won't need to take anything with us, for God will furnish us with blessings beyond imagination. In regard to the second, there will be rest (*Rev 14:13*), but there will also be rewarding service as we reign with God in glory (*Rev 22:3,5*).

IF ONLY THERE WERE SOMEONE TO ARBITRATE! JOB 9:33

Job was joined in his misery by three friends. At first they had the good sense to sit in silence for seven days (*Job 2:11-13*). Then, as Job began to cry out that he had done nothing to deserve all this, they began to refute him. In response to the accusations of Bildad, the second of his friends/opponents, Job lamented that God could not be confronted in court like a mere human. *"If only there were someone to arbitrate between us,"* Job said (*Job 9:33*).

Job recognized the impossibility of confronting God face to face. He also recognized the need for an arbitrator, or perhaps someone to speak in his behalf to God. In two later chapters there will be intriguing comments about this (*Job 16:19-21; 19:25-27*). Still later, Elihu will assure Job that an angel or mediator on his side would be a good thing for him—if he would just confess all his guilt (*Job 33:23-27*).

Today we live in the greater light of what the NT reveals. We know that we have more than an impartial arbitrator—we have a devoted mediator! Jesus is the mediator between God and man (*1Tm 2:5*), the mediator of a new and better covenant that brings forgiveness of sins and hope of heaven (*Heb 8:6; 9:15; 12:24*).

THE LAND OF GLOOM AND DEEP SHADOW JOB 10:21-22

Job's misery was so great and his despair was so deep that he wished he had never been born (*Job 10:19*). He longed for even one moment of relief before he went *"to the land of gloom and deep shadow, to the land of deepest night, of deep shadow and disorder, where even the light is like darkness"* (**Job 10:21-22**). Without the benefit of knowing later revelations, Job had a pessimistic view of the afterlife. He thought it would be a place of gloomy darkness—a land of disorder where chaos once again ruled supreme.

What is more, Job considered death to be the irreversible end of everything. As he said later in reply to Eliphaz, *"Only a few years will pass before I go on the journey of no return"* (**Job 16:22**). Without some ray of hope from God, why should Job think otherwise? He was only voicing a sentiment that in our own time is considered brave and sophisticated. As the famous twentieth-century philosopher Bertrand Russell said, "When I die I shall rot, and nothing of my ego will survive."

IF A MAN DIES, WILL HE LIVE AGAIN?
JOB 14:10-14

But Job was not totally pessimistic about death. At times he seemed to break through the despair of his pain. It is true that he said, *"Man lies down and does not rise; till the heavens are no more, men will not awake or be roused from their sleep"* (**Job 14:12**). But it is also true that after he said this, he immediately turned to another possibility: perhaps God could just hide him in the grave until His anger had passed and then resurrect him (*v. 13*). With this tantalizing possibility in mind, Job cried out with longing, *"If a man dies, will he live again?"* (*v. 14*). While this is not a clear statement affirming life after death, it is a strong hint in that direction. *"You will call,"* Job said to God, *"and I will answer you. You will long for the creature your hands have made"* (*v. 15*).

Many centuries later Augustine said, "Thou hast made us for Thyself, and our hearts are restless, till they rest in Thee" (*Confessions*, Book 1/1). It is the universal longing of mankind to "make peace" with the Creator, and it is often correctly assumed that the Creator desires fellowship with us. The yearnings of Job become the sacred birthright of the Christian.

MY ADVOCATE IS ON HIGH
JOB 16:19-21

At times Job allowed his optimism to break through. In a thrilling bit of insight into his future, Job said:

> Even now my witness is in heaven;
> > my advocate is on high.
> My intercessor is my friend
> > as I pour out tears to God;
> on behalf of a man he pleads with God
> > as a man pleads for his friend. (*Job 16:19-21*)

Job correctly perceived that he needed an intercessor who was a friend. He also correctly deduced that this advocate had to be able to plead Job's case "in heaven" and "on high." He had little evidence on which to base these conclusions, but he increasingly put his trust in God. For this reason the book of James praises Job, saying, *"You have heard of Job's perseverance and have seen what the Lord finally brought about. The Lord is full of compassion and mercy"* (*Jas 5:11*).

I KNOW THAT MY REDEEMER LIVES JOB 19:25-27

The high point of the book of Job comes in Job's second reply to Bildad. While his first response to this "friend" stated the need for *"someone to arbitrate"* (*Job 9:33*), his second response was a marvel of faith. These were the memorable words of Job:

> I know that my Redeemer lives,
> > and that in the end he will stand upon the earth.
> And after my skin has been destroyed,
> > yet in my flesh I will see God;
> I myself will see him
> > with my own eyes—I, and not another.
> > How my heart yearns within me! (*Job 19:25-27*)

With these words Job's hope in the midst of despair reached a remarkable climax. Truly this man *"spoke from God"* as he was *"carried along by the Holy Spirit"* (see *2Pet 1:21*), soaring to previously unreached heights of revelation. Nowhere else in the book is he given such insight. In spite of everything, Job knew that he had a Redeemer. This would be a "vindicator" who would secure justice for him, a "kinsman-redeemer" who would champion his cause (see *Ruth 4:14*). (In Proverbs' *Sayings of the Wise*, a later writer would recognize that God Himself is the Defender of the weak and fatherless; *Prov 23:11*.) Job even claimed a personal relationship by saying "my" Redeemer. Through the eyes of faith Job foresaw a time "in the end" when this

Redeemer would *"stand upon the earth,"* and even though Job's body had decayed, he would see Him. Job's confidence in a real resurrection was emphatic: *"in my flesh," "I myself," "with my own eyes," "I, and not another"* (**Job 19:26-27**). On that last great day the longing of Job's heart would be satisfied: *"I will see God"* (**v. 26**).

With the greater clarity of the NT, we have even greater assurance than Job's cry of faith. We know the name of our Redeemer (see **Rom 3:24; Gal 3:13; Eph 1:7; Heb 9:12; 1Pet 1:18**) and we know that when we see Him we are seeing God (see **John 14:9**). We not only have confidence that the dead in Christ shall rise (**1Cor 15:52; 1Th 4:16**), but that our bodies will be transformed into something far more glorious (**Php 3:21**). Like Job, how our hearts yearn within us until this is completed!

SIDE BY SIDE THEY LIE
IN THE DUST
JOB 21:23-26

Gripped by his misery and tormented by his friends, Job did not always sustain his lofty optimism. In answer to Zophar, who had earlier assured Job that he was guilty of even more than God could remember (**Job 11:6**), Job gave a sad assessment of human life. One man dies well nourished and in full vigor; another man dies destitute and deprived—but *"side by side they lie in the dust, and worms cover them both"* (**Job 21:26**).

While generations of men go to the grave, God is in the heavens above. But where is He when someone needs Him? Job gave this despairing answer: *"Thick clouds veil him, so he does not see us as he goes about in the vaulted heavens"* (**Job 22:14**). Even though Job had earlier expressed hope for a future resurrection and future justice, he had little to hope for on earth.

THE DEAD ARE
IN DEEP ANGUISH
JOB 26:5

One final passage will show the extent of Job's misery and despair. He had earlier spoken of *"the land of gloom and deep shadow"* (**Job 10:21**), and now finally he concluded what the state of the dead must be. *"The dead are in deep anguish,"* he said (**Job 26:5**). Their lives were over; their hopes were frustrated.

What is of special interest in this verse is the word Job used for "the dead." This is its first appearance in Scripture. Literally, "the dead" in this text could be translated as "the shades" (NRSV) or "the departed spirits" (NASB). The idea was that the existence beyond the grave was dark, shadowy, unreal. Other uses of this word include the following (substituting the translation "shades" for emphasis): *"Do you show your wonders to the dead? Do the **shades** rise up and praise you?"* (*Ps 88:10*). *"A man who strays from the path of understanding comes to rest in the company of the **shades**"* (*Prov 21:16*). *"**Sheol** below is all astir to meet you at your coming; it rouses the **shades** to greet you"* (*Isa 14:9*). *"They are now dead, they live no more; those **shades** do not rise"* (*Isa 26:14*).

These OT passages serve as a reminder that God's revealed truths about life after death were not equally scattered throughout the Bible. Especially in the earlier centuries even men of faith described death as dark and ghastly. We who live in the light of greater revelation, however, have no excuse for thinking that the dead exist only as shadowy spirits, as *shades.*

EVERYTHING IS MEANINGLESS ECCLESIASTES 1:2-14

Most of *Ecclesiastes* is just as dreary as *Job* in its view of death. What must be understood, however, is the writer's self-imposed restriction: he set out to examine the meaning and purpose of *"all that is done under heaven,"* which is equivalent to *"all things that are done under the sun"* (*Ecc 1:13-14*). By deliberately factoring life after death out of the equation, he necessarily came up with a negative assessment of life's meaning. Generations come and generations go, but nothing really changes (*v. 4*). The men of old are not remembered, and the people who are yet to come will not be remembered by those who follow them (*v. 11*). Men live, they die, they are forgotten.

Nothing a man acquires in his life will do him any good when he dies. Even wisdom is meaningless, for *"like the fool, the wise man too must die!"* (*Ecc 2:16*). All that a man has gained must be left to someone else—someone who did not work for it! (*Ecc 2:21*). Even Jesus would have agreed that for the man who ignores God, this assessment is true. In Jesus' parable about a rich man, God says to the man,

"You fool! This very night your life will be demanded from you. Then who will get what you have prepared for yourself?" (**Lk 12:20**).

ETERNITY IN THE HEARTS OF MEN ECCLESIASTES 3:11

Perhaps the most positive clue about heaven in Ecclesiastes is found in the third chapter. After listing all the "times" of life (e.g., "a time to be born and a time to die"), the Teacher wrote, *"He has made everything beautiful in its time. He has also set eternity in the hearts of men; yet they cannot fathom what God has done from beginning to end"* (**Ecc 3:11**).

While this verse stops well short of promising heaven, it does recognize the reason for the universal longing in the human heart. We all long for God; we all have a God-shaped void in our souls. Until we rest with God, we will have no final peace. And this is all true because God has *"set eternity in the hearts of men,"* but has not yet given them the ability to fathom it.

MAN'S FATE IS LIKE THE ANIMALS ECCLESIASTES 3:19-21

If life "under heaven" is all there is, then careful observation can come up with only one conclusion—a conclusion held by certain people even today—that man is really no better off than an animal. The Teacher wrote:

> Man's fate is like that of the animals; the same fate awaits them both: As one dies, so dies the other. All have the same breath; man has no advantage over the animal. Everything is meaningless. All go to the same place; all come from dust, and to dust all return. Who knows if the spirit of man rises upward and if the spirit of the animal goes down into the earth? (**Ecc 3:19-21**)

For almost the entire book of *Ecclesiastes* it was the unwavering judgment of the Teacher that death ends everything. He wrote, *"The dead know nothing; they have no further reward, and even the memory of them is forgotten"* (**Ecc 9:5**).

"Dust to dust and ashes to ashes" might have satisfied the Teacher as a conclusion for the meaning of life, but it will not do for the Christian.

While our bodies will decay and return to the dust from which they were made (*Gen 3:19*), we have the promise that our bodies will be raised (*1Cor 15:52; 1Th 4:16*) and glorified (*Php 3:21*). Man is not on the same level as the animals; man is made in the image of God!

THE SPIRIT RETURNS TO GOD
ECCLESIASTES 12:7

Finally, in a brief reversal of everything he had said about death, the Teacher gave one encouraging word. *"The dust returns to the ground it came from,"* he said, *"and the spirit returns to God who gave it"* (*Ecc 12:7*). This, at last, was his answer to his own question, *"Who knows?"* (*Ecc 3:21*). Viewing life and death from his perspective "under the sun," he could observe that the spirit leaves the body and could surmise that it returns to God.

But without God's own revealed truth, this weak conclusion fails to satisfy. Does the spirit return to God as a cup of water returns to the ocean? Is the spirit to be recycled? Does the individual existence of a person's spirit continue? The Teacher does not say. As an observer of life "under heaven," he cannot know.

SUMMARY

The view of the life to come in *Job* and *Ecclesiastes* is almost completely negative. Job wrote from a very early point in the unfolding of God's revelation, and he wrote in deep anguish and despair. The Teacher wrote with self-imposed limitations, reaching only such conclusions as could be reached while excluding heaven. Therefore both saw death as a gloomy end and the possible existence after death as only a *shade* or a spirit. In this swampland of despair, however, there suddenly arose a mountain peak of exultation for Job: *"I know that my Redeemer lives. . . . In my flesh I will see God!"*

WHAT DO YOU SAY?

1. Why is poetry such a good vehicle for conveying information about heaven?

2. Why is the Book of *Job* thought to narrate a very early time in human history?

3. What do we learn about heaven from the meeting of God, the angels, and Satan?

4. What was Job's overall view of what happens after death? What was his greatest moment of inspiration?

5. What was the Teacher's self-limitation in writing *Ecclesiastes*? What people today labor under the same self-limitation?

6. Why did the Teacher say everything is meaningless? Are there people today who also think life has no meaning? What if they are right?

7. What was the Teacher's final conclusion about what happens at death? Is his verdict the Bible's final word on the subject?

CHAPTER SIX

HEAVEN IN THE POETRY OF ISRAEL

PART TWO: *The Psalms*

D avid was a man after God's own heart (*1Sa 13:14*), and David was a singer. He wrote music, played music, sang music. In view of the fact that the Book of *Psalms* is one of the largest books in the Bible, God must love music! Most of the Psalms were written either by David or by various of his appointed musicians. The subject of heaven rises to a new level of intensity in the Psalms, as these writers pour out their hearts in their longing to be with God.

Unlike the history books of Scripture, and unlike *Job* and *Ecclesiastes*, there is no chronological arrangement or sequence to the Psalms. For this reason, a study of what the Psalms say about heaven does not need to begin with *Psalm 1* and proceed onward to the end. It will be more useful to arrange the information from the various Psalms into six headings that seem logical for this particular topic. Within each section, the Psalms will be considered in subgroups according to their author.

The authorship of individual Psalms cannot be proved or disproved. There is an ancient tradition among both Jews and Christians to accept the names cited in the titles of the Psalms, and that is what this book will follow. In any case, the ultimate author of each Psalm is not the human penman, but the Holy Spirit of God. (On this, see especially **Hebrews 3:7**, "as the Holy Spirit says," and **Hebrews 4:7**, "God . . . spoke through David," both in reference to quoting **Psalm 95**. See also **2 Timothy 3:16** and **2 Peter 1:20-21**.

HEAVEN: THE THRONE OF THE ETERNAL GOD

PSALM 90, A PSALM OF MOSES

Moses, the man of God, showed the stark contrast between the brevity of our lives and the eternality of God. The span of our lives is a mere seventy or eighty years, and when those years have quickly passed, then we will *"fly away"* (*v. 10*). Our lives come to an end and we fall asleep (*v. 5*), as our bodies return to the dust (*v. 3*).

There is little hope of heaven expressed in this early psalm. But Moses did express a strong faith in an enduring God as he said, *"From everlasting to everlasting you are God"* (*v. 2*). God is not a prisoner of time in the sense that humans are, for He is ageless. *"A thousand years in your sight are like a day that has just gone by"* (*v. 4*). He sits in His heaven observing each day of the affairs of earth, as the generations of men come and go.

But God is not a mere passive observer. Moses, of all people, knew that God is involved in the lives of His people. So Moses taught Israel to sing this song as they cried out to the eternal God. All too aware of their own insignificance (*v. 12*), they were to make their plea to the Ever Living One who could make them *"sing for joy and be glad"* all their days (*v. 14*).

PSALM 20, A PSALM OF DAVID

David wrote this psalm as a prayer for the people to sing for their king before he led the troops into battle. Their expectation of victory was based on the assurance that God would answer them from heaven in their time of distress. *"Now I know,"* David wrote, *"that the LORD saves his anointed; he answers him from his holy heaven with the saving power of his right hand"* (**v. 6**). People who did not know God would trust in their chariots and horses, but the king and the people of Israel trusted *"in the name of the LORD our God"* (**v. 7**).

These words affirm several things at once about God and heaven. First, heaven is a holy place that is separate and removed from the earth. Second, it is the place from which God watches, hears, and answers His people. Third, it is associated with power—a divine power that is available to those who trust in God.

PSALM 41, A PSALM OF DAVID

Like the psalm of Moses discussed previously, this psalm of David emphasizes the eternal nature of the God of heaven. *"Praise be to the LORD, the God of Israel,"* he wrote, *"from everlasting to everlasting"* (**v. 13**). The everlasting God sits enthroned as the holy one of Israel (see **Ps 22:3**), and therefore the readers of the Psalms increasingly understand that the everlasting God dwells in an everlasting heaven.

PSALM 72, A PSALM OF DAVID

King David was inspired to see into the future when another King would rule over God's people. The coming Messiah would rule *"from sea to sea and from the River to the ends of the earth"* (**v. 8**). Although David's son Solomon ruled over a large kingdom, its borders did not come close to fulfilling this description. Furthermore, none of the later kings of Judah ruled even half the territory of Solomon.

In addition to ruling such an extensive territory, this King would receive honor from all other kingdoms of the earth. Therefore David declared, *"All the kings will bow down to him and all nations will serve him"* (**v. 11**, see also **Ps 2:7-9**). In view of such promises as these, it is not surprising that the Jewish people in the days of Jesus had such expectations of a Messiah who would rule an earthly kingdom. (See **Jn 6:15**, where the people intended to force Jesus to be a king, and **Acts 1:6**, where the disciples still expected Jesus to restore the kingdom to Israel.)

But the fulfillment of the promises of a ruler over all kings and all the earth will be realized only in the new heaven and the new earth. The kings of the earth will be defeated by the armies of heaven (**Rev**

18:9; 19:15), and every nation will bow at the feet of Jesus (*Php 2:10*). Only in eternity—and throughout all eternity—will David's prayer and plea finally come true: *"Praise be to his glorious name forever; may the whole earth be filled with his glory"* (*v. 19*).

PSALM 47, A PSALM OF THE SONS OF KORAH

The "sons of Korah" are cited in the titles of eleven or twelve of the Psalms. (These are *Psalms 42–49, 84–85*, and *87–88*. While *Psalm 43* has no title, it is combined with *Psalm 42* as one psalm in many Hebrews manuscripts.) Korah is named among the Levites who served in the Temple at the request of King David (*1Chr 6:22*).

Psalm 47 is a beautiful picture of God as *"the LORD Most High, the great King over all the earth"* (*v. 2*). Amid the shouts of joy and the sound of trumpets, *"God has ascended"* (*v. 5*). The earthly representation of this took place at the Tabernacle, where the glory of God dwelt (see *Pss 11:4; 68:17,24*), but this was only a shadow of the reality. God *"reigns over the nations"* and is seated *"on his holy throne"* (*v. 8*). There the *"nobles of the nations"* will assemble *"as the people of the God of Abraham,"* a scene which begins in the church (*Rom 4:12,16-18; Gal 3:29*) and finds it ultimate fulfillment in heaven (*Rev 7:9-10*).

PSALM 33, AN ANONYMOUS PSALM

Book I of the Psalms (*Pss 1–41*) has only four psalms that do not ascribe an author in their titles. *Psalm 33* gives a beautiful tribute to the power and eternality of the God of heaven: *"By the word of the LORD were the heavens made, their starry host by the breath of his mouth"* (*v. 6*). He overrules the plans of the nations, *"But the plans of the LORD stand firm forever, the purposes of his heart through all generations"* (*v. 11*). Once more, God is seen as the Creator who is above and beyond the mere confines of the earth, the Ruler who has final authority over what happens here. Men may plot and scheme during their brief lives, but His plans stand firm *forever*.

PSALM 113, AN ANONYMOUS PSALM

One more anonymous psalm will be examined that extols God as the ruler above all nations. He is *"exalted over all the nations"* and His glory is *"above the heavens"* (*v. 4*). Most significantly, this psalm depicts God as *"the One who sits enthroned on high, who stoops down to look on the heavens and the earth"* (**vv. 5-6**, see also **Ps 2:4**). Without attempting to locate the throne of God in any physical site, the writer clearly saw God's throne as removed above and separated from the physical universe. To interact with history God must *stoop down* into the lives of men.

The united testimony of the Psalms, then, is that God is the Creator of the earth and the heavens—both in the sense of "heaven" as the sky and as His eternal dwelling place. From His lofty throne in heaven, God looks down on the affairs of men and puts His own plans into effect. He is greater than all the kings of the earth and deserves their praise. One day, in the culmination of history in the afterlife, the nations will acknowledge the glory of God and give Him praise.

HEAVEN: THE PURPOSE OF MAN

PSALM 2, A PSALM OF DAVID

David extolled God as the Creator of the starry heavens (*v. 3*), who has set His glory above the heavens (*v. 1*). In view of such majesty, what is puny and insignificant man in His sight? (*v. 4*). The answer to this question echoes all the way back to **Genesis 1:26**. God made man to be *"ruler over the works"* of God's hands; He *"put everything under his feet"* (*v. 6*). Beasts of the field, birds of the air, fish of the sea—all other created things were to be subject to men.

But as the writer of Hebrews observed, *"Yet at present we do not see everything subject to him"* (**Heb 2:8**). At first glance, therefore, it would seem that the plan of God for the human race had failed. In two great steps, however, God would rectify this apparent failure. First, God would send His Son to earth to be the perfect Man. In faithful obedience to the point of death, Jesus would fulfill all God's expectations for humans and would be crowned with glory and honor (**Heb 2:9**). Second, Jesus would *"bring many sons to glory"* (**Heb 2:10**), and in heaven they will ultimately be all that God intended them to be in the first place. Just as God said in the beginning, in their final state *"they will reign for ever and ever"* (**Rev 22:5**). Man can never achieve his ultimate purpose this side of heaven.

PSALM 40, A PSALM OF DAVID

David rejoiced that God had rescued him from the slimy pit, from mud and mire, and set his feet on a rock. By such an act of deliverance, God gave him reason to sing. As David said, *"He put a new song in my mouth, a hymn of praise to our God"* (*v. 3*). The idea underlying the "new song" is that there has been yet another instance of God's saving power, yet another incident to be put into words of praise. The emphasis is not that there are new lyrics or a new tune for people to learn; rather, the emphasis is that God continues to provide additional reasons to praise Him.

The "new song" is always found in the context of God's saving acts. The first reference is in the anonymous *33ʳᵈ Psalm (v. 3)*; additional references to singing a "new song" are found in *Psalms 96:1; 98:1; 144:9-10; 149:1*. Likewise Isaiah told the people to sing a new song in praise of God's deliverance *(42:10)*.

The ultimate "new songs" will be sung in heaven. As in the *Psalms* and *Isaiah*, these new songs will have two main characteristics. First, they are in response to God's acts of deliverance and provision. Second, they have new subject matter as their content each time because God provides endless reasons for praising Him. One of the reasons for our very existence in heaven will be to sing "new songs" in worship of our God.

PSALMS 96 & 98,
ANONYMOUS PSALMS

Two anonymous psalms begin with the same words: *"Sing to the LORD a new song"* (*Ps 96:1; 98:1*). (Note that while *Psalm 96* does not list an author, *1 Chronicles 16:7,13-33* credits the lines to David.) Clearly identified in each psalm is the fact that a "new song" is to be sung in response to God's mighty acts of deliverance. *Psalm 96* exhorts *"all the earth"* to sing such a song, to *"proclaim his salvation"* and *"his marvelous deeds among all peoples"* (*vv. 2,3*). The psalm goes on to portray the whole earth trembling before Him (*v. 9*) as He comes to judge the world in righteousness (*v. 13*). It is a clear picture of the God of heaven reigning over His creation.

Psalm 98 repeats the call for a "new song" in praise of God. The song is a natural response to the fact that He *"has done great things"*; His holy arm has *"worked salvation"* (*v. 2*). He has been faithful to His covenant with Israel (*v. 3*), and He will come to *"judge the world in righteousness"* (*v. 9*).

At no point in human history, however, has all the earth joined in praise of the Creator. The rivers have not clapped their hands; the mountains have not sung together for joy (*v. 8*). It will happen in the future, when God *"comes to judge the earth"* (*v. 9*). All creation will be freed from its groaning (*Rom 8:22*); all those who have received the right to be called children of God (*John 1:12*) will sing—just as the two psalms command.

Psalms 148 & 150,
Anonymous Psalms

Two psalms at the end of the Psalter give final glimpses of the glory of God on His throne and the duty of men to praise Him. In a grand panorama of the universe, *Psalm 148* calls for the angels and the heavenly hosts to *"praise the LORD from the heavens"* (*vv. 1-2*). The sun, moon, and stars are to praise Him from their place in the skies (*vv. 3-4*). From the earth all creatures are to praise Him from the land, air, or water where they live (*vv. 7-10*). Kings of the earth and all mankind are to praise Him, acknowledging His *"splendor is above the earth and the heavens"* (*vv. 11-13*).

"Praise the Lord" is all one word in the original Hebrew. It is transliterated in various ways into English. It can be either *Hallelujah* or *Alleluia* or *Hallelu Yah*. The first three syllables are a command to praise; the last syllable is an abbreviation of the divine name. That syllable is the *Jeh* of Jehovah or the *Yah* of Yahweh. (The four consonants of the name were Y or J, H, W or V, H). Since the divine name was not to be pronounced by the people, today we do not know which vowels to put with the Hebrew consonants or how the resulting form should be pronounced.

Psalm 150 calls for the praise of God *"in his sanctuary"* and *"in his mighty heavens"* (*v. 1*). *"Everything that has breath"* is to praise Him for "his acts of power" and "his surpassing greatness" (**vv. 2,6**). Once again, it must be noted that this summons to worship has been honored only partially and imperfectly in all human history. The purpose and privilege of God's children will be to offer Him this praise in the hereafter.

HEAVEN: ESCAPE FROM THE GRAVE

PSALM 6, A PSALM OF DAVID

David acknowledged the universal plight of mortals: they die. As he called out in anguish to the LORD, he asked to be saved from death. He did not want to lose his fellowship with God, but as far as David knew, *"No one remembers you when he is dead. Who praises you from the grave?"* (**v. 5**).

In his despair David did not say anything in this psalm about heaven as an escape from the grave. He did, however, lay out in graphic terms the human predicament. He did not want to lose connection with God; nor did he want to lose the opportunity to praise Him. As other psalms will foresee, the solution for this plight will be found in heaven.

PSALM 16, A PSALM OF DAVID

David found a much more positive tone for this psalm as he recounted his blessings from God and said, *"Therefore my heart is glad"* (**v. 9**). In a prophetic glimpse of the future, David further said, *"My body also will rest secure, because you will not abandon me to the grave [**sheol**], nor will you let your Holy One see decay"* (**vv. 9-10**).

While these words of David could be interpreted as merely a temporary rescue from dying, two considerations point us in the direction of heaven. First, the psalm concludes with the expectation of *"eternal pleasures at your right hand"* (**v. 11**). Second, the psalm is quoted by both Peter and Paul in the book of *Acts* as a prophecy fulfilled in the resurrection of Jesus, the Son of David (see *Acts 2:25-32; 13:34-37*). Although men must go to the grave where their bodies will decay, that is not the end of the story. God will not leave them there. Resurrection from the dead and a home in heaven await those who have accepted salvation in Jesus, who was the firstfruits of those who will rise from the dead (*1Cor 15:20,23*).

PSALM 22, A PSALM OF DAVID

David wrote this psalm as a prayer of anguish. He was surrounded by enemies on all sides (*v. 12*); he felt his life draining from him (*v. 13*). To make matters worse, people mocked him for trusting in God to rescue him (*v. 8*). But even in his distress, David still knew that dominion belongs to the LORD (*v. 28*) and that all the families of the earth will one day bow down to Him (*v. 27*). In the meantime, however, men *"who cannot keep themselves alive"* will inevitably die and *"go down to the dust"* (*v. 29*). At this point, escape from the grave seems impossible despite David's earnest cry in behalf of the people who seek God, *"May your hearts live forever!"* (*v. 26*).

But this psalm has remarkable foreshadowings of the cross and the victory over the grave won by Jesus Christ. The opening words, *"My God, my God, why have you forsaken me?"* are the very words uttered at Calvary (*v. 1*; see *Mt 27:46*). *Verse seven* has mocking insults from people who shake their heads (see *Mt 27:41*), and *verse eight* predicts the exact taunting words of the Temple authorities (see *Mt 27:43*). *Verse fifteen* is a vivid description of Jesus' intense thirst as He was dying (see *Jn 19:28*). *Verse sixteen* anticipates the Roman crucifixion a thousand years ahead of time, with the words, *"They have pierced my hands and feet"* (see *Mt 27:35; Jn 20:25*). There is even a prophecy that the enemies of the Anointed One would *"divide my garments among them and cast lots for my clothing"* (*v. 18*; see *Jn 19:23-24*). In ways unforeseen by David, therefore, this psalm contains great hope for escape from the grave. It is a stunningly accurate portrayal of the cross.

PSALMS 49 & 88,
PSALMS OF THE SONS OF KORAH

As noted previously, the sons of Korah were Levites who served in the Temple at the request of King David (*1Chr 6:22*). In *Psalms 49 and 88* they voiced confidence in God as man's only hope for escape from the grave. Taking *Psalm 88* first, we can read their deep frustration with the tomb as man's ultimate destiny. *"Is your love declared in the grave,"* they asked, *"your faithfulness in Destruction [**abaddon**]?"* (*v. 11*). Since their vocation and their very lives were centered on praising God, how could they be content to be silenced by the grave?

But in *Psalm 49* they provided a more complete answer for this problem. They acknowledged that both the wise and the foolish die alike (*v. 10*) and *"their tombs will remain their houses forever"* (*v. 11*). Men who trust in themselves are like sheep that *"are destined for the grave, and death will feed on them"* (*v. 14*). Even the rich man *"will take nothing with him when he dies"* (*v. 17*). These ancient singers realized that some kind of ransom was necessary to rescue men from this fate, but they also realized the difficulty of their plight.

> No man can redeem the life of another
>   or give to God a ransom for him—
> the ransom for a life is costly,
>   no payment is ever enough—
> that he should live on forever
>   and not see decay. (*vv. 7-9*)

But the sons of Korah knew that God has the answer. Although no man could pay the ransom, *"God will redeem my life from the grave; he will surely take me to himself"* (*v. 15*). The costly ransom would be paid by Jesus (see **Mk 10:45** and **1Pet 1:18-19**). With that divine ransom and redemption, men will indeed *"live on forever and not see decay."*

HEAVEN: MAN'S DEEPEST LONGING

PSALM 27, A PSALM OF DAVID

No man is complete unless he knows God. Better than virtually any other man, David showed an intense longing for the presence of God. This presence was to be found more immediately at the Temple in Jerusalem, but more completely at the throne room of heaven. These two ideas are inseparably intertwined in David's psalms.

Psalm 27 declares total confidence in the LORD's ability to protect David from all enemies. With God on his side, David could confidently say, *"Whom shall I fear?"* (*v. 1*). But even though God continued to provide security for him, David had one final request:

> One thing I ask of the LORD,
>   this is what I seek:
> that I may dwell in the house of the LORD
>   all the days of my life,
> to gaze upon the beauty of the LORD
>   and to seek him in his temple. (*v. 4*)

The immediate interpretation of this verse points to the Tabernacle, where the ark of God still awaited its permanent home to be built later by Solomon. David loved to go to this physical site to feel close to God and to be protected by Him (*v. 5*). The ultimate interpretation of David's yearning, however, will be found only in heaven. There the plea of his heart, *"Seek his face!"* (*v. 8*) will finally be granted.

PSALMS 61 & 63, PSALMS OF DAVID

David knew that he needed the protection that comes from being with God. He also sensed that there is an eternal element involved in this as he said, *"I long to dwell in your tent forever and take refuge in the shelter of your wings"* (*Ps 61:4*). God's tent, of course, was the Tabernacle; however, to dwell in it "forever" draws our eyes upward to God's eternal abode in heaven. This is further developed when David prayed that as Israel's king he might *"be enthroned in God's presence forever"* (*v. 7*).

In a similar psalm David voiced his passionate desire to be with God. He said, *"O God, you are my God, earnestly I seek you; my soul thirsts for you, my body longs for you"* (*Ps 63:1*). For the present, David could only approach God in the tent sanctuary (*v. 2*), but that is not the final answer to a longing as great as David's. The earthly sanctuary is a glimpse of the glory to come in the afterlife.

PSALM 139, A PSALM OF DAVID

This beloved psalm portrays the God of heaven as an all-seeing, all-knowing God. He perceives David's thoughts *"from afar"* and knows David's words before they are even formed on his tongue (*vv. 2,4*). David also portrayed God as everywhere present, saying, *"If I go up to the heavens, you are there; if I make my bed in the depths [**sheol**], you are there"* (*v. 8*).

David yearned to have fellowship with the God who "knit" him together in his mother's womb (*v. 13*), and knew all the days of his life (*v. 16*). His deep longing for companionship with his Maker pointed his thoughts forward to the eternal:

> Search me, O God, and know my heart;
>> test me and know my anxious thoughts.
> See if there is any offensive way in me,
>> and lead me in the way everlasting. (*vv. 23-24*)

PSALM 42, A PSALM
OF THE SONS OF KORAH

The sons of Korah (see *1Chr 6:22*) also knew the deep longing for the presence of God. Especially in times of trouble, taunted by their enemies (*vv. 3,10*), the people of Israel could hear the Temple musicians set their inner feelings to music:

> As the deer pants for streams of water,
>   so my soul pants for you, O God.
> My soul thirsts for God, for the living God.
>   When can I go and meet with God? *(vv. 1-2)*

In the immediate foreground this meeting with God would happen whenever the Israelites joined *"the multitude, leading the procession to the house of God"* (*v. 4*). In a more distant setting, the kind of meeting with God that they really want will only happen in the afterlife. "When can I go and meet with God?" In heaven!

PSALM 73, A PSALM OF ASAPH

Asaph is named among the men that David put in charge of the music in the house of the LORD after the ark came to rest there (see *1Chr 6:31,39*). *Psalms 73–83* carry the name Asaph in their titles. As leader of one of the Tabernacle choirs Asaph penned one of the most beautiful and meaningful passages in all the Book of *Psalms*. Asaph first admitted that he had nearly lost his foothold when he saw the prosperity of the wicked (*Ps 73:3*). But when he entered the sanctuary of God, he understood their final destiny (*v. 17*). Back on solid spiritual ground, he prayed to God, *"You guide me with your counsel, and afterward you will take me into glory"* (*v. 24*). Then, as Asaph considered that final glory he exclaimed, *"Whom have I in heaven but you? And earth has nothing I desire besides you"* (*v. 23*).

People naturally look forward to being reunited with family and friends in heaven, just as David did when his infant son died (*2Sa 12:23*). People also look forward to the splendor and riches of the heavenly city. But this verse is a beautiful reminder of the real treasure of heaven—God Himself! Every other joy and blessing in that eternal land will pale into insignificance when we meet God.

HEAVEN: SPECIFIC PROMISES

PSALM 37, A PSALM OF DAVID

Scattered throughout the psalms are a number of specific promises about the world to come. They appear in prophetic form, with a certain degree of poetic metaphor. Even so, some of these promises are quite specific, especially when understood in the fuller light of what we know from the NT.

In *Psalm 37* David stated his complete trust in the goodness of God as he said, *"Delight yourself in the LORD and he will give you the desires of your heart"* (*v. 4*). What God will provide His people is then expressed in the form of an inheritance. Those who put their hope in the LORD, whom the LORD blesses, *"will inherit the land"* (*vv. 9,22*). In words foreshadowing the Beatitudes, David added, *"The meek will inherit the land and enjoy great peace"* (*v. 11*). (As the context of the Beatitudes clearly shows, this is not speaking just of some real estate in the state of Israel.) In words more clearly emphasizing the eternal nature of this land David said, *"The days of the blameless are known to the LORD, and their inheritance will endure forever"* (*v. 18*). Finally, there is this promise: *"The righteous will inherit the land and dwell in it forever"* (*v. 29*).

PSALM 69, A PSALM OF DAVID

David was aware of the "book of life" that was mentioned by Moses in *Exodus 32:32* and will play a prominent role in John's Revelation (see *Rev 3:5; 13:8; 17:8; 20:15; 21:27*). While he did not elaborate on the exact nature of this book, he was clear about the fact that the wicked have no place in it. *"May they be blotted out of the book of life,"* David said, *"and not listed with the righteous"* (*69:28*).

These words make two specific predictions about heaven. First, there is a book that records the names of the righteous who will be there. Second, the wicked will not have any place in heaven.

PSALM 95, A PSALM OF DAVID

(While not ascribed to David in the title, *Psalm 95* is credited to David in *Hebrews 4:7*, as well as to the Holy Spirit in *Hebrews 3:7*.) The message of this psalm is for the people of God to take advantage of God's invitation while it is still open. *"Today,"* David wrote, *"if you hear his voice, do not harden your hearts"* as the Israelites did in the wilderness (*95:7*). Because their hearts went astray from God, He said, *"So I declared on oath in my anger, 'They shall never enter my rest'"* (*v. 11*).

The promised rest that the Israelites failed to enter was not just the Promised Land. Centuries later, even when they were already living there, the invitation was still open and the warning still stood. Even in the time of the NT, the promised "rest" was not yet attained (see *Heb 4:7-11*). When God offers His rest, where His people will rest from their labors (*Rev 14:13*), it is a specific promise of heaven.

PSALM 46, A PSALM
OF THE SONS OF KORAH

A final specific promise about heaven is found in *Psalm 46*, another psalm of the sons of Korah. They sang of a remarkable vision, one that was impossible for the geography of the mountain citadel, Jerusalem. *"There is a river,"* they wrote, *"whose streams make glad the city of God, the holy place where the Most High dwells"* (*v. 4*).

Most great cities of history were built on the banks of a river, so that they would have a ready source of water. Jerusalem, however, on its lofty heights, had to rely on cisterns and nearby springs. In this prophetic imagery, however, the city where God dwells will be blessed with a river! This image looks back to the river in the Garden of Eden (*Gen 2:10*) and looks ahead to the heavenly river that flows from the throne of God (*Rev 22:1*). This *"river of the water of life"* will water the *"tree of life"* and *"make glad the city of God."*

HEAVEN:
ASSURANCE OF *HESED*

The Hebrew language has a special word that describes the "unfailing love," "lovingkindness," or "mercy" of God. The word is *hesed* (pronounced HESS-ed). In addition to the basic idea of love and mercy, the word also carries the connotation of loyalty. *Hesed* describes God acting with love, out of loyalty to His covenant. The word is found 134 times in the book of *Psalms*, with 54 of the uses written by David. In the context of the afterlife, *hesed* is our assurance that God will keep His promises and will mercifully give us entrance into heaven.

PSALM 23, A PSALM OF DAVID

This favorite psalm is a good example of how Scripture imagery can refer to both a present reality and a future promise. In his shepherd's psalm, David described how he could feel safe even when he walked *"through the valley of the shadow of death"* (*v. 4*). Then he concluded with a boast of confidence in the LORD: *"Surely goodness and love [**hesed**] will follow me all the days of my life, and I will dwell in the house of the LORD forever"* (*v. 6*).

In its immediate context this psalm can be understood as David's trust that God would keep him from dying prematurely, and that he would continue to worship God at the Tabernacle as long as he lived. In the larger context, especially as Christians read this psalm in the light of Jesus as the Good Shepherd (*Jn 10:11-14*), a view of a life beyond the grave is inescapable. The valley of death becomes a portal to heaven, where we will dwell with God in His home forever.

Further, we must not lose sight of the key word *hesed* (NIV "love," or KJV "mercy"). It is this "covenant loyalty" of God that is the basis of our hope of heaven. It is this "lovingkindness" that extends heaven as a gift. All people who are loyal to God and His covenant in Christ can be assured that "goodness and mercy" *will* follow them through the days of this life and into the eternity of heaven.

These are only some of David's verses about God's *hesed*:

Ps 5:7–"But I, by your great **mercy** will come into your house"

Ps 6:4–"Save me because of your **unfailing love**."

Ps 13:5–"I trust in your **unfailing love**; my heart rejoices in your salvation."

Ps 18:50–"He shows **unfailing kindness** to his anointed, to David and his descendants forever."

Ps 36:5–"Your **love**, O LORD, reaches to the heavens."

Ps 51:1–"Have mercy on me, O God, according to your **unfailing love**, according to your great compassion blot our my transgression."

Ps 52:8–"I trust in God's **unfailing love** for ever and ever."

Ps 57:3–"He sends from heaven and saves me. . . . God sends his **love** and faithfulness."

Ps 57:10–"For great is your **love**, reaching to the heavens."

PSALMS 100 AND 136, ANONYMOUS PSALMS

When the armies of Judah marched out to face the armies of the Moabites and the Ammonites, King Jehoshaphat appointed men to sing to the LORD and placed them at the head of the army. They praised God for *"the splendor of His holiness"* and sang as they marched, *"Give thanks to the LORD, for his love [**hesed**] endures forever"* (*2Chr 20:21*). This would perhaps strike some as an unusual battle tactic, but not the children of God who remembered Jericho.

The anonymous author of *Psalm 100* joined this chorus by writing, *"For the LORD is good and his love [**hesed**] endures forever; his faithfulness through all generations"* (*v. 5*). The God of Israel, the faithful God of the covenant, is also the eternal God who will be present in every generation. His lovingkindness, moreover, is not just for this life—it endures forever.

So it is not inappropriate that *Psalm 136* should repeat in every verse, *"His love [**hesed**] endures forever."* As its conclusion, the final verse says, *"Give thanks to the God of heaven. His love [**hesed**] endures forever"* (*v. 26*). No other phrase in Scripture comes anywhere close to this many repetitions, and rightly so. Let us, too, give thanks to the God of heaven for His *hesed*!

HEAVEN:
A GRAND SUMMARY

PSALM 103, A PSALM OF DAVID

If any single psalm comes near to encapsulating the thoughts of all the psalmists, it is David's *Psalm 103*. The great themes—man's mortality, God's eternality, God's reign in heaven, God's unfailing love—are summed up in this psalm. David admitted the brevity of man's life, for man is like dust and his days are like a flower of the field, soon to be blown away and forgotten (*vv 14-16*). But the LORD is *"from everlasting to everlasting"* (*v 17*). He showed Himself in the days of Moses (*v. 7*) and will continue to display His righteous acts to the *"children's children"* in future generations (*v. 17*). He has *"established his throne in heaven, and his kingdom rules over all"* (*v. 19*).

Best of all, the eternal God blesses mortal man with His unfailing love [*hesed*]. God *"redeems your life from the pit and crowns you with love [**hesed**] and compassion"* (*v. 4*). He is *"compassionate and gracious, slow to anger, abounding in love [**hesed**]"* (*v. 8*). *"As high as the heavens are above the earth,"* David wrote, *"so great is his love [**hesed**] for those who fear him"* (*v. 11*). From everlasting to everlasting, *"the LORD's love [**hesed**] is with those who fear him"* (*v. 17*). In conclusion to all this, therefore, David said:

> Praise the LORD, you his angels,
>   you mighty ones who do his bidding,
>   who obey his word.
> Praise the LORD, all his heavenly hosts,
>   you his servants who do his will.
> Praise the LORD, all his works
>   everywhere in his dominion.
> Praise the LORD, O my soul. (*vv. 20-22*)

WHAT DO YOU SAY?

1. What is your favorite psalm? What does it tell you about heaven?

2. Where is the throne of God located? Where is that from your house?

3. How did the worship of God at the Tabernacle/Temple preview the worship of God in heaven? In what ways are there differences?

4. What is man that God is mindful of him?

5. What does Scripture mean by the words *"sing a new song"*? What if we would rather sing the old ones?

6. The sons of Korah wrote, *"God will redeem my life from the grave; he will surely take me to himself"* (**Ps 49:15**). What did they mean by that? How do we understand that today?

7. Do all people have a longing for heaven? How keen is your own longing?

8. What would ancient people have made of God's promise that a river would flow in Jerusalem?

9. What is *hesed*? How does it relate to heaven?

CHAPTER SEVEN

HEAVEN IN THE PROPHETS OF ISRAEL

PART ONE: *Isaiah*

The prophets of Israel can tell us much about heaven and the life to come, but we must be careful to avoid two extremes as we study what they wrote. The first extreme is to take every word as literal and every promise as applying to a restored Jewish kingdom centered in Jerusalem. God has much more in mind for the human race than merely restoring another David to a Palestinian monarchy. As the prophets themselves will repeatedly show us, what God has in mind is a kingdom that is worldwide and eternal. Ruling over this kingdom will be God's own Son. Therefore, to find every prophecy fulfilled in a modern state like Israel is much too small.

The second extreme to avoid is to take every word as figurative and every promise as fulfilled spiritually in the church. The restored kingdom *does* begin to take shape in the church, and we will see many prophecies fulfilled in the resurrection of Christ and the launching of the church. But this is by no means all that the prophets promised. As Peter preached some days after the church had already been started, the Lord Jesus *"must remain in heaven until the time comes for God to restore everything, as he promised long ago through his holy prophets"* (*Acts 3:21*). Scripture itself teaches us, therefore, to

95

expect to find OT prophecies that point to the return of Christ from heaven and the ushering in of the eternal kingdom.

THE LIFE AND MINISTRY OF ISAIAH

God called Isaiah to his prophetic ministry at least as early as 740 BC, *"in the year that King Uzziah died"* (*Isa 6:1*). For the next sixty years Isaiah faithfully proclaimed to Judah a warning of imminent exile and a promise of ultimate restoration. He is often called "the gospel prophet" because of his frequent prophecies about the Messiah and the messianic age. While we do not know the date of Isaiah's death, he lived at least until the death of Sennacherib in 681 BC, which he recorded in *Isaiah 37:38*.

But what did Isaiah say about heaven and the age to come? As we will see, Isaiah's testimony came in two forms. First, he often spoke of the present heaven as the lofty home of God. Second, and in far greater detail, he spoke of wonderful blessings to be enjoyed by God's people in the future. These promises were not fulfilled by the portion of the Jews that returned from Babylonian captivity. Postexilic Judaism was well aware that the glorious promises of the prophets did not match up well with their small efforts at rebuilding the kingdom and their continuous domination by foreign powers.

Neither are the promises of Isaiah fulfilled by the coming of the church. Isaiah spoke of the future as a time when God would *"create new heavens and a new earth"* (*Isa 65:17*), a time when the Messiah will reign over a kingdom forever (*Isa 9:7*). Unless we disregard virtually everything Isaiah said as mere prophetic hyperbole, many of the promises God made through him are yet to be kept. Moreover, as we see repeated parallels in the language of Isaiah and Revelation, we will conclude that Isaiah and John are talking about the same thing: the end of the ages in heaven.

HEAVEN: THE THRONEROOM OF GOD

I SAW THE LORD
ISAIAH 6:1-4

In the tumultuous year of Uzziah's death, Isaiah saw a vision of God seated on His throne. (His vision is remarkably similar to the vision of John in *Rev 4:1-4*.) The King of the universe sat on a throne, high and exalted, in a heavenly temple (*v. 1*). The seraphs flew above the throne in worship of the Lord. Like the "living creatures" of *Revelation 4:8*, each seraph had six wings. One pair covered the face, as if in awestruck reverence. A second pair of wings covered the feet, as if in awareness of the seraph's unworthiness. With the third pair the seraph flew, hovering above the throne (*v. 2*).

The six-winged creatures in heaven are named seraphs only in this passage in the Bible. The plural of the Hebrew word *seraph* is *seraphim*, (so the "seraphims" of the KJV is an unnecessary double plural). The seraphs are not specifically called angels, although it is probably correct to speak of them as angelic creatures. They have the ability to speak, both in eternal praise of God and in carrying God's message to Isaiah or to John.

Strikingly, when the seraphs cried out a dominant trait of God, it was not "love, love, love" or "grace, grace, grace." Their eternal song was, *"Holy, holy, holy is the LORD Almighty; the whole earth is full of his glory"* (*v. 3*, see also *Rev 4:8*). Untouched by any taint of sin, "the Holy One of Israel" (a title used 26 times by Isaiah, but found only 6 times in the rest of the OT) sits on His throne. Perhaps it is true among men that "absolute power corrupts absolutely," but the sovereign God of heaven is completely and incorruptibly pure.

The similarity of *Isaiah 6* to *Revelation 4* is a caution that we must not too quickly dismiss what the prophets say as poetic metaphor or empty imagery. While Isaiah could certainly use a figure of speech, as mountains *"burst into song"* and trees *"clap their hands"* (see *Isa 55:12*), this vision of the LORD should be taken at face value. At a time when the people of Judah needed assurance because their world was crumbling around them, Isaiah reported what he had seen: the all-holy God still sits on His throne. At a time when early Christians faced the onslaught of imperial power, John reported the same truth: the God of power and holiness still rules.

Enthroned above
the Grasshoppers
Isaiah 40:22

After 39 chapters of warning about the coming deportation to Babylon, in *chapter 40* Isaiah looked farther ahead and saw a time of restoration. *"Comfort, comfort my people, says your God"* (*v. 1*), because there will be a voice crying in the desert, *"Prepare the way for the LORD"* (*v. 3*). Even though men perish like wilted flowers (*v. 7*), there is yet good news for Zion: *"The Sovereign LORD comes with power"* (*v. 10*), and He will set things right.

But does He, in fact, care about His people? And is He strong enough to defeat their powerful enemies? As to the first question, Isaiah assured his beleaguered people that God *"tends his flock like a shepherd: He gathers the lambs in his arms"* (*v. 11*). And in a much fuller answer to the second, God will have no problem with the puny nations of the world. *"Before him,"* Isaiah said, *"the nations are as nothing . . . and less than nothing"* (*v. 17*). No doubt remembering the vision that had called him to his prophetic ministry, Isaiah proclaimed that God *"sits enthroned above the circle of the earth, and its people are like grasshoppers"* (*v. 22*). The God of heaven is *"the everlasting God, the Creator of the ends of the earth"* (*v. 28*). The fear of persecution and death fade into nothingness when God's people lift up their eyes to heaven.

The final promise of this chapter was much needed to encourage Judah then, just as it has encouraged God's people ever since:

> *Those who hope in the LORD*
> *will renew their strength.*
> *They will soar on wings like eagles;*
> *they will run and not grow weary,*
> *they will walk and not faint.* (*v. 31*)

Such is the hope of people whose God is the LORD.

The Higher Thoughts of Heaven
Isaiah 55:9 & Isaiah 66:1

As we accumulate our increasing collection of information about God on His throne, two final passages will serve as a caution that we must never think we have God all figured out. Philosophers have often been too quick to define what God must be; theologians have been too quick to explain Him. But it is as God spoke through Isaiah:

"As the heavens are higher than the earth, so are my ways higher than your ways and my thoughts than your thoughts" (**Isa 55:9**). In both senses of the word—the skies overhead and the throne room itself—the "heavens" are higher than the earth. Therefore we must never lose the sense of awe that is appropriately attached to thoughts of heaven, the same awe that Isaiah felt in **chapter six**.

Likewise, the final chapter of Isaiah reinforces the grandeur of God's heaven. *"Heaven is my throne,"* says the Lord, *"and the earth is my footstool"* (**Isa 66:1**). Heaven and earth belong to God: they are *His* throne, *His* footstool. Furthermore, the contrast between a throne and a footstool aptly puts us in our place. Our "footstool" earth, beautiful as it may be, cannot compare with the glory of the heaven that we will one day share with God.

HEAVEN: HIS KINGDOM, OUR HOME

And the Government Will Be on His Shoulders
Isaiah 9:6-7

Messianic prophecies abound in Isaiah. They always point to Jesus; they often point not only to His earthly ministry, but also to His eternal kingdom in heaven. As we examine a number of these prophecies, we will watch for certain indicators that the fulfillment can only be found in the eternal context of heaven.

Thus, in the well-known verses of **Isaiah 9:6-7** there is the promise of the birth of "a child" who will reign on the throne of David. At first glance, this could be applied to the birth of Jesus and to the ultimate establishment of His church. This much is true, but the prophecy requires more. **Verse seven** says, *"Of the increase of his government and peace there will be no end,"* and the Messiah will reign *"from that time on and forever."*

God's people can look forward, therefore, to living in an eternal kingdom where Jesus Christ is king. The Wonderful Counselor who is also Mighty God will establish that kingdom and uphold it with justice and righteousness. While the people of Isaiah's day could perhaps see no further than a restored kingdom in Judea, the promises require us to think heavenward. Heaven is the place—the only place—where Jesus will rule *"from that time on and forever."*

The Wolf Will Live
with the Lamb
Isaiah 11:1-9

In a future age, Isaiah promised, a Branch will sprout from the root of Jesse (David's father). This Ruler (always understood to be the Messiah) will have the Spirit of the LORD on Him and will finally bring righteousness and justice to the earth (*vv. 1-4*). He will not bring judgment based on appearances or hearsay; at last the poor will have a righteous Judge.

Perhaps the most interesting aspect of this coming kingdom is the idyllic scene of predators coexisting in peace with their prey:

> The wolf will live with the lamb,
>   the leopard will lie down with the goat,
> the calf and the lion and the yearling together;
>   and a little child will lead them.
> The cow will feed with the bear,
>   their young will lie down together,
>   and the lion will eat straw like the ox.
> The infant will play near the hole of the cobra,
>   and the young child put his hand into the viper's nest. (*vv. 6-8*; see *Isa 65:25*)

The world is promised a time of peace and harmony unlike anything since the Garden of Eden. Now how should we understand these verses? If they are merely prophetic metaphor, they have a lot of detail that actually means nothing. Why tell about so many kinds of animals and innocent infants when the message is not about animals and infants at all? On the other hand, if these verses describe a future reality, it must be awaiting us in heaven. Neither those who returned from exile nor those who gathered in the church have ever experienced anything like this. But there is every reason to expect that our ultimate paradise will look just like this!

A Banquet on the Mountain
Isaiah 25:6-9

When the people of Judah went off into exile, they were to take heart in the promise of future happiness. Even though the city of Jerusalem would be reduced to rubble, God will bring His people back to the holy hill and restore their fallen fortunes. Even by the time of Jesus, however, the Jews of Palestine realized that this restoration had never happened. In a sense, of course, some of what Isaiah described here is found in the church. But in a larger sense, these words are best fulfilled in the afterlife of heaven.

God promises *"a feast of rich foods for all peoples, a banquet of aged wine—the best of meats and the finest of wines"* (*v. 6*). It will happen *"on this mountain,"* that is, in Jerusalem. And when it happens, the Sovereign LORD will *"swallow up death forever"* and will *"wipe away the tears from all faces"* (*v. 8*). What better preview could there be of heaven? (See *Rev 7:17; 19:7-9; 21:2-4.*) In that day, when all this has finally come to pass, God's people will say, *"This is the LORD, we trusted in him; let us rejoice and be glad in his salvation"* (*v. 9*).

YOUR DEAD WILL LIVE
ISAIAH 26:19

In the day that God spreads the banquet on the mountain of Jerusalem (*Isa 25:6*), He also promises to bring the dead back to life. Why should the faithful of earlier times miss out on this feast of celebration? *"Your dead will live,"* declares God, *"their bodies will rise. You who live in the dust, wake up and shout for joy. . . . The earth will give birth to her dead"* (*26:19*).

This promise is quite specific. Those who are dead will live—and not just in some vague, spiritual sense. Their bodies will rise from the dust of the earth (see *1Cor 15:20-24,52; 1Th 4:14-18*). This can only be a picture of what is yet to come, a prelude to heaven.

WALKING THE HIGHWAY OF HOLINESS
ISAIAH 35:8-10

Isaiah continues to promise a future king who will *"reign in righteousness"* (*Isa 32:1*). The people will *"see the king in his beauty and view a land that stretches afar"* (*Isa 33:17*). Best of all, there is a highway to lead the people back home to their king. This road will be called "the Way of Holiness," because the unclean will not be allowed on it (*Isa 35:8*; see *Rev 21:8,27*). Only *"the redeemed of the LORD will walk there"* (*v. 9*). While the immediate fulfillment of this promise would be for those who return from exile in Babylon, the ultimate fulfillment must be in heaven. It is only there that the rest of the promise can come true: *"They will enter Zion with singing; everlasting joy will crown their heads . . . and sorrow and sighing will flee away"* (*v. 10*, see also *Isa 61:7-8*).

BE SAVED, ALL YOU ENDS OF THE EARTH
ISAIAH 45:22-23

God invites all the earth to walk the Way of Holiness. To ignorant men who carry idols made of wood, He says, *"Turn to me and be saved, all you ends of the earth; for I am God, and there is no other"* (**Isa 45:22**). Some will accept the invitation; most will not. But whether by glad acceptance or in sullen defeat, the day will come when, *"Before me every knee will bow; by me every tongue will swear"* (*v. 23*). Paul will apply these verses to Jesus as Lord (***Php 2:10-11***) and will place the event at the day of judgment (***Rom 14:10-12***).

Similarly, the picture of restoring Israel in **Isaiah 49:8-12** applies both to the immediate future when they return from Babylon, and to the distant future when they go to heaven. In **Revelation 7:16** John quotes several key elements of **Isaiah 49:10** and sees them fulfilled in heaven: no more hunger, no more thirst, no desert heat or burning sun.

HE WILL MAKE HER DESERTS LIKE EDEN
ISAIAH 51:3-8

When God's people walk the Way of Holiness back to God's kingdom, they will enjoy *"an everlasting salvation"* and will not be put to shame *"to ages everlasting"* (**Isa 45:17**). It is interesting to note that God's plan for blessing His people recalls the original garden in **Genesis**. *"He will make her deserts like Eden,"* Isaiah declared, *"her wastelands like the garden of the LORD"* (**Isa 51:3**). As in the preceding paragraph, this promise is also set in terms that take us beyond the return from Babylon to a vista of the afterlife. *"The heavens will vanish like smoke,"* Isaiah continues, *"the earth will wear out like a garment and its inhabitants like flies. But my salvation will last forever"* (*v. 6*). Moreover, *"My righteousness will last forever, my salvation through all generations"* (*v. 8*).

The character of God does not change (see **Mal 3:1**). It would also appear that His ultimate plan for mankind does not change. The bliss of the original garden is promised again in **Isaiah**, and is promised yet again in **Revelation**.

THE SUFFERING SERVANT
ISAIAH 53:7-11

The chapter about the Suffering Servant provided a clear indication that there is life beyond the grave, although there was not a clear understanding as to who would get it. Some of the early Jewish commentators thought the servant who was *"despised and rejected by men"* was the whole nation of Israel. Others thought it would be the Messiah. The continuing confusion was echoed by the Ethiopian eunuch's question to Philip: *"Tell me, please, who is the prophet talking about, himself or someone else?"* (**Acts 8:34**).

The ultimate answer, of course, is that the Suffering Servant is Jesus (**Acts 8:35**). He is the One who was led to the slaughter (**Isa 53:7**). He is the One who was *"cut off from the land of the living"* (**v. 8**) and *"assigned a grave with the wicked"* (**v. 9**). Just as the prophecy said, Jesus died. But He would live again to see another day, for *"after the suffering of his soul, he will see the light of life and be satisfied"* (**v. 11**). While this passage does not provide any specific details about the nature of heaven, it firmly declares that life after death is available.

THE LORD WILL BE YOUR LIGHT
ISAIAH 60:5-21

The final chapters of Isaiah brought to a climax the prophetic pictures of the age to come. There he described the glory of the rebuilt Zion. It will have the wealth of nations (**v. 5**), with much gold and silver (**vv. 6,9,17**). As if immune to any attack, the gates will always stand open (**v. 11**), and any nation that does not serve God's city will perish (**v. 12**). Best of all, they were told that at Jerusalem *"the LORD will be your everlasting light, and your God will be your glory"* (**v. 19**). When all this happens, *"Then will all your people be righteous and they will possess the land forever"* (**v. 21**).

The nation of Israel, from the time of the return from Babylon until this very day, might well complain that none of this ever happened. No gold, no immunity, no light from God, no permanent possession of the land. But these will be fulfilled in the New Jerusalem of heaven. There will be gold (**Rev 21:18**) and wealth delivered by nations (**Rev 21:24**), final victory over enemies (**Rev 19:11-21**), open gates (**Rev 21:25**), the light of God's glory (**Rev 21:11,23**), and a kingdom where the righteous will live and reign forever (**Rev 22:5**).

THEY WILL REBUILD
THE ANCIENT RUINS
ISAIAH 61:1-10

"The LORD has anointed me to preach good news to the poor," said Isaiah—and Jesus! The promise of a restored kingdom (**Isa 61:1-2**)

103

was the text chosen by Jesus at His home synagogue (*Lk 4:18-19*). On that day in Nazareth, Jesus further said, *"Today this scripture is fulfilled in your hearing"* (*Lk 4:21*). Jesus understood completely that the kingdom of heaven that He preached (*Mt 4:17*) would be the way God would restore the fallen throne of David.

The promises of *Isaiah 61* were about more than just ruined cities (*v. 4*). The more important part—the part that the divine Messiah would accomplish—was about what would happen to the people. They will all someday be called *"priests of the LORD"* and *"ministers of our God"* (*v. 6*; compare *1Pet 2:5* and *Rev 1:6*). They will have *"everlasting joy"* (*v. 7*) and an *"everlasting covenant"* (*v. 8*). God will dress every person whom He loves in *"a robe of righteousness"* (*v. 10*; compare *Rev 3:5; 7:14; 19:8*). The imagery of adorning the bridegroom and the bride is even used to describe God and His people (*v. 10*, compare *Rev 21:2*). The "ancient ruins" will indeed be rebuilt—in heaven!

BEULAH LAND
ISAIAH 62:2-8

Exiled in Babylon, the people of Judah could only feel abandoned. Why had their God forsaken them? But Isaiah brought to God's people a word of hope. While the enemies of Judah called her *"Deserted"* and *"Desolate"* (*v. 4*), she will have a new name, a name that the LORD Himself will bestow (*v. 2*). She will be called *"Hephzibah"* (which means "My delight is in her"), and her land will be called *"Beulah"* (which means "Married") (*v. 4*). Then, in words strongly prophetic of Christ's love for the church, Isaiah said, *"As a bridegroom rejoices over his bride, so will your God rejoice over you"* (*v. 5*).

The Jewish nation had only a partial fulfillment of this prophecy when they returned from exile. The church has had only a preliminary fulfillment of this prophecy as the promised—but not yet married—bride of Christ. The ultimate fulfillment of these words is found in *Revelation 19:7 and 9*. *"Let us rejoice and be glad and give him glory! For the wedding of the Lamb has come, and his bride has made herself ready." "Blessed are those who are invited to the wedding supper of the Lamb!"*

NEW HEAVENS AND A NEW EARTH
ISAIAH 65:17-25

God promised through Isaiah that in a glorious future day, *"Behold, I will create new heavens and a new earth"* (*v. 17*; see also *Isa 66:22*). While this never happened following the return from exile, this is the very thing John saw in *Revelation 21:1*. It will be a place of rich prosperity, created specifically by God to be a "delight" to His people (*v. 18*). As in *Isaiah 11*, the animals that were formerly predator and prey will live in peace (*v. 25*). The serpent, however, will eat dust (see *Rev 12:9*).

One more fascinating thing will be true of the new heaven and new earth: *"The former things will not be remembered, nor will they come to mind"* (*v. 17*). For this reason, *"The sound of weeping and of crying will be heard in it no more"* (*v. 19*). This serves us well as a picture of what awaits us in heaven. God will wipe away every tear of regret and sorrow, and after that there will be no more mourning or crying (*Rev 21:4*). In God's new heaven and earth, the old order of things will have passed away.

PEACE LIKE A RIVER
ISAIAH 66:12-24

In his final vision of the age to come, Isaiah saw a time of worldwide peace. *"I will extend peace to her like a river,"* promised the LORD, *"and the wealth of nations like a flooding stream"* (*v. 12*). Yet from the time Judah returned from captivity until now, she has never lived in security and peace. When is this time that God will *"gather all nations and tongues, and they will come and see my glory"* (*v. 18*)? When is the time that God will have His new heavens and new earth, as well as His people who live there, endure permanently (*v. 22*)? It is obviously to be fulfilled in the afterlife.

Isaiah's final chapter also includes a somber note about the last days of the future. The LORD is coming *"with fire,"* to *"bring down his anger with fury, and his rebuke with flames of fire"* (*v. 15*). He will *"execute judgment upon all men, and many will be those slain by the LORD"* (*v. 16*). Viewing the dead bodies of those condemned by God, Isaiah concluded his book with these prophetic words: *"Their worm will not die, nor will their fire be quenched, and they will be loathsome to all mankind"* (see *Mk 9:47-48*).

CONCLUSION

Isaiah brought the word of the LORD to his own people at a time of impending distress. Facing the prospect of defeat and exile at the hands of Babylon, the little nation of Judah needed a strong word of encouragement. The answer for their problems, both short-range and long-range, lay in the truth that God was on His throne. Situated in perfect holiness, God sat above the mere "grasshoppers" of the earth, thinking His higher and loftier thoughts.

Not only would the people of Judah return from their captivity in Babylon, they had an even more exciting prospect in the distant future. The God of heaven is going to make a new heaven and earth, a utopia where His people will live. The dead will rise from the dust to share an eternal banquet in a restored Eden. The animals will live in peace; the people will live in holiness. This kingdom will be ruled by the Messiah, a descendant of David, who will appear first as a little child. Living in the splendor of gold and in radiant light, the people will be called Beulah—the bride of the LORD.

WHAT DO YOU SAY?

1. Why did Judah need to know about Isaiah's vision of the LORD, high and lifted up?

2. How are promises of a future (heavenly) kingdom any help to a people in exile? How are promises of "pie in the sky by and by" any help to you?

3. What did Isaiah say about the coming Messiah? Why did that matter in 600 BC?

4. Will there be animals in heaven? What is the biblical evidence?

5. How is the Suffering Servant (*Isaiah 53*) a proof that there is an afterlife?

6. What is the significance of "Hephzibah" and "Beulah" for you personally?

7. Both Isaiah and Jesus said they were sent to preach good news to the poor. Who were "the poor," and what was the "good news" for them?

8. Why is it necessary to understand many of Isaiah's prophecies as pointing beyond Israel and the church—pointing to heaven?

CHAPTER EIGHT

HEAVEN IN THE PROPHETS OF ISRAEL

PART TWO: *Jeremiah, Ezekiel, Daniel*

THE LIFE AND MINISTRY OF JEREMIAH

The word of the LORD came to Jeremiah in the thirteenth year of the reign of King Josiah, which was 626 BC (see *Jer 1:2*). His prophetic ministry lasted right up to the time the people were carried off into exile in 586 BC (see *Jer 1:3*). Jeremiah's difficult role was to proclaim doom to people who did not want to hear it. Yet even in the midst of such negativity, the "weeping prophet" gave a few glimpses of distant glory.

A CITY INHABITED FOREVER
JEREMIAH 17:25

Through the early chapters of Jeremiah the LORD's judgment was leveled against Judah, a disobedient people and a faithless bride (see *Jer 2:9-13; 3:1-3*). In anguish God foretold the disasters in store for His people (see *Jer 4:19-20; 6:1; 8:13; 9:10*). They had broken their covenant with God (see *Jer 11:8*), so they would face drought, famine, and the sword (see *Jer 14:1-12*). Then, just as the warning of the days of disaster reached a fever pitch in *chapter 16*, Jeremiah presented a word of hope in God's loving appeal.

Even yet, if the people would obey God, there could be a time of great future blessing. *"Then the kings who sit on David's throne,"* Jeremiah promised, *"will come through the gates of this city with their officials"* (*v. 25a*). These descendants of David will rule over the city of Jerusalem, *"and this city will be inhabited forever"* (*v. 25b*).

God's people did, of course, eventually return from Babylonian exile. But no one ever sat on David's throne as a king. Neither did the city of Jerusalem become their home "forever." What Jeremiah fore-saw will come to pass in heaven, when Jesus is the son of David who rules over God's kingdom.

A Righteous Branch, A King
Jeremiah 23:5-6

More chapters of accusation and future punishment follow. Then, like the sun breaking through after a storm, Jeremiah brought a ray of hope:

> *"The days are coming," declares the LORD,*
> *"when I will raise up to David a righteous Branch,*
> *a King who will reign wisely*
> *and do what is just and right in the land.*
> *In his days Judah will be saved*
> *and Israel will live in safety.*
> *This is the name by which he will be called:*
> *'The LORD Our Righteousness'"* (*Jer 23:5-6*).

Like the *"shoot of Jesse"* promised in *Isaiah 11:1*, there will be a Branch to reign in the place of David. Because this King is righteous and wise, the people will be safe. Interestingly, Israel is included with Judah in this promise, even though the northern tribes were carried off and scattered by the Assyrians over 100 years earlier. When this promise is fulfilled in Jesus, we can understand how this King can be called "The LORD," and how He can be "our righteousness." While this prophecy has some degree of fulfillment in the church, it is in heaven that the tribes of Israel—all twelve—will enjoy these blessings (see *Rev 7:4; 21:12*).

I Will Build You Up Again
Jeremiah 31:1-40

Clearly Jeremiah's most dramatic promise of future blessing is *chapter thirty-one*. *"All the clans of Israel"* (*v. 1*) will be included, because

God has loved them *"with an everlasting love"* (*v. 3*). Even though they were decimated and exiled, God promised, *"I will build you up again and you will be rebuilt, O virgin Israel."*

Much of the chapter describes scenes of restored happiness in the Promised Land. With only a small allowance for hyperbole, they can be understood as physical blessings that were enjoyed when the exile was over. But there are two passages that point beyond this return. The first is *verses 31-34*, where the LORD promised to make *"a new covenant with the house of Israel and with the house of Judah."* This will be an internal covenant, written on the minds and hearts of God's people. As *Hebrews 8:8-12* makes clear, this did not happen until Christ came and established the church. The second passage goes even further: *"'The days are coming,' declares the LORD, 'when this city will be rebuilt'"* (*v. 38*). In no uncertain terms God further says, *"The city will never again be uprooted or demolished"* (*v. 40*). This promise is entirely and literally true—in heaven.

DAVID WILL NEVER FAIL TO HAVE A MAN ON THE THRONE
JEREMIAH 33:17

With one final glimpse into the glorious future, Jeremiah made another assertion that never came true for physical Israel. He promised a time of restoration, when the sound of joy and gladness will be heard in the house of the LORD. Once again the people will say, *"Give thanks to the LORD Almighty, for the LORD is good; his love [**hesed**] endures forever"* (*Jer 33:11*). Jeremiah then repeats (from *Jer 23:5-6*) what he said about the Branch of David bringing safety to Jerusalem.

All of this is Jeremiah's prelude to a most audacious statement: *"David will never fail to have a man to sit on the throne of the house of Israel"* (*Jer 33:17*). Jeremiah said this just as the last of the kings of Judah were bringing the line of David to an end. The closing of the Book of Jeremiah, in fact, describes the next-to-last king of Judah as he is imprisoned in Babylon. There the king of Babylon *"gave Jehoiachin a regular allowance as long as he lived, until the day of his death"* (*Jer 52:34*). His successor, the evil king Zedekiah, *"did not humble himself before Jeremiah the prophet, who spoke the word of the LORD"* (*2Chr 36:12*) and died in disgrace. Thus ended the line of the kings of Judah.

But the word of the LORD will not fail; David will yet have his descendant on the throne forever. Jesus, the Shoot from the stump of Jesse, *will* rule over all the true Israel of God. Jesus, the Branch of David, *will* rule throughout the ages. This begins in the church, of course, but only comes to complete fulfillment at the 2nd Coming; then the rule of Jesus will last throughout eternity.

THE LIFE AND MINISTRY OF EZEKIEL

Ezekiel was among an early group of exiles whom King Jehoiachin led to exile in Babylon in 597 BC (*Eze 1:2*). In the fifth year of that exile (593 BC) the word of the LORD came to Ezekiel, and through his early years he proclaimed a harsh message of God's judgment. The city of Jerusalem was destroyed in 587 BC, and some time after that Ezekiel began to offer occasional glimpses of the hope of forgiveness and restoration. He concluded twenty-two years of prophetic ministry with a remarkable image of the New Jerusalem (*Eze 48:30-35*).

FOUR LIVING CREATURES
EZEKIEL 1:5-28

Ezekiel opened his book with a dramatic vision of a great windstorm that contained lightning and fire. In the center of the fire was what looked like *"four living creatures"* (*v. 5*). Each one had the face of either a man, a lion, an ox, or an eagle (*v. 10*). The creatures, later identified as cherubim that were covered with eyes (see *Eze 10:12-14*), extended their wings until their tips touched (*1:11*). Then Ezekiel saw a great sapphire throne above the cherubim, and on the throne was seated a figure that resembled a man (*v. 26*). Shining with a radiance like a rainbow, this was *"the likeness of the glory of the LORD"* (*v. 28*). God, who had for centuries made His presence known through shining glory in the Temple (where golden cherubim spread their wings), was now present with His people in their exile! (See *Ex 25:20-22*.)

This glimpse of God's glory is remarkably similar to the imagery of heaven in *Revelation*. It is a place where a rainbow shines (*Rev 10:1*) and where four living creatures have the face of a man, a lion, an ox, or an eagle (*Rev 4:7*). Like the cherubim of Ezekiel, they are covered everywhere with eyes (*Rev 4:8*). In the center of these living creatures is the throne of God, flashing with lightning (*Rev 4:5*). With the

Father is the Son, seen earlier in Revelation as One whose face blazes with fire and shines with the brightness of the sun (*Rev 1:14-16*). All this combines to show that Ezekiel, without realizing the full extent of his vision, saw a magnificent glimpse of heaven, our eternal home.

AND I WILL BE THEIR GOD
EZEKIEL 11:19-20

Tragically, Ezekiel saw in *chapter ten* another vision of the Temple and the cherubim. In this vision he saw the glory of the LORD above the cherubim, but then that glory moved outward to the threshold of the Temple (*v. 4*). Later the glory moved to the east gate of the Temple compound, as God prepared to leave His house altogether (*v. 19*).

Chapter eleven reveals that the city of Jerusalem was about to be completely destroyed, and that it was going to be God's own judgment that made it happen (*vv. 7-10*). But even in this final pronouncement of doom, there was hope. *"I will gather you from the nations,"* said the sovereign LORD, *"and bring you back from the countries where you have been scattered, and I will give you back the land of Israel again"* (*v. 17*). In that happy future time, God promised that He will *"give them an undivided heart and put a new spirit in them"* (*v. 18*). Best of all, He said, *"They will be my people, and I will be their God"* (*v. 19*).

At the end of the Babylonian exile, the Jews trickled back to live among the ruins of the old city. They lived under the dominance of various foreign powers, never regaining clear possession of their land. The ark of the covenant was never restored; the Holy of Holies was an empty room. Neither then nor now, with the modern secular state of Israel, can this prophecy be said to have come true. The real fulfillment will be in heaven. It is only there that God's fullest blessings will be given. It is only there that it will be truly said, *"Now the dwelling of God is with men, and he will live with them"* (*Rev 21:3*). The glory of God departed from the Temple in Jerusalem, but that glory will be the universal treasure of all the saints in heaven.

I MYSELF WILL TEND MY SHEEP
EZEKIEL 34:15-16

In the twelfth year of Ezekiel's exile (586 BC) word came that Jerusalem had fallen (*Eze 33:21*). It was no longer just a prophetic threat; it was an accomplished fact. God's people knew that He meant what He said and that He had the fortitude to carry it out. When the word of the LORD came to Ezekiel in **chapter 34**, it was God's explanation of why He had rejected the shepherds of His people Israel. The shepherds had not taken care of the flock (*v. 3*). They had not cared about the weak, the sick, the injured (*v. 4*). They had ruled with a harsh, brutal hand (*v. 4*) and now the flock was scattered (*v. 5*). So what will God do? He said,

> *I myself will tend my sheep and have them lie down. I will search for the lost and bring back the strays. I will bind up the injured and strengthen the weak, but the sleek and the strong I will destroy. I will shepherd the flock with justice. (**Eze 34:15-16**)*

But this never happened in the return from exile; neither has it happened at any time since. God has yet to take over the shepherding job Himself. (Even the commitment of Jesus to be the Good Shepherd in *John 10* was primarily fulfilled when He laid down His life for His sheep, not in any direct shepherding of their lives.) But in heaven the Father and Son will live with the sheep, and They will put an end to sickness, injury, and death.

FOR THE SAKE OF MY HOLY NAME
EZEKIEL 36:22-38

Ezekiel promised the people of God that God will be faithful to His covenant promises. The enemies of Israel will be punished (*Eze 36:1-6*), and Israel will be restored to her land (*vv. 8-15*). In fact, Israel will even take over the lands of those who were her enemies (*v. 13*) and will never again be subjected to the scorn of nations (*v. 15*). When God accomplishes this mighty act of restoration, He said it would be, *"Not for your sake, O house of Israel . . . but for the sake of my holy name"* (*v. 22*). Although Israel has profaned the name of God, by this mighty act *"the nations will know that I am the LORD, declares the Sovereign LORD"* (*v. 23*).

This restoration, however, does not resemble what actually happened when the people of Judah returned from Babylon. Neither does it resemble the rest of what Ezekiel predicted: the people will get *"a new heart"* and *"a new spirit,"* and their *"heart of stone"* will be replaced with *"a heart of flesh"* (*v. 26*). In the coming age when all this will happen, Ezekiel said that their wasted land will become *"like the garden of Eden"* (*v. 35*). While none of this happened when they returned from exile, it will happen in heaven. And when it does, *"Then they will know that I am the LORD"* (*v. 38*).

THE VALLEY OF DRY BONES
EZEKIEL 37

Immediately following the prophecies just mentioned, Ezekiel was taken by the Spirit to a valley full of bones (*Eze 37:1*). After Ezekiel saw how very dry the bones were, the LORD asked him, **"Can these bones live?" (v. 3)**. In spite of the obvious answer to this question, God said He will say to the bones, *"I will make breath enter you, and you will come to life"* (*v. 5*).

The immediate application of these words is simply that God promised Israel, virtually dead at the hands of her enemies, that the nation would be brought back to prosperity. But the graphic promises were repeated and emphasized in a way that necessarily lifts our eyes to the afterlife. *"O my people,"* God said, *"I am going to open your graves and bring you up from them"* (*v. 12*). *"I will make one nation in the land. . . . There will be one king over all of them and they will never again be two nations or be divided into two kingdoms"* (*v. 22*). *"My servant David will be king over them, and they will all have one shepherd"* (*v. 24*). *"They and their children and their children's children will live there forever, and David my servant will be their prince forever"* (*v. 25*). *"I will make a covenant of peace with them; it will be an everlasting covenant . . . and I will put my sanctuary among them forever"* (*v. 26*). *"My dwelling place will be with them; I will be their God, and they will be my people"* (*v. 27*). At long last the nations will know who the true God is: the God who makes Israel holy, *"When my sanctuary is among them forever"* (*v. 28*). These beautiful words, so predictive of heaven, hardly need any further explanation!

THE WATER FLOWING
FROM THE TEMPLE
EZEKIEL 47:1-12

Since Ezekiel himself was either a priest or at least the son of a priestly family (see *Eze 1:3* and NIV text note), he had great familiarity with the Temple in Jerusalem. From *Ezekiel 40 through 48*, chapter after chapter gives a detailed description of how the restored Temple will look. Ezekiel's Temple, however, was never built. There was a

Temple built by Zerubbabel and the returning exiles, but even the foundation showed that it would be sadly inferior to Solomon's original Temple (see *Ezra 3:12*). Neither did the rebuilt Temple of Herod the Great fulfill what Ezekiel saw.

Of special note is Ezekiel's statement that he saw *"water coming out from under the threshold of the temple"* (*Eze 47:1*). As the water flowed eastward, it grew into a river he could not cross (*v. 5*). This river brought life—both to the fish in it and to the land around it (*v. 9*). There are fruit trees of all kinds on both banks of this river, bearing a new crop every month (*v. 12a*). *"Their fruit will serve for food,"* Ezekiel prophesied, *"and their leaves for healing"* (*v. 12b*). This wonderful river clearly is a foreshadowing of the river of the water of life that flows from the throne of God (*Joel 3:18; Zech 13:1; Rev 22:1-2*).

This description of the river so closely parallels *Revelation* that it may come as a shock to recall that in John's vision he records, *"I did not see a temple in the city"* (*Rev 21:22*). How then, can Ezekiel's prophecy come true? The answer is that heaven ultimately does not need a temple, because heaven *is* a temple—the very dwelling place of God. The Father and the Lamb *are* the temple, because they live in the midst of their people.

"THE LORD IS THERE"
EZEKIEL 48:35

Ezekiel closed his book with a final picture of the rebuilt Jerusalem and her city gates. After enumerating the three gates on each of the four walls and the measurements of the walls, he stated, *"And the name of the city from that time on would be: 'THE LORD IS THERE'"* (*Eze 48:35*). But when Judah returned and rebuilt Jerusalem, the former glory was missing. The Holy of Holies was empty; the glory of the LORD was *not* there.

Ezekiel's city, like Ezekiel's Temple, are a foreshadowing of heaven. The New Jerusalem will also have three gates on each wall (*Rev 21:12-13*) and those gates are never closed (*Rev 21:25*). In *Revelation* the walls are also carefully measured and are found to be an amazing 1400 miles in each direction (*Rev 21:16*). Best of all, it can be truthfully said in the new heaven and the new earth, *"THE LORD IS THERE"* (*Rev 21:3; 22:3*).

THE LIFE AND MINISTRY
OF DANIEL

Daniel was part of the very first group of exiles to be taken to Babylon, in 605 BC during the puppet reign of Jehoiakim (see *Jer 25:1* and *Dan 1:1*). Nebuchadnezzar, the king of Babylon, had a practice of selecting the most promising young men of a conquered people and then training them to be his deputies. It was during this training that Daniel refused to defile himself with the royal food and wine (*Dan 1:8*). After this training was completed, Daniel showed that his wisdom and understanding were *"ten times better than all the magicians and enchanters"* in the whole kingdom of Babylon (*Dan 1:20*).

Nebuchadnezzar's Dream
Daniel 2:36-44

In the second year of his reign, Nebuchadnezzar had a dream that none of his own wise men could interpret (*Dan 2:1-12*). Daniel, however, was able both to tell the king what the dream was and to tell him what it meant (*vv. 31-36*). The dream was about a great statue made of gold, silver, bronze, iron, and clay. It represented four kingdoms: Babylon, Medo-Persia, Greece, and Rome. According to Daniel's interpretation, in the time of the fourth kingdom, *"God will set up a kingdom that will never be destroyed, nor will it be left to another people. It will crush all those kingdoms and bring them to an end, but it will itself endure forever"* (*Dan 2:44*). Jesus set up this kingdom when He built His church, but the church itself is not the final phase. The point at which all the kingdoms are crushed will come in the end times when *"The kingdom of the world has become the kingdom of our Lord and of his Christ, and he will reign for ever and ever"* (*Rev 11:15*).

Nebuchadnezzar's Second Dream
Daniel 4:3

When Nebuchadnezzar saw how God delivered Shadrach, Meshach, and Abednego from the blazing furnace (*Dan 3:24-29*), he was powerfully impressed. He issued a royal proclamation about this God, saying, *"His kingdom is an eternal kingdom; his dominion endures from generation to generation"* (*Dan 4:3*). With the help of God's people, even a heathen king can figure out that the God of heaven has a kingdom that will outlast all earthly powers.

Nebuchadnezzar included in this proclamation certain details of a second dream, this one about a giant tree. The part that is significant for our study is the king's statement, *"While lying in my bed, I looked, and there before me was a messenger, a holy one, coming down from heaven"* (**Dan 4:13**). The descent of this angel (identified as Gabriel in **Dan 9:21**) "coming down from heaven" clearly links the infinite distances of the open sky with God's heaven. While this does not locate heaven as "up," it suitably conveys the sense that the Most High God (**4:2**) has a dwelling that is higher and greater than anything on earth.

THE DECREE OF DARIUS
DANIEL 6:26

The empire of Babylon was soon overthrown by Darius the Mede. Just as Nebuchadnezzar had learned about God when He delivered the three Hebrews from the fiery furnace, Darius learned God's power when He protected Daniel in the lions' den (**Dan 6:16-23**). He wrote a decree that people throughout the kingdom must *"fear and reverence the God of Daniel"* (**v. 26a**). Specifically, Darius said, *"For he is the living God and he endures forever; his kingdom will not be destroyed, his dominion will never end"* (**v. 26b**). This unending kingdom that cannot be destroyed is God's eternal reign—and ours (**Rev 22:5**)—in heaven.

DANIEL'S DREAM
DANIEL 7:3-28

While Belshazzar was still king of Babylon (before the conquest of Darius the Mede), Daniel himself was given a night vision. In it were four beasts: a winged lion (a cherub), a bear, a winged leopard, and a terrifying beast with ten horns (**Dan 7:4-7**). As Daniel detailed each item of his dream, he unfolded an amazing parallel with John's vision in **Revelation**. Daniel foresaw things that would begin with the establishment of the church, but there were also things that would not fully happen until heaven. The following chart shows the remarkable similarity of the two visions:

Daniel	Revelation
Four winds *(7:2)*	Four winds *(7:1)*
Beasts out of sea *(7:3)*	Beast on shore of sea *(13:1)*
Four beasts *(7:4-7)*	Beast with four natures *(13:2)*
Lion	Leopard
Bear	Bear
Leopard	Lion
Great beast	Enormous dragon
Beast has ten horns *(7:7)*	Dragon has ten horns *(12:3; 17:3)*
Beast speaks boastfully *(7:8)*	Dragon utters proud words *(13:5)*
The Ancient of Days *(7:9)*	The First and the Last *(1:17)*
Hair white like wool *(7:9)*	Hair white like wool *(1:14)*
1,000s attended Him *(7:10)*	1,000s of angels *(5:11)*
10,000s before Him *(7:10)*	10,000 times 10,000 around Him *(5:11)*
Books opened *(7:10)*	Books opened *(20:11-15)*
Beast slain *(7:11)*	Beast thrown into lake of fire *(20:10)*
Son of man in clouds *(7:13)*	Son of man seated on cloud *(14:14)*
Given glory *(7:14)*	Given glory *(5:12-13)*
By all nations *(7:14)*	By all on earth *(5:13)*
Everlasting dominion *(7:14)*	Power for ever and ever *(5:13)*
Saints receive kingdom *(7:18)*	Saints reign with God *(22:5)*
War against saints *(7:21)*	War against saints *(13:7)*
Ten horns are ten kings *(7:24)*	Ten horns are ten kings *(17:12)*
Oppression to last "a time, times and half a time" *(7:25)*	Church sheltered "a time, times and half a time" *(12:14)*
Victory by Ancient of Days *(7:22)*	Victory by the Lamb *(17:14)*

Of special importance is Daniel's vision of *"one like a son of man, coming with the clouds of heaven"* (*v. 13*). In Revelation there is also someone *"like a son of man"* (*1:13*) who was dead and now lives for ever and ever (*1:18*). The picture of **Daniel 7:14** is clearly of Jesus Christ, who will have such authority that *"all peoples, nations and men of every language"* will worship Him. In heaven He will have *"everlasting dominion"* and His kingdom is *"one that will never be destroyed."* This is repeated even more emphatically in **Daniel 7:27-28**, *"Then the sovereignty, power and greatness of the kingdoms under the whole heaven will be handed over to the saints, the people of the Most High. His kingdom will be an everlasting kingdom, and all rulers will worship and* *obey him."* Thus concludes the most extensive preview of heaven anywhere in the OT.

Multitudes Who Sleep
in the Dust Will Rise
Daniel 12:1-13

Daniel closed his prophecy with a final picture of coming events. Part of what he wrote seems to point to Antiochus Epiphanes, the Syrian ruler who precipitated the Jewish revolt under the Maccabees in the 160s BC. But the opening and the close of this chapter clearly point to the end times.

"There will be a time of distress," Daniel was told, *"such as has not happened from the beginning of nations"* (**12:1a**). When that time comes, *"Everyone who is written in the book"* (**12:1b**; see **Rev 20:15**) will be delivered. To confirm that this points beyond the destruction of Jerusalem, Daniel also wrote, *"Multitudes who sleep in the dust of the earth will awake: some to everlasting life, others to shame and everlasting contempt"* (**v. 2**). This is the first (and only!) clear statement in the OT that both the righteous and the wicked will be brought back to life. This prophecy foretells a bodily resurrection from *"the dust of the earth."* It is also a clear statement that a judgment of eternal consequences will follow. God's people—*"those who are wise"*—will *"shine like the brightness of the heavens . . . like the stars for ever and ever"* (**v. 4**). (This statement led Dante to imagine in *The Divine Comedy* that the saints would become actual stars in the sky of heaven; see "Paradise," Canto XII.) Daniel was then told to seal these words *"until the time of the end"* (**v. 4**).

But when will these things happen? The answer seems to be a double prophecy, that is, one that will be fulfilled in two future stages. The initial phase will last for *"a time, times and half a time"* (**v. 7**), beginning from *"the time that the daily sacrifice is abolished and the abomination that causes desolation is set up"* (**v. 11**). This happened in the days of Antiochus Epiphanes (167 BC), when the priests were driven from the Temple and a swine was sacrificed on the altar. This "abomination" happened again when the Romans destroyed the Temple (AD 70), as predicted by Jesus (see **Mt 24:15** and **Lk 21:20**). But even after this event, John still writes about the *"time, times, and half a time"* during which the woman (the church) will be protected from destruction by God (*Rev 12:14*). Then comes the end (*Dan 12:9,12,13*), after which God's people will *"receive your allotted inheritance"* (*v. 13*).

CONCLUSION

Jeremiah prophesied right up to the time that God's people were carried off to Babylon. Daniel was a young man in the first wave of exiles; Ezekiel followed him into captivity shortly afterward. All three wrote things that would sustain the people's hope while they lived as aliens in a foreign land. Despite appearances, God was still in control and God's kingdom would at last be victorious. David's great Son will sit on the throne, and God's resurrected people will be blessed with His presence. A new Jerusalem with a crystal-clear river will be the capital of an everlasting kingdom. We who are Christians, ourselves now living as aliens in a foreign land (see *Php 3:20*), can find strong hope in these same promises.

WHAT DO YOU SAY?

1. Jeremiah promised that Jerusalem would be rebuilt and would never again be uprooted or demolished (*Jer 31:40*). Did this promise hold true AD 70?

2. Jeremiah also promised that David would never fail to have a descendant on the throne. How well did that promise work out?

3. What do we learn about heaven from *Ezekiel 1*?

4. What do we learn about God's future plans from *Ezekiel 34*?

5. *Ezekiel 47* has an amazing picture of a river flowing from the Temple. Why was this physically impossible? What was the point of making such a prediction?

6. What should we make of the remarkable similarities between *Daniel 7* and the Book of *Revelation*? Should either be taken literally?

7. *Daniel 12* has the only clear statement in the OT that both the wicked and the righteous will be resurrected. Why do you think there were not more such references?

CHAPTER NINE

HEAVEN IN THE PROPHETS OF ISRAEL

PART THREE: *The Minor Prophets*

All twelve of the Minor Prophets have something to contribute to the promises of life to come in heaven. Like the Major Prophets, they prophesy events in both the near future and in the distant future. This chapter will focus on selected passages that foretell the glories of heaven in that distant future.

In the OT canon these books are arranged in what the ancient Jews understood to be their chronological order. Some of the books have clear references to events by which they can be dated; others have dates assigned by tradition. Conservative scholars today usually date *Amos* before *Hosea*, but the exact dating of the books is not important in this study. It will be convenient for our purposes to examine these books in three groups: those that deal with the menace of Assyria, those that deal the menace of Babylon, and those that deal with issues after the return from Babylon.

PROPHETS IN THE DAYS OF ASSYRIAN POWER

HOSEA

Hosea is thought to be the only one of the written prophets to come from the northern kingdom. (This is based on his repeated references to northern cities and his unusual Hebrew dialect.) Hosea wrote just before the time when Assyria was about to swoop down on Israel and scatter the ten northern tribes to distant lands. He repeatedly warned of the coming destruction, but pleaded that even yet the nation could turn its heart to God. Moreover, it was not formal lip-service God wanted, but heartfelt worship. *"For I desire mercy, not sacrifice,"* God said through Hosea, *"and acknowledgment of God rather than burnt offerings"* (**Hos 6:6**).

Where, O Grave, Is Your Destruction?
Hosea 13:14

Israel was about to be destroyed because the nation had turned against God, who is its only true helper (**Hos 13:9**). But even in the coming calamity there was a ray of hope. *"I will ransom them from the power of the grave [**sheol**],"* God promised, *"I will redeem them from death"* (**v. 14**). The remainder of the verse provides a cry of victory that mocks death as powerless: *"Where, O death, are your plagues? Where, O grave [**sheol**], is your destruction?"* In nearly identical words this same taunt will be echoed nearly nine centuries later by Paul (see **1Cor 15:55**). The people of the northern kingdom might well perish in the Assyrian invasion; they might be dispersed to the four winds and die in a foreign land. But for those who turned back to God while the door of opportunity still stood open, there would be rescue from death and reward in heaven.

JOEL

While **Joel** cannot be dated with any certainty, the prophecy fits well in the ninth century BC with **Amos** and **Hosea**. Joel wrote after a great swarm of locusts had devastated Israel. His message was that this disaster should call Israel to repentance. If not, an invasion of even worse "locusts" would be coming. When it came, they would *"have the appearance of horses"* (*Joel 2:4*; see *Rev 9:7*) and would create *"a noise like that of chariots"* (*Joel 2:5*; see *Rev 9:9*). The invading army would be unstoppable, because it would be sent by the LORD Himself (*Joel 2:11*).

Rend Your Heart and
Not Your Garments
Joel 2:13

So what could Israel do? How could the nation lay claim to the deliverance God offers? Joel faithfully delivered God's demand: *"Rend your heart and not your garments,"* the LORD said, *"Return to the LORD your God, for he is gracious and compassionate, slow to anger and abounding in love"* (*Joel 2:13*). While this verse does not specifically say anything about heaven, it lays the groundwork for the promises that follow and declares the attitude that is necessary for a person to receive them.

I Will Pour Out My Spirit
on All Flesh
Joel 2:28

After the destruction, after the northern army had been driven far away (*Joel 2:20*), the people of Israel would have reason to rejoice (*v. 23*). God promised to repay them for the years of the locusts (*v. 25*) and *"never again will my people be ashamed"* (*v. 27*).

But the northern tribes did not return; the scattered people did not have reason to rejoice. What can God have meant? The fulfillment of His promise has two stages. The first stage took place on the Day of Pentecost when the church was founded. Peter quoted the words of *Joel 2:28* and said, in effect, "This preaching in foreign languages is what Joel prophesied" (see *Acts 2:14-21*). This is what Joel said: *"And afterward, I will pour out my Spirit on all people. Your sons and daughters will prophesy, your old men will dream dreams, your young men will see visions. . . . And everyone who calls on the name of the LORD will be saved"* (*Joel 2:28,32*). According to the Apostle Peter, this happened at Pentecost. But Joel's prophecy continues.

I Will Gather All Nations
Joel 3:1-21

There is clearly an additional fulfillment of Joel's prophecy that goes beyond the birth of the church at Pentecost. God said, *"I will gather all nations and bring them down to the Valley of Jehoshaphat"* (*Joel 3:2*). The name Jehoshaphat means, "The LORD judges," and what is pictured is the Day of Judgment in the end times. Joel continued, *"The day of the LORD is near in the valley of decision"* (*v. 14*), where God *"will sit to judge all the nations on every side"* (*v. 12*).

Then, when God has judged the nations and has vindicated His people, He promises, *"You will know that I, the LORD your God, dwell in Zion, my holy hill. Jerusalem will be holy; never again will foreigners invade her"* (*Joel 3:17*). Just as **Ezekiel 47:1** had also prophesied, *"A fountain will flow out of the LORD's house and will water the valley"* (*v. 18*; see **Zec 13:1; Rev 22:1-2**). Then *"Judah will be inhabited forever and Jerusalem through all generations"* (*v. 20*). Best of all, Joel gave this closing cry of victory: *"The LORD dwells in Zion!"* (*v. 21*, see **Rev 21:3**).

Joel's short book of prophecy provides hope for the future, not just the future of Israel, but the future of all God's people for all time. This hope is for far more than a repopulated Jerusalem secure from her enemies (which has never yet happened). This hope is a glorious expectation of an eternal habitation in heaven, where God will dwell in the midst of His people.

AMOS

Amos prophesied to Israel during the reign of Jeroboam (793–753 BC) and to Judah during the reign of Uzziah (792–740 BC), as stated in the opening verse of the book (*Am 1:1*). His message to both kingdoms was that God would punish them for their smug complacency (*Am 6:1*) and their abuse of the poor (*Am 8:4-6*). They were quite happy to hear God say, *"For three sins of Damascus, even for four,"* He would bring His wrath upon that city. But they were not as pleased to hear the LORD say through Amos, *"For three sins of Judah, even for four"* (*Am 2:4*) and *"For three sins of Israel, even for four, I will not turn back my wrath"* (*Am 2:6*). Therefore Amos called both kingdoms to repentance. *"Seek the LORD and live,"* Amos proclaimed, *"or he will sweep through the house of Joseph like a fire"* (*Am 5:6*). These were not empty words, for the Assyrian invasion was just over the horizon (722–721 BC).

In That Day I Will
Restore David's Fallen Tent
Amos 9:11-15

When the LORD gave the command, Israel would be slain by the sword and the survivors would be driven into exile (*Am 9:1-4*). This would happen to Israel in mere decades, and the devastation would be so complete that the northern kingdom would never recover. Yet Amos promised restoration. *"In that day,"* declared the LORD, *"I will restore David's fallen tent . . . restore its ruins, and build it as it used to be"* (*Am 9:11*). In those glorious days, *"The reaper will be overtaken by the plowman and the planter by the one treading grapes"* (*v. 13*). In other words, the harvest will be so bountiful that it will be time to plant again before it can all be gathered in, and it will grow to ripeness so quickly that vineyards are no sooner planted than the grapes are ready for treading into wine.

"I will bring back my exiled people Israel," promised the LORD (*Am 9:14*). It must be noted that this promise was not about Judah and its later exile in Babylon; this was about Israel, the northern kingdom, and its forced exile by Assyria. *"I will plant Israel in their own land,"* said God, *"never again to be uprooted from the land I have given them"* (*v. 15*). Like the closing words of Joel, these words of Amos give a final prediction of a paradise. While some might think the modern state of Israel is a sufficient fulfillment of these words, the miraculous harvests and the permanent security will come only in heaven.

OBADIAH

Obadiah is by far the shortest book in the OT. The vision of Obadiah was a warning against Edom, proud with a false sense of security in her rock cliffs at Petra (*v. 3*). Then the warning was expanded: *"The day of the LORD is near for all nations. As you have done, it will be done to you"* (*v. 15*). Some day God will finally bring about justice.

On Mount Zion Will Be Deliverance
Obadiah 17-21

When final justice is handed down, God's people will be redeemed. *"On Mount Zion will be deliverance,"* promised Obadiah, *"it will be holy"* (*v. 17a*). More significantly, the promise of restoration included the northern kingdom as well: *"And the house of Jacob will* possess its inheritance" (*v. 17b*). God's restored people will include both *"this company of Israelite exiles"* and *"the exiles from Jerusalem"* (*v. 19*). When the kingdom is rebuilt and the people are restored, then, Obadiah said, *"The kingdom will be the LORD's* (*v. 21*).

JONAH

Just when Israel was facing the impending peril from Assyria, the prophet Jonah was given the thankless task of helping Assyria escape God's judgment. Sometime during 800–750 BC he was sent to Nineveh, the great city that was soon (700 BC) to be made the capital of Assyria by Sennacherib. If they would listen to his warning and repent, they could avoid destruction. Perhaps Jonah was afraid to go to Nineveh; more likely, he was unwilling to help them (see *Jonah 4:2*). For whatever combination of reasons, he ran from God—right into the mouth of the great fish (*Jonah 1:1-17*).

Should I Not Be Concerned about That Great City?
Jonah 4:11

When Jonah finally did preach to Nineveh and they repented, God did not bring down destruction on them (*Jonah 3:10*). This displeased Jonah. With the help of an object lesson—a large sheltering vine—God let Jonah see inside His heart. There were many souls in Nineveh, including over 120,000 people (young children?) *"who cannot tell their right hand from their left. Should I not be concerned about that great city?"* (*Jonah 4:11*).

This is an indirect glimpse of heaven, to be sure, but it does say something about God's desire. He is *"not wanting anyone to perish, but everyone to come to repentance"* (*2Pet 3:9*). This is why John's vision of heaven includes not only people from all the tribes of Israel (*Rev 7:4-8*), but a great multitude *"from every nation, tribe, people and language"* (*Rev 7:9*). Should we not think that heaven will include all kinds of repentant sinners—even from Nineveh?

MICAH

Micah was a contemporary of Isaiah and Hosea, prophesying during the reigns of Jotham, Ahaz, and Hezekiah (*Mic 1:1*). He predicted the destruction of Samaria, the capital of the northern kingdom (*Mic*

1:6), with disaster approaching the very gates of Jerusalem (*Mic 1:12*). Eventually, Jerusalem herself would be *"a heap of rubble"* and the Temple hill would be *"a mound overgrown with thickets"* (*Mic 3:12*). But that would not be the end of the story; the LORD would yet restore His people and His kingdom.

The Mountain of the LORD's Temple
Will Be Established
Micah 4:1-7

Micah promised that *"in the last days"* the LORD will establish the mountain of His Temple (*Mic 4:1*). People will come to Jerusalem from many nations so they can be taught God's ways (*v. 2*). As we have seen in other prophets, Micah appears to be giving a prophecy with a double fulfillment. In the initial phase, the "last days" refers to the coming of Jesus (see *Heb 1:2; 9:26; 1Pet 1:20*) and the establishment of the church (*Acts 2:17*). Many nations did, in fact, hear the word of God on the Day of Pentecost (*Acts 2:9-11*), and the testimony of Jesus went from Jerusalem to the corners of the earth (*Acts 1:8*).

But as the details of the prophecy multiply, the ultimate fulfillment must be seen in events far beyond Jerusalem in the first century. In that final kingdom, *"Nation will not take up sword against nation, nor will they train for war anymore"* (*Mic 4:3*; see also *Isa 2:4*). God's people will walk in His name *"for ever and ever"* (*v. 5*), and *"The LORD will rule over them in Mount Zion from that day and forever"* (*v. 7*).

The Ruler from Bethlehem
Micah 5:2-6

The ruler of this kingdom of double fulfillment (church and heaven) will be born in Bethlehem. This *"ruler over Israel"* will be the One *"whose origins are from of old, from ancient times"* (*Mic 5:2*). These words of prophecy about the coming Messiah were so well known in the days of Herod the Great that his wise men were able to tell him immediately that the future king would be born in Bethlehem (*Mt 2:4-6*).

Under the leadership of this great Ruler and Shepherd, the people of God *"will live securely"* because their Leader's *"greatness will reach to the ends of the earth"* (*Mic 5:4*) and He *"will be their peace"* (*Mic 5:5*; see also *Eph 2:14*). Even though the Assyrian hordes would invade, the Messiah will deliver His people.

By the time Jesus was born, however, Assyria no longer posed a threat to Israel—or to anyone else! For many of the people of that time, however, it was an easy assumption that the Messiah would deliver them from their current enemy, Rome. But the true work of the Messiah, who was indeed from ancient times (*Jn 1:1*), was to establish the kingdom of heaven. Beginning with the church on earth, Jesus has begun a rule that will reach to the ends of the earth. Reaching its climax in heaven, this kingdom will bring final security and peace to God's people.

You Will Be True to Jacob
Micah 7:12-20

Micah closed his prophecy with a vision of future days when the enemies of Israel will come to Jerusalem in submission (*Mic 7:12*). Enemy nations will tremble before the LORD, but God's people will rejoice in the forgiveness of their sins (*Mic 7:16-19*). The God of heaven, ever true to His covenant promises, will keep His word.

> You will be true to Jacob,
>   and show mercy to Abraham,
> As you pledged on oath to our fathers
>   in days long ago. (*Mic 7:20*)

The honor of God is at stake in the keeping of His word. His promises deal with far more than merely the physical land of Israel and an earthly enemy such as Assyria. God has, in fact, kept the promise to Abraham by bringing his children of faith—not merely of bloodline—into the kingdom. Today all believers, both Jew and Gentile, have been made children of Abraham and heirs according to promise (*Rom 4:12-16; Gal 3:29*). Now we await our inheritance and *"rejoice in the hope of the glory of God"* (*Rom 5:2*). It is no small thing that God is keeping His promise to Abraham and his descendants—through us.

PROPHETS IN THE DAYS APPROACHING BABYLONIAN EXILE

NAHUM

By the time of Nahum, Assyria had brutally destroyed the northern kingdom and had scattered the ten tribes to the winds. God had used Assyria, *"the rod of my anger, in whose hand is the club of my wrath"* (*Isa 10:5*), to punish Israel. Now Assyria herself would be punished. Most of Nahum's prophecy, therefore, was addressed to Assyria as a warning of that punishment.

The LORD Will Not Leave the Guilty Unpunished
Nahum 1:2-3

In the opening words of his oracle, Nahum provided important information about the God of the end times. The LORD is *"a jealous and avenging God"*; He *"takes vengeance and is filled with wrath"* (*Nah 1:2*). He is a Judge of perfect justice, so He *"will not leave the guilty unpunished"* (*v. 3*). Although many nations had trembled before the unstoppable army of Assyria, the whole earth trembles at the presence of God (*v. 5*). This is the verdict of the divine Judge against Nineveh: *"I will prepare your grave, for you are vile"* (*v. 14*). When God brings His perfect peace, it will include the fact that the wicked have been appropriately punished.

But there is good news for God's own people. While God is full of wrath and executes vengeance on His enemies, to those who are faithful to His covenant He is *"slow to anger and great in power"* (*v. 3*). Furthermore, *"The LORD is good, a refuge in times of trouble"* and *"cares for those who trust in him"* (*v. 7*). Therefore, even after Judah has been carried away into her own captivity, there will yet be a runner who brings good news and proclaims peace. Even in exile God's people can look forward to a time when: *"No more will the wicked invade you; they will be completely destroyed"* (*v. 15*).

In the prophetic foreground, Assyria would indeed be destroyed and Judah would come back from captivity in Babylon. But nowhere in this foreground would Judah live securely in peace. It is in the prophetic distance that the more important fulfillment comes. There in eternal heaven God's people will be finally safe; there the wicked will never again invade.

HABAKKUK

Habakkuk, a contemporary of Jeremiah, prophesied around 600 BC. For over a hundred years Israel and Judah had watched in fear as Assyria, Egypt, and Babylon struggled for mastery of the Middle East.

God's people had foolishly tried to create alliances with first one nation, and then another, but there seemed to be no way they could find safety. What was going to happen? To whom could they turn?

Watch—and Be Utterly Amazed!
Habakkuk 1:5-6

Habakkuk's oracle began with a complaint: *"How long, O LORD, must I call for help?"* (**Hab 1:2**). God answered him with these surprising words: *"Look at the nations and watch—and be utterly amazed"* (**Hab 1:5**). God was going to do what no one in Judah would be able to believe. He was going to raise up the Babylonians, *"a ruthless and impetuous people,"* to sweep across the land (**Hab 1:6**). Then Habakkuk understood. God, who is *"from everlasting"* (**Hab 1:12**), had appointed Babylon to execute judgment. God, whose *"eyes are too pure to look on evil"* (**Hab 1:13**) would use Babylon to punish Judah just as He used Assyria to punish Israel.

For the Earth Will Be Filled . . .
Habakkuk 2:14

Through all the coming turmoil, God's people needed to understand that God was still in control. He would use Babylon to punish the unfaithfulness of Judah, and then He would punish Babylon for even greater sins. At that time God would say to Babylon, *"Now it is your turn!"* (**Hab 2:16**). Therefore Habakkuk and all Judah must learn to say, *"Yet I will wait patiently for the day of calamity to come on the nation invading us"* (**Hab 3:16**).

The ultimate lesson of Habakkuk goes well beyond ancient history and an invading nation that no longer exists. The lesson is that God acts in history to move events toward their conclusion. Then, *"the earth will be filled with the knowledge of the glory of the LORD, as the waters cover the sea"* (**Hab 2:14**). This did not happen in 600 BC; it will be the glory of the end times!

ZEPHANIAH

Zephaniah was the great-grandson of good king Hezekiah. He wrote at a time when Jerusalem was being threatened by Babylon, but seemed to have felt a false security that things were going to turn out all right after all. Zephaniah delivered an urgent alarm: God was going to punish *"those who are complacent"* (**Zep 1:12**). *"The great day of the LORD is near,"* he cried, *"near and coming quickly."*

The Whole World
Will Be Consumed
Zephaniah 1:14-18

Zephaniah's forecast of doom was against all nations, both near and far. God's punishment would come upon Philistia (*2:4-7*), Moab and Ammon (*2:8-11*), Cush (*2:12*), Assyria (*2:13-15*), and . . . Jerusalem (*3:1-18*). But the great day of the LORD for those few nations is only a foretaste of more to come. Zephaniah warned, *"In the fire of his jealousy the whole world will be consumed, for he will make a sudden end of all who live in the earth"* (*1:18*). God said He has decided to *"assemble the nations, to gather the kingdoms and to pour out my wrath on them—all my fierce anger"* (*3:8*).

I Will Bring You Home
Zephaniah 3:20

Still, in the midst of unbridled fury, there is a reason for hope. Through times of punishment it is God's intention to *"purify the lips of the peoples, that all of them may call on the name of the LORD and serve him shoulder to shoulder"* (*Zep 3:9*). The people of God will rejoice in that day, because *"The LORD your God is with you. . . . He will take great delight in you, he will quiet you with his love, he will rejoice over you with singing"* (*3:17*). This is the kind of imagery that prepares us for the NT teaching that our Lord rejoices over us as His bride (see *Eph 5:25-27; Rev 19:7-9*).

Then comes the climax of God's promise to a people threatened with exile: *"At that time I will gather you; at that time I will bring you home"* (*Zep 3:20*). This promise stands true, even though Israel never came back from the Assyrian exile and only a minority of Judah ever returned from Babylon (with the majority scattered all over the Mediterranean world). But the day is coming when God will gather all His people from every part of the world. Then He will give us *"honor and praise among all the peoples of the earth"* (*3:21*). Home at last—in heaven!

PROPHETS AFTER THE BABYLONIAN EXILE

HAGGAI

Mighty Babylon herself was conquered by Cyrus and the armies of Persia. In 538 BC Cyrus issued a decree that the Jews should return to Jerusalem and build a Temple to *"the LORD, the God of heaven"* (**Ezra 1:2**). The cost of construction was to be paid out of the royal treasury, and the sacred vessels that were stolen by Nebuchadnezzar were to be returned (**Ezra 6:4-5**). Because of opposition from the Samaritans and indifference among the Jews, however, this project stalled. So in 520 BC Haggai sounded the call for his people to get back to work. He warned them that God was displeased, because His house *"remains a ruin, while each of you is busy with his own house"* (**Hag 1:10**).

I Will Shake All Nations
Haggai 2:6-9

The people who returned from exile had small plans; they just wanted to build their own little houses and plant a few crops. God, however, had big plans. His plans stretched back to the time He brought Israel out of Egypt (**Hag 2:5**); they stretch forward to the end of times. *"In a little while,"* said the LORD Almighty, *"I will once more shake the heavens and the earth. . . . I will shake all nations, and the desired of all nations will come, and I will fill this house with glory"* (**2:6**).

The glory of God never came on the rebuilt Temple however; it did not even have the ark of the covenant in the Holy of Holies. (Speaking of this sacred room in the first century, Josephus said, "In this there was nothing at all." See Josephus, *Wars*, I, 5, 1.) Neither did the promise come true when Jesus taught on the Temple grounds, never entering either the Holy Place or the Holy of Holies. In fact, the prophecy of God's returning glory is yet to be fulfilled. The writer of Hebrews quoted Haggai in reference to the end times, saying, *"Once more I will shake not only the earth but also the heavens. The words 'once more' indicate the removing of what can be shaken— that is, created things—so that what cannot be shaken may remain"* (**Heb 12:26-27**). Therefore, we have Scripture itself affirming that the prophecy of Haggai points to the end of the age, the final judgment, and heaven.

ZECHARIAH

Zechariah's prophetic ministry followed immediately on the heels of Haggai. Like Haggai, he challenged the people to complete the rebuilding of the Temple. Also like Haggai, he foresaw a return of the glory of God to Jerusalem. This was minimally fulfilled in the rebuilt Temple and in the coming of Jesus to Jerusalem, but Zechariah's words point to an ultimate fulfillment in heaven.

The Measuring Line Will Be
Stretched Out over Jerusalem
Zechariah 1:16

Zechariah explained to the people of Jerusalem that the calamities that had come upon them were deserved (*Zec 1:6*). After the calamities, however, God would bring blessings back to His people. *"I will return to Jerusalem with mercy,"* said the LORD, *"and there my house will be rebuilt"* (*1:16*). The "measuring line" would also be stretched out over Jerusalem, meaning that the plans for construction included the entire city. Without the additional prophecies later in Zechariah this could well apply only to physical Jerusalem. But with those prophecies, and with the similarity to the measurements of the city in *Revelation 21:15*, our attention is drawn to the future.

I Am Coming, and I Will Live
among You
Zechariah 2:10-11

Zechariah assured his readers that God had great plans for the future of Jerusalem. The LORD said, *"Shout and be glad, O Daughter of Zion. For I am coming, and I will live among you"* (*Zec 2:10*). These words are strongly predictive of *Revelation 21:3*, *"Now the dwelling of God is with men, and he will live with them."* Later in his prophecy Zechariah will echo these words: *"This is what the LORD says, 'I will return to Zion and dwell in Jerusalem'"* (*Zec 8:3*).

The future fulfillment of *Zechariah 2:10* is also shown by the verse that follows: *"Many nations will be joined with the LORD in that day and will become my people. I will live among you"* (*2:11*). This is how in the end God keeps His ancient promise to Abraham: *"All peoples on earth will be blessed through you"* (*Gen 12:3*). In the ingathering of the nations around the throne of God in heaven, there will be represen-tatives of every nation, tribe, people and language (*Rev 7:9*).

See, Your King Comes to You
Zechariah 9:9-10

Zechariah foresaw a day when *"never again will an oppressor over-run"* God's people (*Zec 9:8*). He told Jerusalem to rejoice, saying, *"Your king comes to you, righteous and having salvation, gentle and rid-ing on a donkey, on a colt the foal of a donkey"* (*9:9*). These words would be fulfilled first, of course, at the triumphal entry (*Mt 21:5*). But their ultimate fulfillment is a picture of a worldwide King, whose dominion is complete. The warhorses and the battle bow will be gone. *"He will proclaim peace to the nations."* Zechariah promised. *"His rule will extend from sea to sea and from the River to the ends of the earth"* (*Zec 9:10*).

King over the Whole Earth
Zechariah 14:8-11

Zechariah promised a rebuilt Jerusalem that will have a fountain opened to the house of David (*Zec 13:1; 14:8*; see *Eze 47:1-12; Joel 3:18; Rev 22:1-2*). Ruling in this new Jerusalem will be God Himself. *"The LORD will be king over the whole earth. On that day there will be one LORD, and his name the only name"* (*Zec 14:9*). The city will be perma-nently inhabited; *"never again will it be destroyed"* (*14:11*). While this has simply not been true of the physical city, it will be eternally true of the heavenly Jerusalem.

MALACHI

The last of the prophets of the OT was Malachi, who wrote around 433 BC. In his days Jerusalem and the Temple had been rebuilt. But the people of the covenant became indifferent to God and lax in their obe-dience to His commands. Perhaps they were resentful because they had not become a mighty empire and God had not come to live among them in all His glory. They questioned whether God had truly loved them (*Mal 1:2*) and whether He was a God of justice (*Mal 2:17*). *"What did we gain,"* they asked, *"by carrying out his requirements?"* (*Mal 3:14*). In response to such charges, Malachi made it clear that it was the peo-ple themselves, not God, who had been unfaithful to the covenant.

For I Am a Great King
Malachi 1:14

God deserved to be praised and honored by all nations. But while
His name should be great, His people had profaned it by treating His
table as defiled and contemptible (*Mal 1:11-12*). They brought animals that were injured, crippled, or diseased as their offering to Him.
As a result, God was outraged. *"I am a great king,"* He declared, *"and
my name is to be feared among the nations"* (*1:14*). God still planned
His worldwide rule, His eternal kingdom, but His people were refusing to let it happen by their failure to keep covenant with Him.

The Distinction between the
Righteous and the Wicked
Malachi 3:16-18

God does not change (*Mal 3:6*). He keeps His ancient promise to
Abraham to bless all nations (*Gen 12:3*), and He resists blotting out
Israel once and for all. Therefore Malachi foresaw a day when there
would be *"a scroll of remembrance"* written down, with the names of
all *"those who feared the LORD and honored his name"* (*Mal 3:16*). In
that future day God promised, *"I will spare them, just as in compassion
a man spares his son who serves him"* (*3:17*). This "scroll of remembrance" (so similar to the "book of life" in *Revelation 20:15*) will
enable God to judge righteously. One that day, the LORD promised,
*"You will again see the distinction between the righteous and the wicked,
between those who serve God and those who do not"* (*3:18*).

CONCLUSION

Every one of the Minor Prophets contributed to the growing body
of knowledge about the end times. They affirmed that there will be
life beyond the grave. They affirmed that God will—in this life and in
the next—restore the fortunes of fallen Israel. In this way God will
keep His promises to Abraham and to David. The restored kingdom
focuses on an earthly empire centered around Jerusalem, with an
additional glance toward things to be fulfilled in the church, but
always ends up with elements projected into a more distant future.
The ultimate empire at the end will be everlasting, have God/Messiah
living with the people as their King, will have a river of life flowing

from the Temple, and will be blessed with abundance beyond human imagination.

The future kingdom will also include Gentiles. God will gather the nations and will show that He has concern for them, as well as for Israel. There will be a day of judgment against the wicked, but the righteous will join Israel in praise of her God. Then the whole earth will be filled with the glory of God.

WHAT DO YOU SAY?

1. When the menace of Assyria and Babylon was looming on the horizon, why did God's people need to be told about a kingdom in the far-distant future?

2. What do you think the typical Israelite thought about Hosea's statement that God would ransom them from *sheol* and redeem them from death?

3. Joel promised that a fountain would flow out of the LORD's house and water the valley. What is that about?

4. Why do so many of the LORD's promises have to do with Jerusalem and Mount Zion? Does this mean anything for the present Jerusalem in the modern state of Israel?

5. If the prophets sometimes prophesied about a near fulfillment and a distant fulfillment in the same verses, how do we tell that a particular prophecy is primarily distant?

6. Do you blame the Jews in Jesus' day for thinking so much about the restored kingdom?

7. When will the LORD be king over all the earth, as Zechariah promised?

CHAPTER TEN

HEAVEN IN THE SYNOPTIC GOSPELS

Jesus spoke often of heaven. It is the home from which He came and the home to which He will return. It is the reward of the Beatitudes, the theme of the parables, and the heart of His promises. Most of all, Jesus spoke about heaven as His kingdom. This kingdom exists on earth, in a fashion, but it will have its ultimate reality in the afterlife.

HEAVEN IN THE GOSPELS

THE BEGINNING AND THE END

Even before Jesus was born, it was clear that He would be the One to fulfill the promises of the long-awaited Messiah. Malachi's prophecy (*Mal 4:5-6*) was fulfilled when an angel announced to Zechariah that his son John the Baptist would go forth to turn the people of Israel back to the Lord (*Lk 1:16-17*). Isaiah's promise (*Isa 40:3-5*) was fulfilled when John went into the desert to *"prepare the way for the Lord"* (*Lk 3:4-6*). Just as nearly all of the old prophets promised, the Messiah came and would be given the throne of His father David and this restored kingdom will never end (*Lk 1:32-33*). At His birth the shepherds were told,

137

"He is Messiah the Lord" (*Lk 2:11*). Then the heavenly host of angels proclaimed, *"Glory to God in the highest, and on earth peace to men on whom his favor rests"* (*Lk 2:14*). Thus, it was clear from the outset that the highest heaven was reaching down to men to establish a kingdom that will never end.

At the beginning of Jesus' public ministry in the Gospel of **Matthew**, heaven was the keynote. *Chapter four* records, *"From that time on Jesus began to preach, 'Repent, for the kingdom of heaven is near'"* (*Mt 4:17; Mk 1:15*). When Jesus carried His ministry into all the towns and villages, He kept preaching *"the good news of the kingdom"* (*Mt 9:35*). When He sent out the Twelve, this kingdom was also to be prominent in their message. Jesus told them, *"As you go, preach this message: 'The kingdom of heaven is near'"* (*Mt 10:7*). What is this "kingdom of heaven"? What do the Synoptic Gospels say? (We will pursue this study through **Matthew**, **Mark**, and **Luke** in chronological order, as found in standard Gospel harmonies.)

TODAY THIS SCRIPTURE IS FULFILLED IN YOUR HEARING
LUKE 4:18-20

Jesus always knew what He was doing. From the beginning of His ministry He knew that He was fulfilling the ancient prophecies about the Messiah and the restored kingdom. When he spoke at the synagogue in His hometown of Nazareth, He chose this passage as His text:

> The Spirit of the Lord is on me,
>   because he has anointed me
>   to preach good news to the poor.

> He has sent me to proclaim freedom for the prisoners
> and recovery of sight for the blind,
> to release the oppressed,
> to proclaim the year of the Lord's favor. (**Lk 4:18-19**)

Then He shocked His audience with these words: *"Today this scripture is fulfilled in your hearing"* (**v. 21**).

The devout students of Scripture in that audience knew the text (**Isa 61:1-2**). As we observed in the study of Isaiah's prophecies, this text promises that the "ancient ruins" will be rebuilt in the days of the Messiah. This work began in the kingdom on earth—the church—but it will find the *"everlasting joy"* (**Isa 61:7**) of bridegroom and bride (**Isa 61:10**) in heaven.

HEAVEN IN THE BEATITUDES
MATTHEW 5:2-12; LUKE 6:20-23

Jesus set the tone for the Sermon on the Mount (**Matthew 5–7**) with promises of heaven. For each group of people whom He congratulates in the Beatitudes, a promise of heaven is given. *"Blessed are the poor in spirit,"* Jesus said, *"for theirs is the kingdom of heaven"* (**Mt 5:3**). As the promises of these verses mount, it becomes clear that their ultimate fulfillment points toward the future. The "blessed" people will enjoy what the prophets foresaw: a restored kingdom, the eternal blessedness of heaven. Jesus (and the prophets) promised the following:

They will be comforted (**Mt 5:4; Isa 40:1**)
They will inherit the earth (**Mt 5:5; Ps 37:11**)
They will be filled (**Mt 5:6; Isa 55:1-2**)
They will be shown mercy (**Mt 5:7; Jer 33:26**)
They will see God (**Mt 5:8; Ps 24:4**)
They will be called the sons of God (**Mt 5:9; Isa 43:6**)
Theirs is the kingdom of heaven (**Mt 5:10**)
Great is their reward in heaven (**Mt 5:12**)

It is striking that such promises are repeatedly seen in connection with the Messiah who will come and rule over an everlasting kingdom. While there may be a certain preview of these promises in the community of the church, the ultimate fulfillment points to heaven.

Two of the promises deserve special comment. First, Jesus said the meek *"will inherit the earth"* (**Mt 5:5**). This promise, quoted from **Psalm 37:11**, is a good example of the double fulfillment of many OT prom-

The Greek word for "blessed" in the Beatitudes is often found in secular documents of the ancient world, describing people who were thought to have found favor with the gods. Specifically, the word was used for people who have just had a baby, people who have been successful in business, or people who have shown how smart they are. Today, when people have a baby, get a promotion, or graduate from college, we buy a card that says, "Congratulations!"

ises. The people of God could expect one aspect of the blessing in their own time by possessing the Promised Land. But God had far more in mind for His children than just that rather mediocre piece of real estate in Palestine. After the earth is purified with fire (*2Pet 3:10-13*), there will be a new heaven and a new earth (*Rev 21:1*). Whether the "new earth" is the same physical planet does not really matter, but it could very well be. Scripture describes the new earth as a real place, with trees and a river and food. This is the earth that the meek will inherit.

The second special promise in the Beatitudes is that the pure in heart *"will see God"* (*Mt 5:8*). Throughout the OT the people were prevented from looking at God's face, because no one could see Him and live (*Ex 33:20; Jn 1:18*). But when the meek inherit the new earth, and God comes to live with His people (*Rev 21:3*), they will *"see his face"* (*Rev 22:4*). God, who has always been unseen and unseeable, will be so no more. Finally, the blessed people *"will see God."*

Thus, the Beatitudes provide an initial glimpse of heaven, a place much like a purified earth. God's children will enjoy the presence of God Himself, and God will give them His mercy and comfort. At long last they will escape the environment of sin and will be filled with the righteousness for which they have always longed. Although they have been poor and hungry and persecuted (*Lk 6:20-23*), theirs is the kingdom of heaven.

YOU WILL NOT ENTER THE KINGDOM OF HEAVEN
MATTHEW 5:19-20

Jesus did not come to abolish the Law or the Prophets; He came to fulfill them (*Mt 5:17*). He came to provide the righteousness demanded by the Law and to fulfill the promises given by the Prophets. To His astonished listeners He said, *"Unless your righteousness surpasses that of the Pharisees and the teachers of the law, you will certainly not enter the kingdom of heaven"* (*v. 20*).

The righteousness that Jesus demands is not merely the external, ritual kind the self-righteous Pharisees had (*Mt 23:5; Lk 18:9-14*). Jesus requires a complete righteousness—that He provides by His atoning death—that becomes the inner desire and inherent behavior of our lives (*Mt 5:21-48*). But significantly, we must have this righteousness before we can enter the kingdom. If the kingdom were only the church, this would mean that we must attain righteousness on our own outside the church, which is impossible. In this verse Jesus clearly treats entering "the kingdom of heaven" as entering heaven itself.

YOUR FATHER IN HEAVEN
MATTHEW 5:45–6:1

Throughout the Gospels Jesus repeatedly spoke of God as *"your Father in heaven"* (*Mt 5:45*) and *"your heavenly Father"* (*Mt 5:47*). These simple words remind us of a profound truth: God is in heaven. It is true that God is present everywhere in the universe (*Ps 139:7-12*), but heaven is His home.

Thus, Jesus called His listeners to turn their eyes upward, away from earthly things. It may be standard practice on earth to hate one's enemies, but as followers of Jesus we should love everyone, just as our Father in heaven does (*v. 45*). In treating all men well, we should aim for nothing less than to *"be perfect,"* as our heavenly Father is perfect (*v. 47*).

Then Jesus introduced a curious concept, one with which we shall wrestle in several other texts. He said that if we do our acts of righteousness (giving, praying, fasting) only to be seen by other men, we will *"have no reward"* from our Father in heaven (*Mt 6:1*). Unfortunately, Jesus did not specify what that reward might be. It could be heaven itself, in which case all faithful people will receive the same reward. Or it could be that God will reward different people in different ways (in degree of honor, in areas of responsibility, etc.) Other texts that hint toward different levels of rewards include *Matthew 10:41-42; 11:11; 13:8; 16:27; 25:21-29; Mark 9:41; Luke 14:14; 19:17-26; 22:29; 1 Corinthians 3:8-14; 9:17*. We will see a much larger number of texts, however, that will speak only of those who are rewarded with eternal life and those who are not.

As we consider the possibility that we will not have identical rewards in heaven, we should also consider Jesus' well-known words in *Matthew 6:20-21*: *"Lay up for yourselves treasures in heaven. . . . For where your treasure is, there your heart will be also."* By committing our treasures to God's work in the earthly kingdom, somehow we are storing up treasures for our future enjoyment in the heavenly kingdom. In this context, however, it should be noted that Jesus did not say that this will cause some Christians in heaven to have more treasure than other Christians.

"OUR FATHER IN HEAVEN . . ."
MATTHEW 6:9-10

At the heart of the Sermon on the Mount is the model prayer that begins, *"Our Father in heaven"* (*Mt 6:9*). We are to pray that His name will be hallowed, and that His kingdom will come. This prayer, for the coming of the long-awaited kingdom, began to be granted when the church was founded, but the ultimate kingdom is heaven.

The next part of the prayer establishes an important fact: God's will is always done in heaven, and it would be highly desirable to have His will always enacted on earth. The very fact that we must pray, *"Your will be done,"* is a constant reminder that things here are not always what God wants. The perfect kingdom—the final kingdom—is heaven, the place where everything is the way God wants it to be. The imperfect kingdom—the temporal kingdom—is on earth, where God's people try to be consistent in letting God have His way with their lives. Much on earth does not go well, however, because in this fallen world the human race did not—and does not—choose God's will.

SEEK FIRST HIS KINGDOM
MATTHEW 6:33

The "heavenly Father" watches over all the earth. He takes care of the birds (*Mt 6:26*) and clothes the grass with flowers (*v. 30*). The "heavenly Father" knows what we need and promises to take care of us. Therefore, we should not focus our efforts on those needs (as the pagans do). We should *"seek first his kingdom and his righteousness, and all these things will be given"* to us (*v. 33*).

If this promise is about life on earth only, then many of God's people have not seen its fulfillment. God's people have sometimes *"gone about in sheepskins and goatskins, destitute, persecuted and mistreated"* (**Heb 11:37**). They have gone hungry; they have been fed to the lions. Clearly God intends to settle accounts at the end—in heaven (as in the context of **Mt 6:20**).

NOT EVERYONE WILL ENTER THE KINGDOM OF HEAVEN
MATTHEW 7:13-14,21-23

Toward the end of the Sermon on the Mount there is a bitter truth: not everyone will go to heaven. Jesus expressed this in two ways. First, He offered the contrast of two paths (**Mt 7:13-14**). The road to life begins through a narrow gate and follows a difficult, constricted path. Few will find and follow it. The other road starts with a wide gate and follows a spacious, roomy path. Many will follow this path, only to find in the end that it leads to destruction.

Second, in a following paragraph Jesus stated plainly, *"Not everyone who says to me, 'Lord, Lord,' will enter the kingdom of heaven, but only he who does the will of my Father who is in heaven"* (**Mt 7:21**). Many will say to Jesus "on that day" that they have done miracles in Jesus' name, but He will send them away as evildoers (**Mt 7:22-23**). The contrast of life vs. destruction (**vv. 13-14**), which will be declared on the day of judgment, (**v. 22**) makes it clear that Jesus is talking about the afterlife.

A small, but growing, number of evangelical writers are embracing an idea called "inclusivism." They believe that people can be saved only by the blood of Christ, but that specific knowledge of Christ may not be necessary. They suggest that God may hold people responsible only for responding to whatever degree of truth they may have been given. In this way, a much larger number of people—perhaps even a majority of the human race—will ultimately be saved. Well-known writers with this view include C.S. Lewis, John R.W. Stott, and Clark Pinnock. However, while we should certainly rejoice for anyone God chooses to save, we must not allow wishful thinking to overthrow the clear teaching of Jesus that only "few" will travel the road that leads to life.

THE FEAST WITH ABRAHAM
IN THE KINGDOM OF HEAVEN
MATTHEW 8:11-12

On one occasion in Capernaum, a centurion came to Jesus and asked that his servant might be healed (*Mt 8:6; Lk 7:3*). Impressed with the soldier's faith, Jesus granted his request. Then He used the incident to show how God will honor the faith of Gentiles, as well as Jews. He described a day when *"many will come from the east and the west, and will take their places at the feast with Abraham, Isaac and Jacob in the kingdom of heaven."* (*Mt 8:11*; Jesus repeated this same prediction on another occasion in *Lk 13:28*.) From His statement we can draw at least three truths: (1) There is a wideness in God's mercy, extending far enough to include Gentiles. (2) The "kingdom of heaven" often refers to the afterlife where we will join the saints of past ages. (3) Heaven can be well described as a "feast."

The following verse, however, has a bleak prediction for those who are not included in the feast. Many who had considered themselves "subjects of the kingdom" will be thrown outside. (This picture of doom for Jews who do not accept their Messiah is a recurring theme in Jesus' sermons and parables. See *Mt 8:10; 9:13; 10:33; 11:20-25; 21:28-32,33-44; 22:8-10; 23:37-39; Lk 4:24-27; Jn 4:21-24; 5:39-40; 8:24; 10:16; 16:1-3*.) Outside, in the darkness, *"there will be weeping and gnashing of teeth"* (*8:12*). Inside, the faithful people of God—both Jews and Gentiles—will enjoy the banquet of eternity with Abraham, Isaac, and Jacob.

THE KINGDOM OF HEAVEN
IS ADVANCING
MATTHEW 11:11-14

Jesus said there was no one born of woman who was greater than John the Baptist, yet the least in the kingdom of heaven is greater than John (*Mt 11:11*). The point is not so much on differing levels of greatness in heaven, as on the great blessing that all in the new covenant have received.

Now that the Messiah had come, the kingdom of heaven was *"forcefully advancing"* (*v. 12*). The restored kingdom, the promise of the ages, was coming. Jesus said, *"All the Prophets and the Law prophesied until John,"* and John himself was the fulfillment of the very last prophecy of the OT (*Mal 4:5*). The rebuilding of the ancient kingdom of David was already beginning during Jesus' lifetime. When He cast out demons, for instance, He could say, *"The kingdom of God has come upon you"* (*Mt 12:28*). This kingdom would find greater expression in the church, and would finally reach completion in heaven.

PARABLES OF THE KINGDOM
MATTHEW 13
(PARALLELS IN MARK 4 AND LUKE 8)

The parables of the kingdom of heaven lift our imaginations to another world. It is a world where crops are abundant, where beggars feast like kings, and where angels dance for joy. This kingdom has a wonderful blend of the "now" and the "not yet." It is a kingdom that *"many prophets and righteous men longed to see"* (*Mt 13:17*), but until Jesus came, they could not. Now the disciples with Jesus—and His disciples of all generations since then—can catch a glimpse of the wonders that are and the wonders that are to come. As Jesus said, *"The knowledge of the kingdom of heaven has been given to you"* (*v. 11*).

The first parable is a picture of failed crops and, finally, an amazing harvest (*Mt 13:1-23*). While the seed does not thrive in some soils, when it falls into good ground it bears thirty, sixty, even one hundred times the amount that was planted. (With the primitive farming methods available in the first century, a typical harvest would be sevenfold.) The abundance promised by the prophets was going to happen after all, but in a way they did not expect.

In the second parable, the people are not the soil, but the seed (*Mt 13:24-30,37-43*). The *"kingdom of heaven is like"* a man who has good seed growing into fine wheat and bad seed growing into weeds. At the time of harvest, the weeds are gathered first and put in bundles to be burned (*v. 30*). Then the wheat is harvested and put into the master's barn. Jesus Himself provides the correct interpretation for this parable:

> The one who sowed the good seed is the Son of Man. The field is the world, and the good seed stands for the sons of the kingdom. The weeds are the sons of the evil one, and the enemy who sows them is the devil. The harvest is the end of the age, and the harvesters are angels. (*vv. 37-39*)

Interestingly for "secret rapture" theorists, the bad are collected first. They are thrown into *"the fiery furnace, where there will be weeping and gnashing of teeth" (v. 42)*. But the righteous will shine like the sun in the kingdom of their Father (*v. 43*).

A third parable says *"the kingdom of heaven is like"* a tiny mustard seed (*Mt 13:31*). It was the smallest of the garden seeds that men planted, yet it grew spectacularly and became *"the largest of garden plants" (v. 32)*. The obvious teaching is that with a small beginning, the kingdom would grow to a phenomenal size. The same truth about the kingdom of heaven is taught in the next brief parable, about the explosive influence of a small amount of leaven in a large amount of dough (*Mt 13:33*).

> The mustard seed not only grows into something big, it also grows into something messy. Because it could easily spread unwanted into nearby areas, the *Mishnah* (recording Jewish traditions from AD 200 to 500) prohibited planting mustard seeds in certain areas (*Kilaim* 2.9 and 3.2). The fact that mustard plants were not always welcome adds an ironic twist to Jesus' parable of a spreading kingdom.

Finally, four more brief parables tell about *"the kingdom of heaven."* The kingdom is like a treasure in a field, bought with all a man had and then possessed in joy (*Mt 13:44*). The kingdom is like a fine pearl, bought with all that a merchant had (*v. 45*). (Obviously, the kingdom of heaven is a prize that *must* be attained, at whatever cost!) The kingdom is like a net that caught all kinds of fish. The good fish are kept; the trash fish are thrown away (*v. 48*). As Jesus explained, *"This is how it will be at the end of the age. The angels will come and separate the wicked from the righteous and throw them into the fiery furnace, where there will be weeping and gnashing of teeth" (vv. 49-50)*. The kingdom (and the one who teaches it) is like the owner of a house who goes to his storeroom and brings out treasures old and new (*v. 52*). This is a picture of two covenants, old and new, bringing people into the kingdom.

THE KEYS OF THE KINGDOM OF HEAVEN
MATTHEW 16:19

In the third year of Jesus' ministry, events were moving toward the inevitable climax. The betrayal, the trials, and the cross awaited in

Jerusalem. Therefore Jesus led His disciples to the region of Caesarea Philippi, far north of their usual territory, to pose a pivotal question to them: *"Who do you say that I am?"* (*Mt 16:15*). Simon Peter rose to the challenge first, answering, *"You are the **Messiah**, the Son of the Living God"* (*v. 16*). By translating "the Christ" as "the Messiah," we can focus on what this would have meant to His disciples. They were faithful Jews who believed the promises of the restored kingdom (see *Mt 20:21-23; Lk 22:29-30; Acts 1:6*).

Jesus commended Peter for his answer. He called him "a rock" (*petros*) and said that His church (or kingdom) would be built on "this rock" (*petra*). The foundation rock was not Peter himself, of course, but the truth that Jesus is the Messiah. Even so, Jesus gave Peter an important promise: *"I will give you the keys of the kingdom of heaven; whatever you bind on earth will be bound in heaven, and whatever you loose on earth will be loosed in heaven"* (**16:19**).

When Peter preached the gospel on the Day of Pentecost, he used the keys to open the way to the kingdom of heaven. Significantly, this meant two things. First, entrance into the kingdom of heaven meant becoming a part of the church, the kingdom on earth (*Acts 2:41,47*). Second, this same act of entering the kingdom had eternal consequences. To become part of the kingdom on earth is to have a share in the kingdom in heaven.

The promise made to Peter in **Matthew 16:19** was that whatever he bound or loosed on earth would be bound or loosed in heaven. The same promise was extended to all the apostles in **John 20:23**. The sins that were forgiven on the basis of their gospel (*Jn 17:10; Acts 2:38*), or not forgiven because of rejection of that gospel (*Acts 4:12*), would be forgiven or not forgiven in heaven. Peter, as an apostolic spokesman, had great prominence; however, Scripture does not depict him as the judge of humanity at the pearly gates.

SAVING YOUR LIFE, LOSING YOUR SOUL
MATTHEW 16:25-28 (MARK 8:35-38)

Jesus knew that "crunch time" was fast approaching. After Peter's confession, Jesus began to explain the sufferings and death that awaited Him (*Mt 16:21*). Even so, on the third day He would be raised to life again. Sufferings—and ultimate resurrection—also awaited the disciples.

According to Jesus, a man can try to save his life now, but will lose his soul later (*vv. 25-26*). *"For the Son of Man is going to come in his Father's glory with his angels,"* the Lord said, *"and then he will reward each person according to what he has done"* (*v. 27*). This is a clear promise that heaven will be the reward that will more than make up for whatever losses a man may incur for the sake of the kingdom. Ultimately life beyond the grave is the only thing that makes sense of life before the grave!

When Jesus promised to reward each person according to what he has done, there are two ways to understand what He meant. First, it could indicate different degrees of rewards that will be given to different individuals based on the amount of their good works (see comments on *Mt 6:1*). Second, it could just as well indicate that the reward is simply heaven or hell, depending on what the person has done with the gospel. Since there is no emphasis here on what the different degrees of reward would be, it is preferable to understand His words in this second sense.

Jesus concluded His warning with a surprise: some of those hearing Him would *"see the Son of Man coming in his kingdom"* in their own lifetimes (*v. 28*). This obvious reference to the beginning of the church is a reminder of how the present kingdom and the eternal kingdom are intertwined in Scripture. Coming in judgment with the angels (*v. 27*) is clearly at the end of time; coming in His kingdom (*v. 28*) is clearly an event in the first century.

THE TRANSFIGURATION
MATTHEW 17:1-9
(MARK 9:2-10; LUKE 9:28-36)

Six days later, Jesus took Peter, James, and John up a high mountain (*Mt 17:1*). As they watched in amazement, His face shone like the sun and His clothes became as white as light (*v. 2*; see *2Pet 1:17* and *Rev 1:13-16*). The glory of His natural state gives us at least a partial glimpse of our own future life, after He transforms our bodies to be like His glorified body (*Php 3:21*) and we shine like the sun in the Father's kingdom (*Mt 13:43*).

Suddenly, Moses and Elijah appeared and they also were *"in glorious splendor"* (*Lk 9:31*). Even though they had been dead for centuries, they were there—alive! They were somehow recognizable (or at least were introduced to the disciples by Jesus). They had visible bodies, they had their own identities, and they had things to talk about with Jesus (*Lk 9:31*). What a nice snapshot of heaven!

WHO IS GREATEST IN THE KINGDOM OF HEAVEN?
MATTHEW 18:1-4

As the disciples looked toward the long-awaited restoration of David's kingdom, they thought in human terms. Who will be greatest? Who will be given special treatment? (And perhaps, who will have greater degrees of reward?) To straighten matters out, Jesus stood a little child among them and said, *"Unless you change and become like little children, you will never enter the kingdom of heaven. Therefore, whoever humbles himself like this child is the greatest in the kingdom of heaven"* (*Mt 18:3-4*; see also *Mt 19:14*).

The core nature of the kingdom of heaven, therefore, is humility. The old nature, always grasping for more and struggling to get ahead of others, is not suited for the afterlife. Moreover, this is not a temporary, pretended humility. It is not a clever ruse by which one can sneak to the front of the line. For those who seek to have more rewards than their brothers and sisters, this passage puts an end to their ignoble quest.

HE WILL NOT LOSE HIS REWARD
MARK 9:41

In the Gospel of Mark, there are also words of Jesus on the subject of rewards. He said, *"Anyone who gives you a cup of water in my name because you belong to Christ will certainly not lose his reward"* (*Mk 9:41*). Again, the focus is on humility. The mere act of giving a cup of water does not seem very meritorious, but it qualifies the giver for his reward. Heaven is not won by great works of merit, therefore, but by gracious reception of those who bring the gospel message.

THE PARABLE OF THE UNMERCIFUL SERVANT
MATTHEW 18:23-25

"The kingdom of heaven," said Jesus, *"is like a king who wanted to settle accounts with his servants"* (*Mt 18:23*). One servant in Jesus' story

owed his king ten thousand talents, an obviously ridiculous amount. (Since a talent was 75 pounds, ten thousand talents would have been 750,000 pounds. If these were silver talents, on the day I write this in 2009, the value would be $140 million. If these were gold talents, today's value would be $10.5 billion.) To think that a king would have loaned such a staggering sum to a servant must have made Jesus' audience chuckle. But then, when the servant fell on his knees and begged, the whole debt was forgiven!

That same servant went right out and found a fellow servant who owed him a mere 100 denarii (average wages for 100 days). Although the first servant had been forgiven so much, he was unwilling to forgive so little. And this, Jesus said, teaches us something about "the kingdom of heaven." The point is that God requires people who are forgiven to be forgiving toward others. The obvious consequence is that heaven will be full of generous, grateful people.

REJOICE THAT YOUR NAMES ARE WRITTEN IN HEAVEN
LUKE 10:20

Sometime during the latter half of the third year of Jesus' ministry, He sent out seventy-two of His disciples to proclaim the coming kingdom (*Lk 10:1*). When they returned, they proudly announced, *"Lord, even the demons submit to us in your name"* (*v. 17*). In reply, Jesus said, *"I saw Satan fall like lightning from heaven"* (*v. 18*). While this could refer to some earlier occasion, it likely means that Jesus could see Satan's defeat happening right then as the kingdom was proclaimed (see *Jn 12:31; 16:11; Rev 12:7*).

But this, Jesus said, was not the main point. Rather than rejoicing about their victory over the demons and Satan, they should rejoice that their *"names are written in heaven"* (*Lk 10:20*). As early as *Exodus 32:32* it could be observed that God has a book in which the saints are saved and the sinners are blotted out. As late as *Revelation 20:12-15* and *21:27* it can still be read that those whose names are in the Lamb's book of life will go to heaven. The greatest joy on earth is to know that your name is on record in heaven.

At an Hour When You Do Not Expect
Luke 12:40-46

Another theme that Jesus began to emphasize in the final year of His ministry was His second coming. It will be good for servants whose master finds them watching when he comes (*Lk 12:37*). But Jesus did not here, or elsewhere, intend to give clues by which clever servants could figure out when that would be. *"You must also be ready,"* He said, *"because the Son of Man will come at an hour when you do not expect him"* (*v. 40*). As in the case of an abusive servant who tries to take evil advantage of his master's absence, the master *"will come on a day when he does not expect him and at an hour he is not aware of"* (*v. 46*).

There is a sharp contrast between the tone of this passage and the tone of rejoicing in *Luke 10:20*. The difference lies entirely in the attitude of the servants. In *Luke 10* the disciples rejoice to be with Jesus and to see the kingdom arriving. In *Luke 12* the wicked servant is glad the master is not around. Thus, the people of God should look forward to the second coming with eager anticipation, while the wicked should dread it.

Repaid at the Resurrection of the Righteous
Luke 14:14

In the home of a Pharisee, Jesus noticed how the guests competed for places of honor at the table (*Lk 14:7*). So He told His host, *"When you give a banquet, invite the poor, the crippled, the lame, the blind, and you will be blessed. Although they cannot repay you, you will be repaid at the resurrection of the righteous"* (*vv. 13-14*). As in our first notice of "rewards" in *Matthew 6:1*, there is a promise that God will repay the saints for their faithful service. There is no indication here, however, that various levels of repayment are to be expected. Jesus' point is that no act of kindness will go unnoticed; for all the kindness we extend, God will abundantly repay—and more.

It should also be noted how Jesus referred to *"the resurrection of the righteous"* in this verse. The "righteous" are not merely those whose sins are covered by the sacrifice of Jesus on the cross. To be included among "the righteous" also means to do acts of kindness and goodness (see *Mt 25:37,46*). That is why the Apostle John would later write, *"He who does what is right is righteous"* (*1Jn 3:7*).

MORE REJOICING IN HEAVEN
LUKE 15:7,10,18,21

The Pharisees were always offended that tax collectors and "sinners" gathered around Jesus (*Lk 15:1*). That is why Jesus told the parables of the Lost Sheep, the Lost Coin, and the Lost (Prodigal) Son. In the first two parables, when the lost sheep and the lost coin were found, everyone rejoiced. Then Jesus said there will be rejoicing in heaven (*v. 7*) and rejoicing among the angels (*v. 10*) when just one sinner repents. While the main point is how we should all be glad when "tax collectors and sinners" repent, there is also the intriguing indication that the saints in heaven will know when wonderful news happens. (This will be explored further in *Heb 12:1* and *Rev 6:10*.)

In the third parable, another point arises. When the prodigal son realized his sin, he determined to say to his father, *"I have sinned against heaven and against you"* (*v. 18*). When he wasted his life in wild living, he was living in defiance of everything that heaven stands for. Like those who lived in excessive luxury in Babylon the Great (*Revelation 18*), by his lifestyle the prodigal son was toying with destruction. Those whose lives are impure and shameful will not be in heaven (*Rev 21:27*).

THE PARABLE OF
THE SHREWD MANAGER
LUKE 16:1-9

One parable of Jesus seems to commend dishonesty. In Jesus' story a shrewd manager found devious means to cheat his master and buy friends for himself, knowing that he was about to lose his position (*Lk 16:1-7*). Then the master found out that the manager had settled accounts with various debtors for only pennies on the dollar. Surprisingly, the master commended the manager. As one of *"the people of this world"* (*v. 8*), at least he had to admire the way the manager looked out for himself. In this case, one crook commended another.

But shrewd dishonesty is not the point. Jesus said, *"Use worldly wealth to gain friends for yourselves, so that when it is gone, you will be welcomed into eternal dwellings"* (*v. 9*). Since we cannot serve both God and Money (*v. 13*), we should use our money in ways that will be to our advantage in heaven. This is not at all to say that we can buy our way into heaven, but that we should *"store up treasures in heaven"* (*Mt 6:20*) and *"seek first his kingdom"* (*Mt 6:33*), trusting that God will reward us.

LAZARUS AND THE RICH MAN
LUKE 16:19-31

Jesus told the story of Lazarus and the rich man as an actual event. (It is different from the parables, since none of the parables ever gives a name to the people in the parable.) In this well-known story Jesus revealed several specific details about the afterlife. First, when Lazarus died, the angels came and carried him to Abraham's side (*Lk 16:22*). God's children do not need to fear that they will have to enter the corridor of death alone. Second, the wicked rich man also went immediately to his reward—a place of fiery torment (*v. 23*). Third, there was conscious awareness in the case of Abraham and the rich man (*vv. 23-31*). This is presumably the case with Lazarus as well, because Jesus has already indicated that going to be with Abraham is like going to a banquet (*Lk 13:28-29*). Fourth, simultaneous with what is happening with Abraham and the rich man, life continues for the people on earth. The rich man has brothers who need to repent (*v. 27*). It is also fair to draw the conclusion for this situation that no people in hell would ever want to have their family come to join them there. Fifth, there is "a great chasm" that separates those who are saved from those who are condemned, and there is no crossing back and forth. No one will ever escape the fire and go to heaven; no one will ever be sent from heaven to be punished in the fires of hell. Sixth, the afterlife will be a place of righting the wrongs and administering justice. The poor beggar has all his misfortunes more than made up to him; the rich man suffers for his selfish indifference. The Judge of all the earth will finally make everything right.

The NIV says the rich man was *"in hell, where he was in torment"* (*Lk 16:23*). The actual Greek word here is *hades*, which simply meant the place of the dead, whether good or bad. This is the only place the NIV translates *hades* as "hell." (The regular word for "hell" is *gehenna*.) In all the NIV translates *hades* five times as "Hades" (*Mt 16:18; Rev 1:18; 6:8; 20:13,14*; twice as *"the grave"*

THE RICH YOUNG RULER
MATTHEW 19:21-24
(MARK 10:24-25; LUKE 18:22-25)

One day a man asked Jesus what he could do to get eternal life (*Mt 19:16*). (From Matthew and Mark we know the man was young and rich; from Luke we know the man was also a ruler.) When Jesus told him to sell his possessions and give to the poor, he could not bear to do it (*vv. 21-22*). So Jesus taught His disciples a great truth: *"It is hard for a rich man to enter the kingdom of heaven"* (*v. 23*). In fact, Jesus said, it is *"easier for a camel to go through the eye of a needle than for a rich man to enter the kingdom of God"* (*v. 24*). While it is not impossible for rich people to go to heaven (*v. 26*), what the Bible says must not be minimized. Jesus said, *"Woe to you who are rich, for you have already received your reward"* (*Lk 6:24*), and His brother James said, *"Now listen, you rich people, weep and wail because of the misery that is coming upon you"* (*Jas 5:1*). Those who grow rich with the excessive luxuries of Babylon the Great will pay a terrible price for their indulgence (*Revelation 18*). How foolish to have the treasures of earth, but lose the treasures of heaven!

As a word of encouragement to His disciples, Jesus added these words: *"At the renewal of all things"* everyone who has given up wealth or family for Jesus *"will receive a hundred times as much and will inherit eternal life"* (*Mt 19:29*). When this "renewal" or "restoration" happens, the Son of Man will sit on His glorious throne and the apostles will sit on twelve thrones, judging the twelve tribes of Israel (*v. 28*; see *Lk 22:30*). The new covenant of Jesus will fulfill and replace the old covenant of Israel.

THE PARABLE OF
THE WORKERS IN THE VINEYARD
MATTHEW 20:1-16

"The kingdom of heaven is like" a man who hires workers for his vineyard. All through the day he continues hiring, even up to the last

hour before sundown (*Mt 20:1-6*). When it comes time to pay the workers, he gives a full denarius—the usual pay for a full day's work—to the "last hour" workmen. When the "full day" workmen also receive the same pay, they grumble. *"You have made them equal to us,"* they complain, *"who have borne the burden of the work and the heat of the day"* (*v. 12*). Then comes a very important lesson about what "the kingdom of heaven is like" (as in *v. 1*). When the landowner is generous with those who came late, he is not being unfair to those who came early.

The first application of this parable fits Israel and the Gentiles. If God wants to give the same reward to the new Gentiles as to the old Israelites, there is no unfairness. There is neither Jew nor Gentile in God's final view (*Rom 9:8; 11:22-24; Gal 3:28; Eph 2:14-17; 3:6; Col 3:11*); the faithful from all the earth will share the heavenly reward. A second application may also be drawn from this parable. It is wrong to hope to earn greater rewards than others in heaven. If God is so generous as to give everyone the same abundant blessings, who can complain?

To Sit at His Right and His Left
Matthew 20:21-23
(Mark 10:37-40)

As Jesus was making His final journey to Jerusalem to face the cross, James and John came with their mother to make an unworthy request (*Mt 20:20*). They wanted to push ahead of the other disciples and claim the seats of power in the new, restored kingdom (*v. 21*). When the other disciples found out what James and John had done, they were "indignant" with the two brothers (*v. 24*). (Was it because they knew such grasping for power was wrong, or because they were sorry they had not grasped for it themselves?)

Jesus refused the request of James and John, with a follow-up lesson on greatness and servanthood (*Mt 20:23-28*). The kingdom is not about personal importance; it is about serving one another. Thus, the picture of a restored kingdom emerges in which every citizen is eager to make every other citizen happy. Different positions of responsibility may well be assigned in heaven, but it is all in the hands of the Father (*v. 23*; see also *Mt 25:14-30*).

The Parable of
the Wedding Banquet
Matthew 22:2-14

Once again, Jesus used a parable to tell His disciples what *"the kingdom of heaven is like"* (*Mt 22:2*). A king prepares "a wedding banquet" for his son. When the invited guests (the people of Israel) refuse to come, he brings in people who otherwise would have been outsiders (the Gentiles). One man even tries to get in without wedding clothes (*v. 11*), that is, without the invitation and approval of the king. This man is thrown outside *"into the darkness, where there will be weeping and gnashing of teeth"* (*v. 13*).

This parable of heaven divides the human race into three parts. First, there are those in the old covenant who were first to be invited but who decided for themselves to be left out. Second, there are those in the new covenant who have been invited to fill the empty places (see *Rom 11:17-21*). Third, there are those who are not a part of either covenant, who may try (too late!) to make entrance for themselves. At the end, Jesus offered this summary: *"Many are invited, but few are chosen"* (*v. 15*). It should not be overlooked that God invites many, but only those who accept are called "chosen."

"At the Resurrection,
Whose Wife Will She Be?"
Matthew 22:23-32
(Mark 12:18-27; Luke 20:27-40)

As opposition mounted in the Final Week, Jesus faced a question from the Sadducees, *"who say there is no resurrection"* (*Mt 22:23*). Their rather absurd question supposed that a widow marries a whole succession of brothers, each fulfilling his role in the ancient practice of levirate ("brother-in-law") marriage (see *Deu 25:5-6*). Since she has rightly been married to each of the seven brothers, whose wife will she be at the resurrection?

> The Sadducees denied the validity of any of the OT except the Pentateuch, the books from **Genesis** to **Deuteronomy**. Using only these five books as Scripture, they rejected the following: the undying soul, the resurrection, angels and demons, heaven and hell. See **Acts 23:8**.

Knowing that the Sadducees accepted only the Pentateuch as Scripture, Jesus quoted *Exodus 3:6*, *"I am the God of Abraham, the God of Isaac, and the God of Jacob."* It is noteworthy that He did not say, "I was" or "I used to be" the God of Abraham. He said, "I am." From this the Sadducees should have understood that centuries after these men died, they were still alive with God.

More directly in answer to their question about the widow and her husbands, Jesus explained role relationships in heaven. *"At the resurrection,"* He said, *"people will neither marry nor be given in marriage; they will be like the angels in heaven"* (*Mt 22:30*). The marriage union, where two people separate themselves from all others, will not exist in heaven. Instead, everyone will live together as brothers and sisters. A man and a woman who were married on earth will certainly know and love each other in heaven, but not in an exclusive sense. Just as a woman can have several brothers and love them equally and completely, so could this woman love all of her seven former husbands as dear brothers. The close affection of husband and wife will not be diminished; it will be enlarged to include all the rest of God's family.

WHAT ABOUT THE CHRIST?
WHOSE SON IS HE?
MATTHEW 22:41-45
(MARK 12:35-37; LUKE 20:41-44)

When everyone had finished asking their questions of Jesus, He had a question for them. *"What do you think about the Christ?"* Jesus said, *"Whose son is he?"* (*Mt 22:42*). They knew the answer, of course. The Christ—the Messiah—was the son of David. But how, Jesus asked, could David call his own descendant his "Lord"? Jesus reminded them of David's familiar words, *"The LORD said to my Lord: 'Sit at my right hand until I put your enemies under your feet'"* (*v. 44*, quoting *Ps 110:1*). Everyone knew this was a messianic passage, promising the restored kingdom to the Messiah. What everyone did not know was that David's descendant, the long-awaited Messiah, would also be more than human and would deserve to be called "Lord" even by David.

Psalm 110, quoted in the NT more than any other OT passage, is a clear picture of what is to come. At the end of earthly life, when every knee will bow to Jesus (*Php 2:10*), all His enemies will be conquered.

Jesus will sit at the right hand of the Father; all the ancient promises will be kept; the eternal kingdom will endure.

SIGNS OF THE END OF THE AGE
MATTHEW 24
(MARK 13, LUKE 21)

When the day of questioning was finished (Tuesday of the Final Week, see *Mt 26:2*), Jesus led His disciples past the magnificent Temple. *"Do you see all these things?"* He asked. *"Not one stone here will be left on another; every one will be thrown down"* (*Mt 24:2*). By the time they reached the Mount of Olives, the astonished disciples were full of questions: *"When will this happen, and what will be the sign of your coming and of the end of the age?"* (*v. 3*). In their bewilderment, the disciples rushed to a confused conclusion. They assumed that the Temple could never be destroyed until the 2nd coming and the end of the age. When Jesus responded to their questions, He interwove His answers regarding one part and then another, leaving them (and us today) a bit uncertain as to how it all works out. He did not seem to care whether they (or we) could construct a prophetic timetable and know in advance how everything would happen. What did matter to Jesus was that the final day would come, the wicked would be judged, the elect would be gathered into the restored kingdom, and He wanted His disciples to be ready!

Scholars disagree on how to interpret what Jesus said. Which parts refer to the destruction of Jerusalem in AD 70? Which parts refer to the 2nd coming? Do some parts refer to both? Since no prophecy of Scripture is a matter of private interpretation (*2Pet 1:20* NASB), we all must label our understanding as tentative. The prophecies will turn out as God intends, regardless of what we may have thought.

Some of what Jesus said seems to be in clear reference to the destruction of Jerusalem in AD 70. The "abomination" (*Mt 24:15*) is explained as *"Jerusalem surrounded by armies"* (*Lk 21:20*). When the people saw this happening, they were to flee to the mountains (*Mt 24:16-22*). Likewise, the statement that "these things" would happen in that generation (*Mt 24:32-35*) seems to point to AD 70.

Some of what Jesus said, on the other hand, seems to be in clear reference to the 2nd coming and the consummation of the age. The coming of the Son of Man will be as visible as the lightning that shines across the whole sky (*Mt 24:27*) and at the trumpet sound all the elect will be gathered by His angels (*v. 31*). The day and hour cannot be known, not by angels or even Jesus Himself (*v. 36*). The Son of Man will come at an hour when people do not expect (*v. 45*).

Much of what Jesus said seems to be for every generation of believers. There will be wars, earthquakes, persecution, betrayal (*Mt 24:4-13*). But stay faithful. There will be false messiahs (*vv. 23-26*). But do not be misled. Most people will be caught unprepared (*vv. 37-44*). So be ready. Those who are not ready will be like the wicked servant who is *"cut to pieces"* and assigned *"a place with the hypocrites, where there will be weeping and gnashing of teeth"* (*v. 50*). This theme of readiness carries right on into the parable of the Ten Virgins (*Mt 25:1-13*). When the Bridegroom comes, only those who are ready for Him will be allowed to enter the wedding banquet (*v. 10*).

THE PARABLE OF THE TEN TALENTS
MATTHEW 25:14-30
(SIMILAR TO LUKE 19:11-27)

Jesus continued immediately into another parable, where readiness, responsibility, and reward are the themes. A man left his servants in charge of his property and went away. Some of them put his money to work; one did not. When the master returned, the *"good and faithful"* servants were rewarded (*Mt 25:20,23*), but the wicked, lazy servant was not (*v. 26*). He was to be thrown *"outside, into the darkness, where there will be weeping and gnashing of teeth"* (*v. 30*).

It is possible to see this parable as supporting the idea of degree of rewards. The servant who was faithful with five talents got five more talents in return. The servant who was faithful with two talents got two in return. (In *Luke 19:11-27*, the servant who was faithful with ten minas got ten cities; the servant who was faithful with five minas got five cities.) It is also possible, however, to see this parable as simply teaching that the Lord will be very generous in rewarding everyone who is faithful and ready.

THE SHEEP AND THE GOATS
AT JUDGMENT
MATTHEW 25:31-46

One of the clearest pictures of Judgment Day is given by Jesus in *Matthew 25*. The Son of Man comes in glory with His angels, sits on

His throne, and all the nations are gathered before Him (*vv. 31-33*). Just as a shepherd has no difficulty telling sheep from goats, the Lord will separate mankind into two groups.

"*Come,*" Jesus will say to those on His right. "*Take your inheritance, the kingdom prepared for you since the creation of the world*" (*v. 34*). Heaven is that "inheritance." It is the "kingdom" God has intended for His beloved children from the very beginning. The Garden of Eden was a foretaste, but was then lost. At last, in the final Day, everything is restored. Adam's garden, Abraham's promises, David's kingdom—everything rightly belongs to the sheep of the Shepherd. They will have "*eternal life*" (*v. 46*).

"*Depart,*" Jesus will say to those on His left, "*into the eternal fire prepared for the devil and his angels*" (*v. 41*). The people on this side have not been conspicuously wicked, just indifferent and uncaring about others (*vv. 42-45*). When they did not care about the Lord's "least" ones, they did not care about the Lord. For their callous disregard they will go away to "*eternal punishment*" (*v. 46*).

It is troubling to some that in this passage the basis for salvation is not faith, but acts of kindness. The very fact that these deeds were done almost unknowingly helps us understand that they are not "points" that we accumulate toward a ticket to heaven. Instead, they are the natural activity of those who have chosen to be on the Lord's side, to live the Lord's kind of life, to love the Lord's people. These acts of kindness were done with no thought of merit whatsoever. At the same time, this passage does serve to keep us away from the error of thinking that "faith" as an idle opinion about Jesus is enough to save.

Until That Day I Drink It Anew with You
Matthew 26:29

Jesus celebrated His final Passover meal in the Upper Room with His disciples. At the conclusion of the meal He took bread and said, "*Take and eat; this is my body*" (*Mt 26:26*). Then He took a cup, saying, "*This is my blood of the covenant, which is poured out for many for the forgiveness of sins*" (*v. 28*). A "*new covenant*" (*Lk 22:20*) was in the making; a new blood sacrifice was going to seal it (*Heb 8:8; 9:12-15*).

Then Jesus said something intriguing: "*I will not drink of this fruit of the vine from now on until that day when I drink it anew with you in my*

Father's kingdom" (*v. 29*). The Lord's Supper, like the original Passover meal, was to become a memorial to the past and a glimpse into the future. The first Passover was not only about deliverance from Egypt, but also about entrance into the Promised Land. The Lord's Supper is not only about deliverance from condemnation, but also about entrance into the eternal kingdom of heaven. Thus, to participate in the Lord's Supper is to *"proclaim the Lord's death until he comes"* (*1Cor 11:26*). The Lord's Supper is a foretaste of the messianic banquet.

TODAY YOU WILL BE WITH ME IN PARADISE
LUKE 23:43

The men who were crucified with Jesus were called *"robbers"* (violent, armed attackers) in **Matthew** and **Mark**, and *"criminals"* (evildoers) in **Luke**. At first they joined the mockery of Jesus as a false claimant to the throne of David (*Mt 27:42-44*). Then one of them pleaded, *"Aren't you the Messiah? Save yourself and us!"* (*Lk 23:39*). The other criminal rebuked him and then said to Jesus, *"Remember me when you come into your kingdom"* (*Lk 23:42*). Everywhere, it seems, there was acute awareness that the Messiah was supposed to come and restore the kingdom.

Jesus' reply was loaded with information about the afterlife: *"I tell you the truth, today you will be with me in paradise"* (*Lk 23:43*). First, what Jesus said was a solemn truth, not a wishful hope or a theological speculation. Second, it was going to happen *"today."* This verse adds its voice to a number of passages that indicate that when believers die they go immediately to be with the Lord (*Lk 16:25; Jn 11:25-26; Acts 7:55-59; 2Cor 5:1-8; Php 1:23; Heb 12:22-23; Rev 6:9-11*). Third, the robber himself would be with Jesus Himself. Individual identities continue in the afterlife. Fourth, the place immediately beyond death is called "paradise."

> The word "paradise" comes from an ancient Persian word for an enclosed pleasure garden. The word is used only three times in the NIV Bible. *"Today you will be with me in paradise"* (*Lk 23:43*). Paul knew a man *"who was caught up into paradise"* (*2Cor 12:4*). Those who overcome are promised the right *"to eat from the tree of life, which is in the paradise of God"* (*Rev 2:7*).

In the Septuagint, the Greek translation of the Hebrew OT, the same word "paradise" is used 27 times and is regularly translated "garden" (**Gen 2:8,9,10, etc.**) The Jewish writers Philo and Josephus also used this word in reference to the Garden of Eden. Interestingly, Isaiah promised that the day will come when God will make the wastelands of Israel *"like the garden ['paradise'] of God"* **(Isa 51:3)**. God's original plan was—and His ultimate plan will be—to put His people in a splendid garden.

There is frequent speculation that our immediate home after death is a place called "paradise," while our final home after Judgment Day is a place called "heaven." While this idea may be correct, there are not many verses to support it. At any rate, there seems to be little practical difference between the two. We will investigate the concept in more depth at *Philippians 1:23*.

Two on the Road to Emmaus
Luke 24:13-32

On the day of Jesus' resurrection He met up with two disciples returning to their home in Emmaus (*Lk 24:13*). They were quite sad about the crucifixion, because they *"had hoped that he was the one who was going to redeem Israel"* (*v. 21*). Now their hopes for a restored kingdom were crushed. But Jesus began to explain to them how the Messiah had *"to suffer these things and then enter his glory"* (*v. 26*). Jesus gave them a "crash course" on God's eternal plan for the Messiah and His kingdom, beginning with Moses and then all the prophets (*v. 27*). Finally, in the act of breaking bread with Jesus at their home, their eyes were opened and they recognized the risen Lord.

These two shared the common expectation that the Messiah would come and "redeem Israel." Jesus confirmed their expectation, but with the explanation that the Messiah would first suffer and then *"enter his glory."* All through the OT there was preparation for this great event. Now Jesus sits at the right hand of God, ready to welcome each of us to share that glory (*Rom 5:2; 8:18; 9:23; Heb 2:10*).

Appearance in the Closed Room
Luke 24:36-45

On the evening of the first day of the week, Jesus suddenly appeared to the disciples who were gathered behind closed doors (*Lk*

24:36; Jn 20:19). They were startled and frightened to see the man they thought was dead, so they thought it must be a ghost. (The people at Mark's house had a similar thought when Rhoda saw Peter in *Acts 12:15*.) Jesus was very careful to prove that He was alive in a physical body. *"Look at my hands and my feet,"* He said. *"Touch me and see; a ghost does not have flesh and bones, as you see I have"* (*Lk 24:39*). He also asked for and ate a piece of broiled fish in their presence. He was very much alive, in a very real body.

Was the resurrection body of Jesus the same as what our resurrection bodies will be? Possibly. Paul used Christ's resurrection as a proof that we also will be raised from the dead and called Jesus *"the firstfruits"* of those who have fallen asleep (*1Cor 15:20,23*). At the same time, our promise is not merely that we will be restored to the same body, but that our bodies will be transformed to be like His glorious body (*Php 3:21; 1Jn 3:2*). After Jesus is exalted to heaven, the pictures of Him are much more grand (*Rev 1:13-17*). Therefore, we should more likely conclude that the postresurrection body of Jesus was intentionally ordinary, but that the ultimate body of Jesus (and our own bodies) will be much more.

After Jesus had demonstrated that He had risen bodily from the grave, He explained to the disciples how the OT had pointed to all this. *"This is what I told you while I was still with you,"* Jesus said. *"Everything must be fulfilled that is written about me in the Law of Moses, the Prophets and the Psalms"* (*v. 44*). It was important that they understand how it had all been the plan of God, from beginning to end.

THE ASCENSION OF JESUS
LUKE 24:51; ACTS 1:9

For forty days following His resurrection, Jesus taught His disciples *"about the kingdom of God"* (*Acts 1:3*). This "kingdom" fulfillment was so much on the minds of His disciples that they asked Him on the final day, *"Lord, are you at this time going to restore the kingdom to Israel?"* (*v. 6*). But just as He had told them earlier (*Mt 24:36*), it was not for them to know the times or dates the Father has set. The church would be launched when God determined; the eternal kingdom would replace the old heavens and earth whenever God chooses. Their job was not to calculate numbers and solve prophetic mysteries; their job was to wait for the Holy Spirit and then evangelize (*v. 8*).

Then, as the disciples looked on with amazement, Jesus had His "liftoff." He was taken up into the sky until finally a cloud hid Him from their sight (*Lk 24:51; Acts 1:9; 1Tm 3:16*). But the story was not over. As the angel told them, *"This same Jesus, who has been taken from you into heaven, will come back in the same way you have seen him go into heaven"* (*v. 11*). Visibly, on the clouds, with the angels—Jesus is coming back!

CONCLUSION

In the Synoptic Gospels there is much that Jesus said about the afterlife. More than anything else, it is the long-awaited fulfillment of what the OT promised. The kingdom would indeed be restored, beginning on earth and culminating in heaven. Believers can look forward to sitting at a banquet with Abraham, receiving their inheritance and final reward. The kingdom will be a place of humility, righteousness, abundance, and rejoicing. All this will finally happen at a time when God alone chooses; our job is to be ready.

WHAT DO YOU SAY?

1. How often did Jesus teach about the "kingdom"? How do we know it was not just about the church?

2. How does each Beatitude tell us something about heaven?

3. How would things change if God's will really was done on earth as it is in heaven?

4. What can we learn about heaven from the Parables of the Kingdom (*Matthew 13*)?

5. What does the Transfiguration teach us about heaven?

6. When sinners repent, there is rejoicing in heaven. Does this mean that people in heaven know what is going on back on earth?

7. What did Jesus teach about marriage in heaven?

8. What can we learn from the reply of Jesus to the thief on the cross?

9. Why were the disciples still expecting Jesus to "restore the kingdom to Israel" right up to the day He ascended?

CHAPTER ELEVEN

HEAVEN IN JOHN AND ACTS

J ohn wrote his Gospel two or three decades after the Synoptic writers, and deliberately avoided repeating the same information. About 90% of the material in John is new. Therefore, we will consider John separate from the others, as we investigate what he records about Jesus and the life to come.

Acts, of course, tells how the work of the kingdom proceeded after Jesus ascended into heaven. The apostles faithfully carried the gospel into all the world, proclaiming the message of the only name under heaven by which men can be saved (*Acts 4:12*). Even the very last verse of Acts shows Paul carrying on this good work, boldly preaching *"the kingdom of God"* (*Acts 28:31*).

HEAVEN IN THE GOSPEL OF JOHN

THE WORD BECAME FLESH
JOHN 1:14

In the beginning, before the universe was created, Jesus was with God in what we would understand as heaven (*Jn 1:1-3*). As we learn new information from the NT, we must adjust our OT pictures of God on His throne (*Isa 6:1*, for instance) to see Jesus at His side. The eternal Father has a Son.

Then God's Son became a man. In the single most important event in the history

165

of the human race, *"the Word became flesh and made his dwelling among us"* (*v. 14a*). John and the other apostles were privileged to see *"his glory, the glory of the One and Only, who came from the Father, full of grace and truth"* (*v. 14b*). When John wrote that Jesus *"made his dwelling"* among humans, he chose the Greek word that recalls the glory of the Tabernacle of old. It could be translated, *"Jesus 'tabernacled' among us."*

When Moses prepared the Tabernacle in the wilderness, the glory of God entered it; God made His dwelling among men. For much of the next thousand years, the presence of God was associated in this way with the Holy of Holies in the Tabernacle/ Temple. (When the Temple was destroyed by the Babylonians and then rebuilt, the Holy of Holies sat empty. For 400 years there was no ark of the covenant, and presumably, no presence of God.) Now, in the incarnation of Jesus, the presence of God would become personal. God was no longer shut off behind a curtain in a forbidden room; for thirty-three years God in Christ walked among us! One last chapter in this grand story remains. As John will tell us in his *Revelation*, in heaven God will make His dwelling among men—for good (*Rev 21:3*).

You Are the King of Israel
John 1:49-51

Jesus began to call men to be His disciples. When He called Philip, Philip quickly found Nathaniel and told him, *"We have found the one Moses wrote about in the Law, and about whom the prophets also wrote"* (*Jn 1:45*). After so many centuries, the people of Israel were still waiting for God to keep His promises. When Nathaniel met Jesus, he exclaimed in a burst of enthusiasm, *"Rabbi, you are the Son of God, you are the King of Israel"* (*v. 49*). The people of Israel were still expecting their king.

Jesus then gave Nathaniel and the others a preview of what was to come: *"You shall see heaven open, and the angels of God ascending and descending on the Son of Man"* (*v. 51*; see *Gen 28:12*). Heaven, the final kingdom, would be open. Jesus, the Son of God and of Man, would be the access. He was indeed a King.

You Must Be Born Again
John 3:3-5

As Jesus preached, worked miracles, and cleansed the Temple (*John 2*), He began to attract the attention of the authorities. One night Nicodemus, a member of the ruling council, came to see Him and declared Him to be a teacher sent from God. In a rather surprising response, Jesus told him, *"No one can see the kingdom of God unless he is born again"* (*Jn 3:3*). When Nicodemus objected that rebirth is impossible, Jesus stated it even more emphatically: *"No one can enter the kingdom of God unless he is born of water and the Spirit"* (*v. 5*).

Entering the kingdom is about more than just joining the church. In just a few verses Jesus indicated that He was speaking of *"heavenly things"* (*v. 12*). Furthermore, He was supremely qualified to speak of heavenly things, because *"no one has ever gone into heaven except the one who came from heaven—the Son of Man"* (*v. 13*).

For God So Loved the World
John 3:15-16

Jesus continued His conversation with Nicodemus. He had come to throw open the doors to eternal life, and there was only one way that could be done. Just as Moses put a bronze snake on a pole as the remedy for fatal snakebites (*Num 21:8-9*), *"the Son of Man must be lifted up"* on a cross as the remedy for fatal sin (*Jn 3:15*; see also *8:28*; *12:32-33*). All people who put their faith in the Son who died for them will have eternal life.

This is the first of seventeen verses in John that speak of "eternal life" (*Jn 3:15,16,36; 4:14,36; 5:24,39; 6:27,40,47,54,68; 10:28; 12:25,50; 17:2,3*). God will give this life to everyone who believes in Jesus (*v. 16*). The same God who created life in the beginning (*Gen 2:7*), lovingly offers life forever in heaven. But if anyone rejects the Son and His sacrifice, he will not receive this life and *"God's wrath remains on him"* (*v. 36*).

The Greek language has a way of showing where "continuing" action (as opposed to a one-time action) is indicated. When a participle, for instance, is in the present tense, it specifies "continuing" action. A careful study of all the promises of eternal life in John will show a consistent pattern: it is promised to "the one believing," "the one coming to me," "the one eating and drinking my flesh," etc. These are all present participles, requiring continuing action.

MY FATHER IS WORKING UNTIL NOW
JOHN 5:17

Sickness is not man's natural, nor ultimate, state. So when Jesus saw a lame man by the Bethesda pool in Jerusalem, He asked him, *"Do you want to get well?"* (*Jn 5:6*). Although the man thought healing would someday come through a bubbling in the water (*v. 7*), Jesus said, *"Get up! Pick up your bed and walk"* (*v. 8*). Immediately the man was completely healed.

But that was not good; it was the Sabbath. Therefore, the Jews objected to the man carrying his bed (*v. 10*), and even more so to Jesus healing on the sacred day. By their detailed listing of actions that were forbidden on the Sabbath, both the man and Jesus were in serious violation of the rules. Jesus responded, *"My Father is always at his work to this very day, and I, too, am working"* (*v. 17*).

Jesus' comment gives us accidental insight into a facet of heaven. When God made the universe in six days and then "rested," He still went on working. Without God constantly supporting our life and existence, no life would be possible. In that sense, God never has a day off. In a somewhat similar fashion, we will both rest and work in heaven. Those who die in the Lord *"will rest from their labor"* (*Rev 14:13*), but they will also be His servants and *"will serve him"* (*Rev 22:3*). The old life—struggling to wrest a living from a fallen world—will be over. The new life—serving God and reigning in His behalf—will begin.

ALL WHO ARE IN THEIR GRAVES
WILL COME OUT
JOHN 5:28-29

The Jewish authorities were horrified. Jesus had just called God His own Father, making Himself equal to God (*Jn 5:18*). Rather than smoothing ruffled feathers, however, Jesus proceeded to make matters worse. In fact, He went on to say, *"Whatever the Father does the Son also does"* (**v. 19**). The Father can raise the dead; so can the Son. The Father has the authority to judge; He has given it to the Son (**vv. 21-22**).

Whoever believes in Jesus *"has eternal life and will not be condemned"* (**v. 24**), thus indicating that "eternal life" is a present reality for believers. *"Do not be amazed at this,"* Jesus continued, *"for a time is coming when all who are in their graves will hear his voice and come out—those who have done good will rise to live, and those who have done evil will rise to be condemned"* (**vv. 28-29**). These words echo the ancient prophecy of **Daniel 12:2**, *"Multitudes who sleep in the dust of the earth will awake: some to everlasting life, others to shame and everlasting contempt."* God's plan for the ages has not changed.

You Are from Below;
I Am from Above
John 8:23

At the Feast of Tabernacles in the final year of Jesus' ministry, He told the Pharisees that He was going to a place where they could not come (**Jn 8:21**). He further explained, *"You are from below; I am from above. You are of this world; I am not of this world"* (**v. 23**). To anyone who was willing to listen, Jesus made it perfectly clear that He had come to earth from heaven.

This is the sense in which we should understand His frequent references to *"the One who sent me."* Thirty-four times Jesus spoke of being "sent" in the Gospel of John. He knew that He was sent not merely as the prophets or John the Baptist had been sent; He was sent from heaven. He was the One *"whom the Father set apart as his very own and sent into the world"* (**Jn 10:36**).

In My Father's House
John 14:1-3

What Jesus said in **John 14:1-3** has already been treated in chapter one of this book. In the ongoing flow of information about heaven in John's Gospel, it would be good to remind ourselves briefly of what Jesus said here. He promised that there are *"many rooms"* in the Father's house, and that He would prepare *"a place"* specifically for His followers. He solemnly affirmed that this was all true, and that He would come again to take His disciples home.

I Am the Way and
the Truth and the Life
John 14:6

Jesus continued, *"You know the way to the place where I am going"* (*Jn 14:4*). But they did not know the way, and Thomas said so (*v. 5*). How can anyone know where heaven is, or the way to get there? So Jesus said, *"I am the way and the truth and the life. No one comes to the Father except through me"* (*v. 6*).

Several truths here should be emphasized. First, Jesus knows all about heaven and the way to get there. Second, He Himself is the true avenue—the only way—to this life. Third, to go to heaven can be expressed as *"come to the Father."* Heaven is indeed a place, but even more, it is an eternal relationship with our Creator.

If You Have Seen Me,
You Have Seen the Father
John 14:9

At this point Philip interrupted. *"Lord, show us the Father and that will be enough for us"* (*Jn 14:8*). Jesus had spoken about coming to the Father; Philip wanted to see Him. Perhaps in Philip's mind this was also connected with the restoration of the kingdom and God dwelling in their midst. Then Jesus said something truly earthshaking: *"Don't you know me, Philip, even after I have been among you such a long time? Anyone who has seen me has seen the Father"* (*v. 9*).

In fact, it has always been God's desire to reveal Himself to men. From Adam to the patriarchs to the prophets, God has been revealing Himself in a variety of ways. Now, at last, God is seen in the person of Jesus, His Son. When we think of seeing God's face in heaven, it should be no more frightening than it was for the little children to crawl up on Jesus' lap. To see Jesus—in all the attributes that made people love Him—is to see God, who will similarly reveal Himself to us in heaven.

The Glory I Had with You
before the World Began
John 17:5

In *John 17* Jesus prayed as the great High Priest of the human race. Just as the high priest in the OT would first sanctify himself and then the people, Jesus prayed first for Himself, then for the disciples and those who would believe through their word. In His prayer for Himself, Jesus prayed, *"Father, glorify me in your presence with the glory I had with you before the world began"* (*v. 5*). Likewise, near the end of the prayer, He spoke of *"the glory you have given me because you loved me before the creation of the world"* (*v. 24*).

Jesus not only knew that He had been sent to earth from heaven, He remembered the glory that had once been His. Before the creation of the world, Jesus already shared the splendor of heaven with His Father. Incredibly, He came to earth to give glory to believers as well (*v. 22*). The ultimate fulfillment of this will be our eternal state in heaven. Paul wrote that when He comes again, we *"will appear with him in glory"* (*Col 3:4*).

My Kingdom Is Not of This World
John 18:36

By Friday morning of the final week, Jesus stood on trial before Pilate. Prompted by the accusations of the Jewish leaders, Pilate asked Jesus, *"Are you the king of the Jews?"* (*Jn 18:33*). Jesus gave a forthright answer: *"My kingdom is not of this world. If it were, my servants would fight to prevent my arrest by the Jews. But now my kingdom is from another place"* (*v. 36*). Jesus confirmed to Pilate that He was a king, that He had been born for this, that He had come into the world for this (*v. 37*).

The kingdom over which Jesus reigns is, first of all, the church: all those who name Him as Lord also honor Him as King. But ultimately and fundamentally, Jesus' kingdom is *"not of this world,"* but *"from another place."* Earthly kingdoms like Rome would rise and fall, but the kingdom of the Messiah will last forever. It is "of" and "from" another place, and that place is heaven.

Do Not Hold On to Me!
John 20:17

Mary Magdalene was the first to see the risen Lord. She had come early on resurrection morning to the garden tomb, but the stone was rolled away and the grave was empty (*Jn 20:1*). She ran to tell the others; Peter and John ran back to see for themselves; and after they left, she wearily returned. Angels spoke to her, but she could only lament that the body of her Lord was gone (*v. 13*). Then she turned, and Jesus was standing there. After He convinced her that He was indeed alive, she grabbed Him with excitement and adoration (just as the other women *"clasped his feet"* a few minutes later, *Mt 28:9*).

"Do not hold on to me," Jesus said to her, *"for I have not yet returned to the Father"* (*Jn 20:17*). Mary was clinging to Jesus as if never to let Him go, but it was not necessary. Jesus would indeed *"return to the Father"* (*v. 17*) after forty days, but He was not gone yet. When He did ascend to the Father, He would prepare heaven for all the believers of all generations to come. There we will embrace Him just as Mary Magdalene did.

The wording of the King James Version has given rise to fanciful notions about the resurrected Lord. In **John 20:17** of that version Jesus says, *"Touch me not, for I am not yet ascended to my Father."* Some have supposed from this that Jesus did not yet have a material body. Therefore, He would have to make a quick trip to heaven and back before He met up with the other women, who then *"came and held him by the feet"* (**Mt 28:9**, KJV). Actually, the prohibition of the Greek verb in **John 20:17** is best understood as, *"Stop clinging to me."*

WITH THE DOORS LOCKED . . .
JESUS CAME AND STOOD AMONG THEM
JOHN 20:19

On the evening of resurrection day, Jesus appeared to ten of His disciples. They were gathered behind locked doors, fearful that the persecution by the authorities might now be turned toward themselves. In spite of the locked doors, Jesus came and stood among them (*Jn 20:19*). The text does not explain just how Jesus could pass through solid walls or locked doors, but neither did the text earlier explain how He could walk on water (*Jn 6:19*).

Jesus was certainly not a ghost. He was in a body, one with nail prints in the hands and a spear hole in the side (*Jn 20:20*). Luke's Gospel adds here that Jesus had *"flesh and bones"* and that He ate a piece of broiled fish in their presence (*Lk 24:39,42*). Even more emphatically, the following week He ordered a doubtful Thomas, *"Put your finger here; see my hands. Reach out your hand and put it into my side. Stop doubting and believe"* (*Jn 20:27*).

The resurrected body of Jesus is our confirmation that our bodies, too, will be raised from the grave (*1Cor 15:12-49*). But that is not the end of the story. Our bodies will then be *"changed"* (*Php 3:21*) and *"the perishable must clothe itself with the imperishable, and the mortal with immortality"* (*1Cor 15:53*). In our imperishable bodies we may not walk through walls, but we will walk on streets of gold.

"COME AND HAVE BREAKFAST"
JOHN 21:4-14

The final appearance of Jesus in the Gospel of *John* was at a breakfast in Galilee. In one last confirmation that He really did rise from the grave, Jesus stood by the seashore roasting fish over a charcoal fire (*Jn 21:9*). He handed bread and fish to the seven disciples who were there that morning, and shared a sunrise breakfast.

Four of the final appearances of Jesus were at a meal: in Emmaus (*Lk 24:30*), in the closed room (*Lk 24:43*), at this breakfast in Galilee (*Jn 21:13*), and prior to His ascension in Jerusalem (*Acts 1:4*). When Jesus comes again (as He promised Peter that He would in *John 21:23*), He will once again be the host of a banquet. It will be the wedding supper of the Lamb, and this time all His disciples will be there (*Rev 19:9*).

HEAVEN IN THE ACTS
OF THE APOSTLES

HE SHOWED HIMSELF ALIVE
ACTS 1:3-6

The chronicle of the actions of the apostles begins with a farewell to Jesus. For a period of forty days after the resurrection Jesus showed Himself alive, proving His power to bring life after death. With *"many convincing proofs"* He provided them the material and the confidence for the sermons they would preach, and spoke about *"the kingdom of God"* (*Acts 1:3*).

At the end of this forty days, on the occasion of another meal with His disciples, Jesus instructed them to await being baptized with the Holy Spirit (*v. 5*). Sensing that something big was about to happen, the disciples asked, *"Lord, are you at this time going to restore the king-*

dom to Israel?" (*v. 6*). The kingdom would be restored, but on the Father's timetable (*v. 7*). (It would seem odd if *"the times or dates the Father has set by his own authority"* referred only to the beginning of the church ten days later. Jesus is clearly speaking in the context of the 2ⁿᵈ Coming, just as in *Mt 24:36*). In the meantime, they were to take the power of the Holy Spirit and carry the good news to the ends of the earth (*v. 8*). As always, the work of the church is a preliminary part of restoring the kingdom, but the climax of the ages will come when the prophecies are fulfilled in heaven.

"THIS SAME JESUS . . . WILL COME BACK"
ACTS 1:9-11

Jesus ascended into heaven. As the disciples watched Him disappear into a cloud, suddenly two angels appeared with a message: *"This same Jesus, who has been taken from you into heaven, will come back in the same way you have seen him go into heaven"* (*v. 11*). Two key truths emerge in this event. First, Jesus ascended into heaven. He came from heaven, and He was going back to that same place. Rising into a cloud was a symbolic representation of this, since we have seen "the heavens" as sky and "heaven" as God's throne interconnected throughout Scripture. Second, Jesus is coming again. Just as He ascended to heaven, *"in the same way"* (*v. 11*) He will return to earth surrounded by clouds and angels (see *Mt 24:30; 1Th 4:16-17*). Then the restored kingdom, for which the disciples were so eager, will be complete.

HE WAS NOT ABANDONED
TO THE GRAVE
ACTS 2:31-33

Ten days after the Ascension, Peter stood up to preach on the Day of Pentecost. He told the crowd that the ancient prophecies were being fulfilled in Jesus the Messiah (*Acts 2:16-21*, see *Joel 2:28-32*). The work of building an everlasting kingdom had begun. Then he directed their attention to the man they had killed. Again in fulfillment of ancient prophecy, this man was not abandoned to the grave (literally *hades*), nor did this man's body see decay (*Acts 2:27,31*; see *Ps 16:8-11*). Instead, God raised Jesus to life again (*v. 32*). In keeping His ancient oath to David, God would now place one of his descendants on the throne (*v. 30*), and that throne was in heaven (*v. 33*). This was in fulfillment of a third ancient prophecy, where God said to the Messiah, *"Sit at my right hand until I make your enemies a footstool for your feet"* (*v. 34*, see *Ps 110:1*). They had crucified a lowly Galilean; God had crowned Him as Lord and Messiah (*v. 36*). All those who accepted Jesus that day (*vv. 38-41*) could expect to join Jesus eventually in heaven.

HE MUST REMAIN IN HEAVEN
UNTIL THE TIME COMES
ACTS 3:21

Some days later, Peter and John healed a lame man at the Temple gate (*Acts 3:1-10*). When a crowd came to see the sight, Peter seized the opportunity to proclaim Jesus to them. He repeated the themes of his Pentecost sermon: they killed, God raised, now they must repent and turn to the Holy and Righteous One whom they had disowned (*vv. 13-19*). In Jesus, God was fulfilling the prophecy of Moses (*v. 22*, see *Deu 18:15*) and indeed the prophecies of all the prophets since Samuel (*v. 24*).

For now, Jesus must remain in heaven (*v. 21*). When *"the time comes for God to restore everything"* as He had promised, then He will send Jesus (*v. 20*). This is clear confirmation that the prophecies of the restored kingdom will remain unfulfilled until Jesus comes again. When He ushers in eternity, then the everlasting kingdom of heaven will finally be a reality.

NO OTHER NAME UNDER HEAVEN
ACTS 4:12

Heaven continued to be a theme of apostolic preaching. When Peter and John were arrested and called before the Sanhedrin, Peter reminded them that the authorities themselves had killed Jesus, but God raised Him from the dead (*Acts 4:10*). What is more, Jesus is the capstone—the crowning glory—of the kingdom that God has built. Then Peter threw down the gauntlet: *"Salvation is found in no one else, for there is no other name under heaven given to men by which we must be saved"* (*v. 12*).

The affairs of men are conducted under the watchful eye of heaven. Sin will be punished; only one escape is possible. The God of heaven gives one name, Jesus Christ of Nazareth, through which deliverance is possible. He is the only means of salvation—under heaven.

THE BELIEVERS SHARED
EVERYTHING THEY HAD
ACTS 4:32-34

As a summary to the events following Pentecost and the birth of the church, *Acts* gives a fortuitous preview of heaven. Since the believers were *"one in heart and mind"* (*Acts 4:32*), they were unwilling to let any of their number go hungry. (It should be remembered that people had come from many nations to celebrate Pentecost. Naturally, those who became Christians wanted to stay, even though their resources would quickly run out.) Everyone, both local and immigrant, shared everything they had.

This text does not address the topic of room and board in heaven, but that early experience is surely a preview. When people love each other enough and have the same mind about what is important, it becomes easy to be generous. With God's abundant provisions in heaven and with this willingness to share, heaven will be a delight.

STEPHEN LOOKED UP TO HEAVEN
ACTS 7:49-55

Stephen, one of the deacons in the early church, was soon proclaiming Christ in spite of opposition. Like the apostles, he was arrested and called before the Sanhedrin. In a long sermon reviewing their history of stubbornness, Stephen also recounted how Solomon built a house for God (*Acts 7:47*). But Stephen said the God of heaven does not dwell in houses made by man. As Isaiah had given the word of the Lord, *"Heaven is my throne, and the earth is my footstool"* (*Acts 7:49; Isa 66:1*).

What is most interesting here is not just the statement that God lives in heaven. That has been a familiar theme throughout the Scriptures. Here, however, it precedes by only a few verses the stoning of Stephen. As they gnashed their teeth at him in fury, he *"looked up to heaven and saw the glory of God, and Jesus standing at the right hand of God"* (*Acts 7:55*). When they heard him describe this, they dragged him out of the city and stoned him. But whether they liked it or not, certain facts were true. Heaven is the home of God in His glory; Jesus is at His right hand; Jesus welcomes His faithful followers into heaven at their death.

This incident also raises a controversial question. As Stephen died he prayed, *"Lord Jesus, receive my spirit"* (*v. 59*). Does this mean that, for the present time at least, only the spirit of a man goes to be with

Jesus? What about the body? Is there an intermediate "spirit" existence now, followed by a later resurrection of the body in preparation for the ultimate place called heaven? (And is it even reasonable to expect Stephen to know exactly what is going to happen here?) As noted in the comments on *Luke 23:43*, we will attempt a more complete answer at *Philippians 1:23*.

A LIGHT FROM HEAVEN
FLASHED AROUND HIM
ACTS 9:3-16

As the history of the Book of *Acts* continues, the Lord continues to reach down from heaven to interact with the affairs of earth. When Saul neared Damascus on his mission to exterminate Christians, suddenly *"a light from heaven"* flashed around him (*Acts 9:3*). The Lord spoke to Saul (*vv. 4-6*) and then spoke to Ananias (*vv. 10-16*). In these special circumstances, at least, heaven is the source of instructions for the servants of God. So, as Paul later told King Agrippa, *"I was not disobedient to the vision from heaven"* (*Acts 26:19*).

THE HOLY AND SURE BLESSINGS
PROMISED TO DAVID
ACTS 13:34-38

When Paul preached the gospel in Pisidian Antioch on his first missionary journey, he emphasized the good news of the restored kingdom. He said that the very fact that God raised Jesus from the dead was prophesied in these words: *"I will give you the holy and sure blessings promised to David"* (*Acts 13:34*). God's promise, as quoted from Isaiah, includes *"an everlasting covenant"* in which the Chosen One would be endowed with splendor and the nations of the world would hasten to obey Him (*Isa 55:3-5*). The certainty that God was beginning to fulfill that prophecy in Jesus was shown when God raised Him from the dead and did not let His *"Holy One see decay"* (*Acts 13:35; Ps 16:10*).

When Paul finished his preaching, some of his audience gladly accepted the gospel message. The conclusion of the matter was that *"all who were appointed for eternal life believed"* (*Acts 13:48*). (While some see predestination in this verse, it can also mean that those "who were so disposed" believed.) What is significant for this study is that the preaching of life after death and the restored, everlasting kingdom go hand in hand.

The Lord of Heaven and Earth
Acts 14:15; 17:24-31

In the city of Lystra, later on that same missionary journey, Paul preached to men who worshiped idols devoted to Zeus. He called for them *"to turn from these worthless things to the living God, who made heaven and earth and sea and everything in them"* (**Acts 14:15**). Then in Athens on the second missionary journey, he repeated this theme to the idol-worshipers there. *"The God who made the world,"* he said, *"is the Lord of heaven and earth and does not live in temples made by hands"* (**Acts 17:24**). Now this God has *"set a day when he will judge the world with justice by the man he has appointed,"* and He has *"given proof to all men by raising him from the dead"* (**v. 31**). The God of heaven has returned His Son to heaven and will someday declare who will join them there.

"Because of My Hope in the Resurrection of the Dead"
Acts 23:6-8

After the three missionary journeys were over, Paul was arrested in Jerusalem (**Acts 21:27-28**). When he was brought before the Sanhedrin, he made a speech that was calculated to divide the council against itself. Knowing that the Sadducees did not believe in a resurrection and that the Pharisees did, Paul said, *"My brothers . . . I stand on trial because of my hope in the resurrection of the dead* (**Acts 23:6-8**). But it was not just a clever ploy; it was the truth. Paul's whole ministry was based on his faith in the risen Christ and his hope of the final resurrection.

Soon Paul was taken to Caesarea, where he stood trial before Felix. There Paul repeated his theme: *"It is concerning the resurrection of the dead that I am on trial before you today"* (**Acts 24:21,25**). After two years, Paul presented his case to Festus and King Agrippa: *"It is because of my hope in what God has promised our fathers that I am on trial today"* (**Acts 26:6**). The ancient hope of the restored kingdom was motivating Paul throughout his ministry. Its connection with heaven is shown as Paul goes on to say, *"Why should any of you consider it incredible that God raises the dead?"* (**v. 8**). This twin hope—a restored kingdom and life beyond the grave—never left Paul. The book of **Acts** ends with him still preaching the kingdom of God *"boldly and without hindrance"* (**Acts 28:31**).

CONCLUSION

John stresses the truth that Jesus was sent from heaven, would return to heaven, and is Himself the only way to heaven. Heaven is a place He prepares for His followers, where they will enjoy eternal life. His physical resurrection from the dead shows that there is life beyond the grave.

Acts stresses the truth of the restored kingdom. The church is the first, but not final, phase. The generous sharing of all possessions in the church is a preview of the unity and camaraderie we will enjoy in heaven. The preaching of Acts stresses the fact of the resurrection as proof that God is fulfilling many prophecies and beginning an eternal kingdom with Christ as Lord. God is in heaven, and through Christ, men and women can join Him there.

WHAT DO YOU SAY?

1. Did God dwell in the Temple in Jerusalem during Jesus' lifetime? Did this help to create a desire and expectation?

2. What is "eternal life"? Do we have it now or later?

3. What did Jesus mean when He said, *"My kingdom is not of this world"*?

4. Why was it so important for John to demonstrate that the risen Jesus had a real body? Will our eternal bodies be anything like His?

5. At the time of Jesus' ascension to heaven, why were the disciples still asking about restoring "the kingdom" to Israel?

6. *Acts 3:21* says Jesus must stay in heaven until the time comes for the Father *"to restore all things."* What will be restored?

7. When the early Christians had everything in common, how was that a preview of heaven?

CHAPTER TWELVE

HEAVEN IN PAUL'S EPISTLES

Heaven was a favorite theme for Paul. He was educated in the rich Hebrew Scriptures and shared the Pharisees' belief about the world to come (*Acts 23:6-8; 24:15; 26:5*). Then he encountered Jesus, who spoke to him directly from heaven (*Acts 9:5; 22:8; 26:15*). Paul often made resurrection the theme of his teaching, even saying that without it his preaching was pointless (*1Cor 15:14*). He was a man who had caught a glimpse of heaven (*2Cor 12:2-4*), and pressed on toward the goal of joining Christ there (*Php 3:11-14*). More than most, Paul knew that for the Christian, "to die is gain" (*Php 1:21*).

HEAVEN IN THE BOOK OF ROMANS

Romans is Paul's most complete explanation of how God saves us. It is noteworthy that this book, heavy in "doctrine," is saturated with the hope of heaven. That is where God's children will share in His glory (*Rom 8:17*).

181

THE DAY WHEN GOD WILL JUDGE MEN'S SECRETS ROMANS 2:16

Paul opens his epistle to the Roman church with a universal condemnation of the human race. Jews and Gentiles alike are sinners. In the coming day of wrath God will show no favoritism (*Rom 2:5-11*). All this will take place *"on the day when God will judge men's secrets through Jesus Christ, as my gospel declares"* (*v. 16*). For Paul, then, preaching the gospel was not complete without a warning of judgment to come.

TO BRING ETERNAL LIFE THROUGH JESUS CHRIST ROMANS 5:21

The good news of the gospel is that God justifies believers through faith (*Rom 3:21-26*). This is the God in whom Abraham believed—the God *"who gives life to the dead"* (*Rom 4:17*). This is the God in whom Paul believed—the God *"who raised Jesus our Lord from the dead"* (*4:24*). This is the God who sent Christ to die for us and to save us from the coming wrath (*Rom 5:8-9*).

Just as Adam introduced sin and death into a fallen world, now Christ brings righteousness and life in heaven (*Rom 5:16*). In Adam the garden paradise was lost; in Christ the eternal paradise is regained. God's grace reigns triumphantly through the righteousness that has been credited to us *"to bring eternal life through Jesus Christ our Lord"* (*v. 21*).

THE GIFT OF GOD IS ETERNAL LIFE IN CHRIST JESUS

ROMANS 6:23

In baptism, Christians are united with Christ in a death like His. Raised from the watery "grave," Christians begin the pilgrimage to heaven, energized by the expectation that they *"will certainly also be united with him in his resurrection"* (*Rom 6:5*). Dead to the old penalty and power of sin, Christians are set free to become "slaves" of righteousness (*vv. 11,18*). This new life *"leads to holiness, and the result is eternal life"* (*v. 22*). Sin pays its terrible wages in death, but *"the gift"*—not the wages—*"of God is eternal life in Christ Jesus our Lord"* (*v. 23*).

THAT WE MAY SHARE IN HIS GLORY
ROMANS 8:17-18

God promises to give life to our mortal bodies through His Spirit, just as He raised Jesus from the dead (*Rom 8:11*). Raised with Christ, we are co-heirs with Christ. In the present life we share His sufferings, but in the life to come we will share in His glory (*v. 17*). Paul notes that whatever the present sufferings may be, they are *"not worth comparing with the glory that will be revealed in us"* (*v. 18*). Thus, God's ultimate plan is to share His glory with us (see comments at *Rom 8:30*).

CREATION ITSELF WILL BE LIBERATED
ROMANS 8:19-22

God's ultimate plan includes the redemption of the physical universe. He will fix the fallen world. Under the curse of the Fall, all creation has been doomed to decline and die (*Gen 2:17; 3:17-18; 1Cor 7:31*). But along with the God's people, the created world will be *"liberated from its bondage to decay"* and *"brought into the glorious freedom of the children of God"* (*Rom 8:20-21*). Other Scriptures that also point to this purging and restoring of fallen creation include *Colossians 1:20* and *2 Peter 3:10-13*. Paul even sees the whole creation *"groaning as in the pains of childbirth right up to the present time"* (*Rom 8:22*),

Chapter 12

Heaven in Paul's Epistles

eagerly awaiting the final chapter of God's plan. When it is all accomplished, it will not just be a slightly spruced up universe; it will be fitly called *"a new heaven and a new earth"* (**Rev 21:1**).

THE REDEMPTION OF OUR BODIES
ROMANS 8:23

As part of the created universe, our physical bodies also await redemption and purification. Just as the whole creation "groans" as in childbirth, believers also *"groan inwardly as we wait eagerly for our adoption as sons, the redemption of our bodies"* (**Rom 8:23**). In one sense, we are already adopted into God's family. However, the full benefits have not yet been received. It is in that sense that we *"wait eagerly for our adoption."*

Many of the Greek philosophers taught that the human body was somehow a debased prison from which we will gratefully escape. Scripture, however, shows that the body was originally proclaimed "good" and will ultimately be redeemed. When all God's creation—including our physical bodies—is liberated from its downward spiral, then the world will be what God wanted in the first place.

THOSE HE JUSTIFIED,
HE ALSO GLORIFIED
ROMANS 8:30

God does not share His glory. At least that is what He said to Israel in the OT (**Isa 42:8**). In that context, He was speaking of the false gods to whom people wrongly gave praise that belonged to God. But now, in the NT, an incredible truth emerges: God's children will share in the divine glory!

Promises in **Romans** that the believer will share God's glory:

"We rejoice in the hope of the glory of God" (**Rom 5:2**)
"Co-heirs with Christ . . . in order that we may also share in his glory" (**Rom 8:17**)
"The glory that will be revealed" (**Rom 8:18**)
"Those he justified, he also glorified" (**Rom 8:30**)
"Theirs is the adoption as sons; theirs the divine glory" (**Rom 9:4**)
"Whom he prepared in advance for glory" (**Rom 9:23**)

It is the Father's good pleasure to invite sinners into His kingdom to share His glory. He has "foreknown" these people and has "predestined" that they should be conformed to the image of His Son (*Rom 8:29*). These people are "called" through the gospel, "justified" by their faith in Christ's sacrifice, and will ultimately be "glorified" in heaven. This does not mean that humans will become divine (as Mormons teach). It does, however, underscore the reality that we will reign with God (*Rev 22:5*), be in a position over the angels (*1Cor 6:3*), and will in ways that we cannot yet fathom share some portion of God's glory.

CHRIST JESUS . . .
IS AT THE RIGHT HAND OF GOD
ROMANS 8:34-38

Paul concludes *Romans 8* with a cry of triumph. In spite of whoever might try to condemn us, we have Jesus to speak up for us. He who died and *"was raised to life"* is even now *"at the right hand of God and is also interceding for us"* (*Rom 8:34*). One of the most important truths about heaven, then, is that Jesus is already there opening the way for us (see *Jn 14:1-3*).

No power in heaven or on earth can tear us away from God's love. Death cannot hold us down; life cannot keep us away. Neither angels nor demons, now or in the future, can do anything that would divide us from our Father. Nothing in all creation, short of our own refusal to want Him, can *"separate us from the love of God that is Christ Jesus our Lord"* (*Rom 8:38*).

WE WILL ALL STAND
BEFORE GOD'S JUDGMENT SEAT
ROMANS 14:10-12

In *Romans 9–11* Paul addresses a primary purpose for writing the book of Romans: Jew and Gentile belong in the same church (see *Rom 1:17; 15:7-9*). In order to fulfill the ancient promise of a restored kingdom, a kingdom great enough to include the nations of the world (*Rom 15:9-12; 16:26*), God has broken off "natural" branches and grafted in "wild" branches, accepting all people who put faith in Christ Jesus (*Rom 11:11-25*).

This equality of Jew and Gentile before God leads up to a very important section in *chapter 14*. No one lives—or dies—to himself;

"whether we live or die, we belong to Christ" (**Rom 14:8**). That is why Christ *"died and returned to life"*; so that He would be *"Lord of both the dead and the living"* (**v. 9**). Since we belong to Christ, we have no right to pass judgment on one another. Instead, *"we will all stand before God's judgment seat"* (**v. 10**, see **2Cor 5:10**). When this happens, it will be the time when the OT prophecies of the everlasting kingdom will be fulfilled. Just as Isaiah foretold, that is when *"every knee will bow before me; every tongue will confess to God"* (**v. 11**, see **Isa 45:23; Php 2:10-11**).

THE KINGDOM OF GOD NOT A
MATTER OF EATING AND DRINKING?
ROMANS 14:17

Paul wrote to a church that was divided over what foods were allowed or disallowed to Christians. Some boldly ate; others were scandalized by their audacity; both sides condemned the other (**Rom 14:13-15**). Paul sternly wrote, *"Do not by your eating destroy your brother for whom Christ died"* (**v. 15b**). After all, food was not that important.

It was in this context, then, that Paul made a statement that is often misunderstood: *"For the kingdom of God is not a matter of eating and drinking, but of righteousness, peace and joy in the Holy Spirit"* (**v. 17**). Some have mistakenly thought this means that there will be no food or drink in God's eternal kingdom. For good measure they have also thrown in: *"Food for stomach and the stomach for food—but God will destroy them both"* (**1Cor 6:13**). How do these verses harmonize with all the texts that speak about eating and drinking in that kingdom?

It is vital to observe that Paul's point is about who is in and who is out of God's kingdom. In being so eager to pass judgment on each other, some of the Roman Christians were missing the point. Neither eating nor abstaining has anything to do with deciding who gets in. That is not the basis for judgment; thus, the kingdom of God "is not a matter" of such things. It should be noticed, further, that **Romans 14:17** needs the following verse to complete the sentence (and the thought): *"because anyone who serves Christ in this way is pleasing to God and approved by men"* (**v. 18**). So will we eat and drink in heaven? Certainly (**Rev 2:7,17; 19:9; 22:1-2**). But that is not the basis of what gets us in.

THE GOD OF PEACE
WILL SOON CRUSH SATAN
ROMANS 16:20

The final good news of Romans is that God will ultimately destroy the devil. He will not do this *for* the Christians; He will do this *through* the Christians. The promise is that God will *"crush Satan under your feet"* (*Rom 16:20*). Our ancient foe will be forever defeated (*Rev 20:10*) because God will enable us to crush him under our feet.

Then the plan of the ages will be complete. The truth revealed *"in the prophetic writings"* (*Rom 16:26*) will come to pass, *"that all nations might believe and obey him"* (*v. 27*). Jew and Gentile—both condemned by sin, both redeemed by Christ—will share the everlasting kingdom.

HEAVEN IN 1 CORINTHIANS

Paul's *first epistle to the Corinthians* contains his most detailed information about the life to come. Some themes are repeated from *Romans*; these will be noted briefly. The ideas of *1 Corinthians 15*, on the other hand, will deserve careful attention.

NO EYE HAS SEEN, NOR EAR HAS HEARD
1 CORINTHIANS 2:9

Paul proclaimed a timeless message when he planted the church in Corinth: *"Jesus Christ and him crucified"* (*1Cor 2:2*). Christ was the core of God's hidden wisdom, a plan destined *"for our glory"* before time began (*v. 7*). In confirmation of the fact that God has been planning to establish this kingdom for the saints, Paul then quoted this passage: *"No eye has seen, nor ear has heard, no mind has conceived what God has prepared for those who love him"* (*v. 9*, see *Isa 64:4*). In the context of the original prophecy, what God has prepared includes *"a new heaven and a new earth"* where He will *"create Jerusalem to be a delight"* (*Isa 65:17-18*). This fulfillment of God's plan includes the church, to be sure, but it is finalized in heaven.

HE WILL RECEIVE HIS REWARD
1 CORINTHIANS 3:12-15

People in Corinth were creating divisions in the church, lining up with Paul or Apollos (*1Cor 3:4*). To correct their error, Paul showed that he and Apollos were simply servants in God's field. One plants, another waters, and both will be rewarded for their labor by God. To make his point more sure, Paul then used another image. Men build on Christ as the foundation, using gold, silver, costly stones—or perhaps only wood, hay, or straw (*v. 12*). But like a house that goes through a fire, the works of some men will not last. *"If what he has built survives, he will receive his reward. If it is burned up, he will suffer loss; he himself will be saved, but only as one escaping through the flames"* (*vv. 14-15*).

Possibly this shows degrees of reward in heaven. Of those who are saved, some will have gold, silver, and jewels, but others will have nothing. More likely, this shows that our life's work is sometimes valuable to the kingdom, and sometimes not. (A person can be saved, even though his pet projects and ambitions have done little that matters in eternity.) Seen in this light, some will have the reward of knowing that they spent their years on earth doing things that contributed to the kingdom. The satisfaction of having done that will be reward enough. In this sense Paul later told this church that some ran *"to get a crown that will not last; but we do it to get a crown that will last forever"* (*1Cor 9:25*).

THE SAINTS WILL JUDGE THE WORLD AND THE ANGELS
1 CORINTHIANS 6:2-3

The Corinthian church had a problem of members taking each other to court to stand before a pagan judge. Paul said they should be able to solve such legal differences among themselves. After all, did they not know that the saints will judge the world? (*1Cor 6:2*). And even more, *"Do you not know that we will judge angels?"* (*v. 3*).

In the age to come God's children will reign with Him in heaven (*Rev 22:5*). Exercising some form of delegated authority as representatives of God's rule, Christians will participate in judging the unsaved world. In addition, the saints will help pronounce judgment on the fallen angels that have been kept in chains for that day (*2Pet 2:4,9; Jude 6*). This is just one of the ways in which we will serve our Creator.

EAT AND DRINK . . . FOR THE GLORY OF GOD
1 CORINTHIANS 10:31; 11:26

The church in Corinth, like the church in Rome, was divided over the issue of whether to eat meat that had been sacrificed to idols. Paul taught them that there were times when they should eat and times when they should not (*1Cor 10:27-30*). The main thing was that when they ate or drank, they should *"do all to the glory of God"* (*v. 31*). Eating and drinking, then, is an activity that can be done to God's glory. It is not a carnal, unworthy endeavor (see notes on *Rom 14:17*).

This becomes even clearer in the next chapter of *1 Corinthians*, where Paul addressed the Lord's Supper. In this sacred meal, to be shared by both rich and poor, eating and drinking take on a deeply spiritual significance. Paul said, *"Whenever you eat this bread and drink this cup, you proclaim the Lord's death until he comes"* (*1Cor 11:26*). In this weekly community meal Christians state publicly that they believe in heaven. They believe in a Lord who is coming again—to welcome them to a grander meal, His wedding banquet! (*Rev 19:9*).

THERE ARE DIFFERENT KINDS OF GIFTS
1 CORINTHIANS 12:4-7

Yet one more division in the church in Corinth concerned spiritual gifts. Paul explained at length that different people have different gifts, but they all share the same Spirit (*1Cor 12:4*). Just as different parts of the body have their own functions (*vv. 12-27*), so Christians have different gifts and responsibilities in the body of Christ. What was important was that *"to each one the manifestation of the Spirit is given for the common good"* (*v. 7*).

Surely this principle will also be true in heaven. There is no reason to think that we will all have identical skills and talents in heaven. Instead, there will be a wonderful diversity of interests and personalities, of talents and abilities. As in Corinth, what will be important is that every person in heaven will contribute his or her part to the total functioning of God's community *"for the common good."*

NOW I KNOW IN PART;
THEN I SHALL KNOW FULLY
1 CORINTHIANS 13:12

More important than individual spiritual gifts in Corinth was the supreme virtue: love. In his beautiful "love chapter" Paul contrasted the imperfection of present gifts with the perfection of what was to come. *"Now we see but a poor reflection as in a mirror,"* he said, *"then we shall see face to face. Now I know in part; then I shall know fully, even as I am fully known"* (*1Cor 13:12*).

Two vital truths come to light here. First, we will see God *"face to face"* (see *Mt 5:8; Heb 12:14; Rev 22:4*). What is presently so dim and obscured will come radiantly into focus in heaven. Second, and more controversially, we will *"know fully."* Some have taken this to mean that we will know everything in heaven. In this view, we would become omniscient like God Himself. However, that was not Paul's point. The context is about knowing God, not becoming God. We will see God *"face to face"* and we will know God *"fully,"* just as He knows us. We will know God then, just as He knows us now—fully and completely.

1 CORINTHIANS 15

The *15th chapter of 1 Corinthians* is Paul's longest discourse on heaven. Based on the truth of Christ's resurrection, Paul established three fundamental truths. First, there will be a resurrection for all of us (*vv. 12-23,29-34*). Second, when Christ returns He will place the triumphant kingdom in the Father's hands (*vv. 24-28*). Third, we will have bodies that are imperishable and immortal (*vv. 35-54*).

How Can You Say
There Is No Resurrection?
1 Corinthians 15:12-23

Incredibly, some Christians in Corinth denied that any persons except Christ would rise from the dead. Paul explained, however, that the very fact of His resurrection gave them assurance of their own (*1Cor 15:21*). Otherwise, his preaching was useless and their faith was, too (*v. 14*). Moreover, if their faith was thus "futile," then they were dead in their sins (*v. 17*). But Christ, as they had to admit, was in fact raised (*v. 20*), and all who are in Christ will be raised as well (*v. 22*). Jesus has shown us that we can be absolutely sure of this truth: there is life beyond the grave.

But we are not absolutely sure of the timing. There is a certain tension in what Paul has written about the resurrection. Are dead Christians already being raised, or must they sleep in their graves for the 2nd coming? Part of what he said would cause us to lean toward the first understanding, that the dead are already in heaven. In *verse 16* the present tense of the verb would be well translated, *"the dead are being raised."* Later, however, it sounds very much as if the dead are not raised until Christ returns (*vv. 23,52*). A more detailed analysis of the options in interpretation will be found in our consideration of *Philippians 1:21-23*.

Then . . . He Hands Over the Kingdom to God
1 Corinthians 15:24-28

Christ will return and *"then the end will come"* (*1Cor 15:24*). All of human history, from the Garden to each man's grave, will reach its grand conclusion. All that God planned for the redemption of Creation will come to its climax. In this grand finale, Jesus *"hands over the kingdom to the Father"* (*v. 24*). All other power and dominion will have been destroyed; every enemy of the kingdom will have been put under His feet (*v. 25*). Since this will be an everlasting kingdom (*2Sa 7:13; Isa 9:7*), death itself will be eliminated.

Death is our enemy. It is a violation of everything God stands for, since He is the great I Am, the eternally existing One. It is a contradiction of the very nature of Jesus, since He is life *(Jn 1:4; 14:6)*. There would have been no death if Adam and Eve had not sinned, but with their rebellion death spread its ugly tentacles over all their descendants *(Rom 5:12)*. So death is our enemy—the last enemy to be destroyed *(1Cor 15:26)*.

Paul found it necessary to clarify what Scripture meant when it said that He has *"put all things under his feet"* (*Ps 8:6*; see *Heb 2:8*). When "everything" is subjected to Jesus, that does not, of course, include God the Father (*1Cor 15:27*). In the age to come, Jesus Himself will be subject to the Father, *"so that God may be all in all"* (*v. 28*). The Son will rule at the right hand of the Father, and their kingdom will last forever.

How Are the Dead Raised?
With What Kind of Body?
1 Corinthians 15:35-54

Some of the Corinthians apparently thought the resurrection could not be possible because the dead body rotted and decayed into dust. But as Paul explained, that is precisely what is necessary. When a seed is planted, for instance, it must first "die" (*1Cor 15:36;* see *Jn 12:24*). A dry, preserved seed will never sprout. A moist, "rotting" seed will fall apart and cease to exist in its former configuration. Then, when the seed comes to life, it is not just a seed, but a stalk of wheat or something else. In a somewhat similar fashion (since all analogies are limited), the body that is planted in the grave is not the body that it will be (*v. 37*).

God determines what the resurrection body will be like. The God who made the various kinds of flesh—animal, bird, fish—is certainly capable of coming up with a new kind of body for heaven (*1Cor 15:38-39*). And just as God gave different degrees of splendor to the earth, the moon, the sun, and the stars, He will give a whole new kind of splendor to our resurrected bodies (*vv. 40-42*). A perishable body is planted; an imperishable body is raised. What is sown in dishonor and weakness will be raised in glory and power (*v. 43*). It goes down into death *"a natural body,"* but it is raised as *"a spiritual body"* (*v. 44*). Just as a lowly seed sprouts into a full-grown plant, so shall our bodies be transformed into something far more glorious (*Php 3:21*).

Our tired, old physical bodies will not be abandoned, but they will be *"changed"* (*1Cor 15:51*). The perishable body *"must clothe itself with the imperishable"* and *"with immortality"* (*v. 54*). Thus, the earlier analogy of the seed and this language of putting on an imperishable nature help us to understand what Paul said in *verses 44-50*. The changes that will take place do not eliminate a certain continuity from the old body to the new. The purely material body is only corruptible flesh and blood. As such, it cannot inherit the kingdom of God (*v. 50*). The "natural body" of Adam must become the "spiritual body" that will *"bear the likeness of the man from heaven"* (*v. 49*). Therefore, our bodies will be raised and transformed, made imperishable and immortal. Then death, the final enemy, is swallowed up and defeated by the final victory in Jesus (*vv. 54,57*).

HEAVEN IN 2 CORINTHIANS

THE GUARANTEE OF WHAT IS TO COME
2 CORINTHIANS 1:22

God always keeps His word. All His promises find their "Yes" in Christ (*2Cor 1:20*). In this context Paul told the believers in Corinth that God has given His guarantee that the promises of heaven will be fulfilled. God has anointed Christians, set His seal of ownership on them, and has put His Spirit in their hearts as a *"deposit, guaranteeing what is to come"* (*vv. 21-22*, see *2Cor 5:5; Eph 1:13-14*).

The Greek word for "deposit" or "earnest" (KJV) was used in everyday life for the down payment or first installment on a purchase. Like "earnest money" in real estate transactions today, it was a guarantee that the buyer would follow through on his agreement. When God puts the Holy Spirit in the heart of the believer, that is a first installment of His personal presence with us in heaven.

> The ancient Greek word for "deposit" is used in modern Greek as a term for an engagement ring. When a young man is serious about his intentions toward his girl friend, he gives her this token of commitment. Since the church is the bride of Christ, the analogy of the Holy Spirit as our engagement ring is a beautiful picture.

TRANSFORMED WITH EVER-INCREASING GLORY
2 CORINTHIANS 3:18

In *chapter three* Paul enlarges on the truth of the indwelling Spirit as a foretaste of heaven. The Spirit's presence gives us a freedom in access to the Lord, an access that is in some ways even superior to what Moses enjoyed (*2Cor 3:13*). Now, when the promises of the old covenant are read, the veil of limited understanding is taken away. Where the Spirit of the Lord is, there is freedom. Thus, *"with unveiled faces"* we reflect the Lord's glory and are being transformed into God's likeness even now *"with ever-increasing glory"* (*v. 18*). It is the Father's pleasure to share His glory with us (*Rom 8:30*), and what we enjoy now with the Holy Spirit in us is a foretaste of heaven.

AN ETERNAL GLORY THAT FAR OUTWEIGHS OUR TROUBLES
2 CORINTHIANS 4:14-18

Our present bodies are inferior jars of clay (*2Cor 4:7*). Though we are dying, *"We know that the one who raised the Lord Jesus from the dead will also raise us"* (*v. 14*). Outwardly we are wasting away, but inwardly we are renewed by the presence of Christ and the prospect of heaven. As Paul said, *"Our light and momentary troubles are achieving for us an eternal glory that far outweighs them all"* (*v. 17*).

As we have seen before in *2 Corinthians*, God promises to share the glory of heaven with believers. This future glory—though unseen for now—is the motivation that sustains Christians through whatever troubles they presently experience. Holding firmly to the promise of heaven, *"We fix our eyes not on what is seen, but on what is unseen. What is seen is temporary, but what is unseen is eternal"* (*v. 18*).

AN ETERNAL HOUSE IN HEAVEN
2 CORINTHIANS 5:1-10

So the lowly body, like a fragile jar of clay, was wasting away, and the Corinthians were to look to the future glory that God would provide. But having said that, Paul was not done. In that unseen eternity, he said, God would provide them new bodies. If their "earthly tents" wore out or even were violently "destroyed," so what? They had *"a building from God, an eternal house in heaven"* (*2Cor 5:1*).

At least six significant truths are established in this passage. First, the present body is like a tent that will perish (*vv. 1,4*). Second, that temporary "tent" is to be replaced by a stronger, permanent "building" from God and what is mortal will be swallowed up by life (*vv. 2,4*). Third, from the beginning God made the human race for this purpose and has given the Spirit as a "deposit" to guarantee that He will carry out His grand plan (*v. 5*, see *2Cor 1:22; Eph 1:13-14*). Fourth, as long as a person lives in the present body (the "tent"), he is away from the Lord (*v. 6*). Fifth, it is preferable to leave the body and be at home with the Lord (*v. 8*). This is one of the verses that strongly support the idea that when the body perishes, the person goes right on to a new body in heaven (see *Php 1:21-23*). Sixth, everyone—living or dead—will stand before the judgment seat of Christ. Therefore, whether we are at home in the earthly body or away from it (and with the Lord), it must be our desire to please Him (*vv. 9-10*).

WE ARE THE TEMPLE OF
THE LIVING GOD
2 CORINTHIANS 6:16

The believers in Corinth needed to be warned that they should not be yoked together with unbelievers (*2Cor 6:14*). In support of that warning, Paul said, *"We are the temple of the living God"* (*v. 16*), and what agreement can God's temple have with the temples of idols? Then Paul quoted a text that appears more than once in the OT, *"I will live with them and walk among them, and I will be their God, and they will be my people"* (*v. 16*). This was God's symbolic intention for the Tabernacle in the wilderness (*Lev 16:12*); this was God's ultimate intention for the restored kingdom in eternity (*Jer 32:38; Eze 37:27*). Finally in heaven, God will walk among His people and the ancient promises will all be true (*Rev 21:3*).

A Man Caught Up
to the Third Heaven
2 Corinthians 12:2-4

Paul said mysteriously, *"I know a man in Christ who fourteen years ago was caught up to the third heaven"* (*2Cor 12:2*). In the parlance of the time, the first sky/heaven was the atmosphere of birds and clouds; the second sky/heaven was the level of planets and stars; the "third heaven" was beyond all that, where God Himself dwelt. Paul also called this third heaven by another name, *"paradise"* (*v. 3*, see *Lk 23:43; Rev 2:7*). This apparently puts paradise into a time frame simultaneous with Paul himself. More significantly, this *"man in Christ"* heard *"inexpressible things, things that man is not permitted to tell"* (*v. 4*). Whatever dying people may or may not see and hear in the oft reported tunnel of brilliant light, the truths of heaven are not disclosed outside the Bible.

Was this man Paul? He wrote **2 Corinthians** AD 55 or 56, so "fourteen years ago" would have been AD 42 or 43 (by Jewish inclusive counting of years), which would have been during the ten "silent years," AD 35-45 in Syria and Cilicia *(Gal 1:21)*. Even though it is too early to connect this event with the stoning in Lystra *(Acts 14:19*, about AD 47), it is still likely that Paul was speaking about himself. His intimate knowledge of the details and his reluctance to boast, plus the connection with his own thorn in the flesh *(2Cor 12:7)*, point to Paul himself as the man.

HEAVEN IN GALATIANS

HEIRS ACCORDING TO PROMISE
GALATIANS 3:29

Judaizers were attacking the churches in Galatia, teaching that people had to keep the OT laws in order to be saved. To address this error Paul demonstrated that God's people are saved through faith (*Gal 2:16*), just as Abraham was (*Gal 3:6-9*). People become children of God through faith and clothe themselves with Christ through baptism (*Gal 3:26-27*). The grand climax to Paul's argument is reached in *verse 29*: *"If you belong to Christ, then you are Abraham's seed and heirs according to promise."*

As we saw in *Genesis 12*, God began the long process of reclaiming the fallen race of man. *"You will be a blessing,"* God promised Abraham, *"and all peoples on earth will be blessed through you"* (*Gen 12:2-3*). Throughout Abraham's life he had faith in God and kept *"looking forward to the city with foundations, whose architect and builder is God"* (*Heb 11:10*). But it would be through Abraham's descendant, Jesus Christ, that the doorway to heaven would be opened. Believers in Christ become Abraham's descendants themselves, and therefore they are co-heirs of God's promise. That is why going to heaven is described as going to Abraham's side (*Lk 16:23*) and as sitting with him at the banquet (*Mt 8:11*).

WILL REAP ETERNAL LIFE
GALATIANS 6:9

Having shown the Galatians that they were saved by faith in Christ and not by works of the law, Paul then had to show them how living for God does matter. The key is *"faith expressing itself through love"* (*Gal 5:6*). Therefore, the believer will shun the acts of the sinful nature (*vv. 19-21*) and produce the fruit of the Spirit (*vv. 22-24*). Faith and lifestyle cannot be separated.

Paul's line of thought leads to this stern maxim: *"God cannot be mocked. A man reaps what he sows"* (*Gal 6:7*). The man who lives for pleasure in this life will reap a harvest of destruction. But the man who lives to please the Spirit *"will reap eternal life"* (*v. 8*). As with the fruit of the Spirit in chapter five, a man cannot claim credit for this harvest. It is God's gift for those whose faith is "working" (*Gal 5:6*, NRSV) through love.

HEAVEN IN EPHESIANS

THE HEAVENLY PLACES
EPHESIANS 1:3,20; 2:6; 3:10; 6:12

God has blessed Christians with every spiritual blessing *"in the heavenly realms"* (**Eph 1:3**). The *"heavenly realms"* are mentioned a total of five times in the epistle to the **Ephesians**, but nowhere else in Scripture. This is Paul's expression for the unseen realm in which Christians already begin to live when they are part of Christ and His church. Specifically, the *"heavenly realms"* are where:

God has already blessed us with every spiritual blessing (*1:3*).

Christ sits at the right hand of God (*1:20*).

We presently sit with Christ (*2:6*).

God shows His wisdom to angels ("rulers and authorities") (*3:10*).

We battle against spiritual forces of evil (*6:12*).

In the same way that the "kingdom of heaven" is both the church now and heaven later, the "heavenly realms" link together this life and the life to come. In the church we have the spiritual blessings and sit with Christ (*1:3; 2:6*). Through the church God demonstrates His wisdom to rebellious angels (*3:10*), whom we battle (*6:12*). (Our struggle against the "rulers" and "authorities" in this realm is *"not against flesh and blood,"* but against the spiritual forces of evil). Reigning over it all, Christ sits at the right hand of God (*1:20*). Thus, in "the heavenly realms" we already have one foot in heaven.

GOD'S PLAN: ALL THINGS
UNDER ONE HEAD
EPHESIANS 1:10

From the beginning it has been God's plan *"to bring all things in heaven and on earth together under one head, even Christ"* (**Eph 1:10**). Thus, after Christ died for our sins, God *"raised him from the dead and seated him at his right hand in the heavenly realms, far above all rule and authority, power and dominion, and every title that can be given, not only in the present age but also in the one to come"* (*vv. 20-21*). Christ reigns supreme in heaven, with all things subjected under His feet (*v. 22*).

In the Coming Ages
Ephesians 2:6-10

The continuing plan is for God to seat us with Christ in the heavenly realms (*Eph 2:6*). In one sense this is already accomplished in the church; in another sense, there is far more yet to come. In *"the coming ages"* God will *"show the incomparable riches of his grace, expressed in his kindness to us in Christ Jesus"* (*v. 7*). This means that God will spend eternity finding new ways to express His love to us. How could heaven possibly get boring?

One of the ways God shows His love to us is by providing work for us to do. This was true in Eden (*Gen 2:15*), and it is true in the church. We are God's workmanship, *"created in Christ Jesus to do good works, which God prepared in advance for us to do"* (*Eph 2:10*; see *Eph 1:19; 3:20-21*). This will also be true in heaven, where we will serve God in an infinite variety of ways (*Rev 22:3*).

The Church Is the Bride of Christ
Ephesians 5:25-32

Christ loves the church. He died to make her holy (*Eph 5:25-26*), and He washes her with water and the word to make her clean (*vv. 26-27*). In the context of how a husband loves and provides for his wife, Paul showed how Christ presents the church to Himself as a radiant bride, without stain or wrinkle or any other blemish. Paul next quoted God's original statement about marriage: *"For this reason a man will leave his father and mother and be united to his wife, and the two will become one flesh"* (*v. 31*, see *Gen 2:24*). Then comes the surprise: *"This is a profound mystery—but I am talking about Christ and the church"* (*v. 32*).

The beauty of marriage as God designed it is a preview of Christ and His church in eternity. Christ has done everything necessary to redeem His bride and prepare her for the wedding. The grand scene of heaven in *Revelation 19* opens with the wedding supper of the Lamb: *"Hallelujah! . . . For the wedding of the Lamb has come, and his bride has made herself ready. Fine linen, bright and clean, was given her to wear"* (*Rev 19:6-8*). *"Blessed are those who are invited to the wedding supper of the Lamb!"* (*v. 9*).

Paul found it necessary to remind slaves to be obedient to their masters, and to warn masters to be fair to their slaves. Slaves could take heart in the fact that *"the Lord will reward everyone for whatever good he does, whether he is a slave or free"* (**Eph 6:8; Col 3:24**). Even if they were not fairly compensated on earth, God will make it up to them in heaven. Masters could take warning in the fact that *"he who is both their Master and yours is in heaven, and there is no favoritism with him"* (**v. 9**, see **Col 3:25**). Just as God will reward those who deserve it, He will also punish others (see **Eph 5:5**). On judgment day, when the Judge of all the earth does the right thing (see **Gen 18:25**), there will be no favoritism or partiality. (The Greek word for "favoritism" is literally "face-taking.") God does not have one standard for slaves and a different standard for masters; He sees all men alike. For those who have done the Lord's will, heaven will be a place a great reward.

HEAVEN IN PHILIPPIANS

COMPLETION AT THE DAY OF CHRIST
PHILIPPIANS 1:6

Paul thanked God for the Philippian church. The small band of believers became his partners in the gospel, opening their homes and loosing their purse strings from their very first meeting with Paul (**Acts 16:15; Php 4:15-16**). In his opening prayer of thanksgiving for them Paul said, *"He who began a good work in you will carry it on to completion until the day of Christ Jesus"* (**Php 1:6**).

Like the rest of us, the Christians in Philippi were a work in progress. Like Paul himself, they were growing in the Lord and reaching new levels of maturity, but they had not yet become what they wanted to be (**Php 3:12**). The wonderful promise is that at the day of Christ Jesus (whether He returns or they die and go to Him) it will all be finished. Their striving, their growing, their occasional failing—all will be carried to completion by God Himself. Having hungered and thirsted for righteousness, finally they will be made into the kind of people fit for heaven.

To Live Is Christ and
to Die Is Gain
Philippians 1:21-23

Paul wrote this epistle from imprisonment in Rome, kept in chains until Caesar decided what to do with him (*Acts 28:30; Php 1:13*). The question of living or dying was therefore a very real issue for him. To go on living in the earthly body would be fruitful labor (*1:22*), so he could say, *"To live is Christ"* (*v. 21*). To be put to death would be a quick ticket to heaven, so he could say, *"To die is gain"* (*v. 21*). Paul summed this up in powerful words: *"To depart and be with Christ"* would be *"better by far"* (*v. 23*). (Interestingly, the Greek word used here for "depart" was the word used for a ship to "untie from its moorings, weigh anchor, and sail away.") As he told the Corinthian church, to be in the body is to be away from the Lord; to leave the body is to be at home with the Lord (*2Cor 5:6-8*).

But not everything Paul wrote seems to agree with this. It will be necessary at this point, therefore, to consider three different views on what happens when the Christian dies. The first view is derogatorily called "soul sleeping." According to this view, when a person dies his soul "sleeps" in a state of suspended animation. Unaware of the passing centuries, he awakes at the 2nd Coming and stands before the judgment seat of Christ. Scriptures that seem to support this view include *1 Corinthians 15:52; 1 Thessalonians 4:16; 5:10; Revelation 20:5*. If these were the only Scriptures on the subject, the case would be closed. But many more Scriptures point to immediate life in "paradise" or an intermediate heaven following death.

A second view attempts to reconcile "sleeping" until the 2nd Coming with going immediately to be with Jesus. We will call this view "joint resurrection." Perhaps in eternity, this view suggests, time is irrelevant. Perhaps God can see all of human history at one glance, so that people die in different centuries, but cross over into eternity simultaneously. To our eyes the times are different, but to God all these people pass through death into resurrection together. Scriptures that seem to support this view include the passages about resurrection at the 2nd Coming, plus *2 Corinthians 4:14 and Hebrews 9:27*. (*Revelation 10:6*, which says *"time will be no more"* in the KJV, does not apply. That verse does not say time will not exist in heaven. Rather, it means, "Time's up!" and there is no more delay as the panorama unfolds.)

While the "joint resurrection" view has some things to commend it, it cannot explain how people are already in paradise/heaven while others are still on earth (*Lk 16:25; Heb 12:22-23; Rev 6:10-11*).

The third view, and one which has the most to commend it, is that the dead go immediately into the presence of Jesus. We will call this view "paradise" or "intermediate heaven." Upon death, people go to heaven, while their old bodies decay in the ground. At the 2nd Coming the physical body is raised (as in *1 Corinthians 15* and *1 Thessalonians 4*) and changed to be imperishable. (Whether the saints in heaven have a temporary body in the meantime is not clear; see below.) Scriptures that support this view are numerous.

1. God is the God of the living—Abraham, Isaac, Jacob—even after they have died (*Mt 22:32*; see *Ex 3:6*).
2. Lazarus is with Abraham and the rich man is consciously suffering in Hades, while at the same time his five brothers are still alive on earth (*Lk 16:22-28*).
3. Jesus told the thief on the cross, *"Today you will be with me in paradise"* (*Lk 23:43*).
4. Jesus told Martha, *"Whoever lives and believes in me will never die"* (*Jn 11:26*). This seems to say that death is only an immediate passage into greater life.
5. Stephen saw heaven open and the Son of Man standing at God's right hand (*Acts 7:55*). This seems to indicate that Jesus was welcoming him into heaven at that moment.
6. When the earthly tent of our body is destroyed, we have a building in heaven. To be absent from the body is to be present with the Lord (*2Cor 5:1,4,6,8*).
7. To live is Christ and to die is gain. To depart and be with Christ is better by far (*Php 1:23*).
8. Christians have approached the heavenly Jerusalem, where joyful angels celebrate with *"the spirits of righteous men made perfect"* (*Heb 12:22-23*).
9. The martyrs in heaven cry out, *"How long, Sovereign Lord, holy and true, until you judge the inhabitants of earth and avenge our blood?"* (*Rev 6:10-11*). These saints are alive in heaven, aware of the passage of time, and aware that those on earth have not yet been punished.

10. In the controversial passage upon which millennial theories are based, the souls of the beheaded *"came to life and reigned with Christ a thousand years"* (**Rev 20:4**). Regardless of whether the thousand years is a literal millennium or a symbolic length of time equaling the church age, there are dead people reigning with Christ prior to the final judgment.

Such a preponderance of Scriptures indicates that the third view must be correct. The first view has too few passages to support it; if anything "sleeps" it is the earthly body, not the soul. The second view requires mental gymnastics that can be neither proved nor disproved. Therefore, as the third view holds, when a believer dies, he goes to be with God. He appears to have a body already (**Lk 16:27**) called a "building" from God (**2Cor 5:1**) so that he does not go into eternity *"unclothed"* (**2Cor 5:4**). The saints in Revelation are given white robes to wear and are told to wait a little longer (**Rev 6:11**). At the 2nd Coming the old body is raised (and united with the heavenly one?) and made immortal. For those who have already been in paradise/heaven, Judgment Day is merely the time when their fate is publicly announced. They have already been in the presence of their Lord, and they will continue to be with Him forever.

I PRESS ON TO WIN THE PRIZE
PHILIPPIANS 3:11-14

Everything Paul knew as a promising young rabbi had turned to dust. After he met Jesus and took inventory of what his previous life had accomplished, it was nothing—even worse than nothing; it was rubbish and sewage (**Php 3:8**). Now his highest goal in life was to follow Jesus, to become like Him in every way (**v. 10**), and somehow to attain to the resurrection from the dead (**v. 11**).

So Paul pressed on. Like all sincere Christians, Paul wanted to become what Jesus wanted him to be. Literally he wanted to *"lay hold on that for which Christ laid hold on me"* (**Php 3:12**). Like a runner stretching forward to win the race, Paul pressed on *"toward the goal to win the prize for which God has called me heavenward in Christ Jesus"* (**v. 14**). Such is the goal of every Christian life—to join the Lord in heaven.

HE WILL TRANSFORM
OUR LOWLY BODIES
PHILIPPIANS 3:20-21

Since Philippi was a Roman colony, the believers there would keenly understand what it meant to have the privilege of imperial citizenship. But Paul said, *"Our citizenship is in heaven"* (**Php 3:20**). Heaven is the land of our primary allegiance; heaven is the home that calls to our hearts. From heaven we await the Savior who is coming to take us to the land where we belong. When He does come to get us, He will of necessity change our physical bodies, since flesh and blood cannot inherit the heavenly kingdom (see **1Cor 15:50**). So He will *"transform our lowly bodies so that they will be like his glorious body"* (**v. 21**).

What will that body be like? It is certainly too little to think only of the body of Jesus following the resurrection. That body was still *"flesh and bones"* (**Lk 24:39**), the kind of body that does not inherit the kingdom of God (**1Cor 15:50**). Neither should we think that we will carry all our scars and mutilations to heaven, as the body of Jesus still had the scars of His crucifixion (**Jn 20:27**). A better image would be how Jesus appeared at the Transfiguration (**Mt 17:2**) or the picture of Jesus in John's revelation (**Rev 1:13-16**). Scripture has already told us that at the resurrection the *"wise will shine like the brightness of the heavens"* (**Dan 12:3**) and that the *"righteous will shine like the sun in the kingdom of their Father"* (**Mt 24:43**).

The transformation of our bodies might be more like the metamorphosis of a caterpillar into a butterfly, or the change of a seed into a plant. There is some continuity from the old to the new, but the new is far more glorious. Whatever the heavenly body may be, several things must certainly be true: (1) The same God who made the body in Eden is going to give us our bodies in heaven. (2) God pronounced that body "good"; the heavenly body will be better. (3) God made the appetites of the first body and the pleasures that satisfy them. We will eat and drink (and what else?) in heaven. (4) God can improve on all the five senses; He has already done so on most of the animal kingdom. (5) God surely did not use up all His good ideas when He fashioned the bodies of Adam and Eve. (6) The final, transformed body will be "glorious" (**Php 3:21**).

WHOSE NAMES ARE IN
THE BOOK OF LIFE
PHILIPPIANS 4:3

Paul spoke of Clement and the rest of his fellow workers, *"whose names are in the book of life"* (**Php 4:3**). Scripture mentioned the book of life as early as *Exodus 32:32*; it is a book in which the saints are saved and the sinners are blotted out. Jesus told His disciples to rejoice that their names were written down in heaven (**Lk 10:20**). The final mention of the book of life (**Rev 20:12-15 and 21:27**) says that those whose names are in the Lamb's book of life will not go into the lake of fire.

HEAVEN IN COLOSSIANS

HE CREATED ALL THINGS
IN HEAVEN AND ON EARTH
COLOSSIANS 1:15-20

Paul wrote to the church in Colosse to correct a budding heresy. One doctrine they needed to get straight was the place of Jesus in regard to creation. Christ is the image (the "making visible") of the unseen God; He holds first rank over all creation (**Col 1:15**). Everything—in heaven and on earth—was made by Him and for Him (**v. 16**). Resurrected to be the firstborn from the dead, Jesus reigns supreme over the church (**v. 18**). With all God's "fullness" dwelling in Him, Jesus made peace by shedding His blood on the cross. In this triumphant act Jesus reconciled all things to the Father, *"whether things on earth or things in heaven"* (**v. 20**).

The heart of the Greek word for "reconcile" is a stem that means "change." God is never reconciled to man in Scripture, because God does not change. It is always man that is reconciled to God. This is more than just having forgiveness; it is more than just a free pass to heaven. At the cross Jesus won back the alienated and hostile heart of man (**v. 21**). It was there that He said He would *"draw all men"* to Himself (**Jn 12:32-33**). Two conclusions must be drawn. First, those who go to heaven are changed individuals. No longer is their heart resistant and rebellious toward God. Second, not every being "on earth or in heaven" is included. Jesus Himself discounted this kind of universalism, saying that *"only a few"* find the road that leads to life (**Mt 7:14**). Similarly, the devil and his angels are not included in this reconciliation. Defiant angels are held in chains awaiting Judgment Day (*Jude 6*). The devil and his angels are destined for the *"eternal fire"* that was prepared for them (*Mt 25:41*). They are the very ones Christ has defeated and disarmed (*Col 2:15*). All those—and only those—in heaven and on earth whose hearts are reconciled and whose sins are covered will have eternal life in Christ Jesus.

THE WORSHIP OF ANGELS
COLOSSIANS 2:18

Angels are such glorious creatures that men have naturally wanted to worship them (*Jdg 13:16; Rev 19:10; 22:8-9*). But the worship of angels is wrong (*Col 2:18*). Incredible as it may seem, in some ways mankind has a position better than the angels. Men, not angels, were created in God's image (*Gen 1:26*). Jesus died for sinful men, not for sinful angels (*Heb 2:16*). At the last day mankind will judge angels (*1Cor 6:3*). Scripture says that men, not angels, will reign with God in heaven (*Rev 22:5*). Angels rejoice over every redeemed sinner; we will rejoice to share heaven with them.

YOU WILL APPEAR WITH HIM IN GLORY
COLOSSIANS 3:1-4

Paul urged the Colossians, *"Set your hearts on things above, where Christ is seated at the right hand of God"* (*Col 3:1*). Likewise he said, *"Set your minds on things above, not on earthly things"* (*v. 2*). This is a clear admonition for Christians to focus their attention on heaven. It is not acceptable to brush off every thought of heaven, since we supposedly cannot know for sure what it will be like. We are to take what we do know and focus our emotional and mental energies there.

Then one day Christ will return for His own. Paul told his readers, *"Then you also will appear with him in glory"* (*v. 4*). It is the Father's pleasure to share His glory with His children (see *Rom 8:30*). A large part of that glory will lie in the fact that when we see Jesus, we will be made like Him (*1Jn 3:2*).

HEAVEN IN 1 THESSALONIANS

The problem in the church at Thessalonica was an excited, but misguided, enthusiasm for the Lord's return. It was a good thing to be eager for that day, as Paul said in the first three chapters. But it was not a good thing to be upset about those who died before that day came, or to worry about when that day would come, as Paul said in chapters four and five.

AND TO WAIT FOR HIS SON
FROM HEAVEN
1 THESSALONIANS 1:10

The Thessalonians had turned from their idols to worship the living God and to *"wait for his Son from heaven . . . Jesus, who rescues us from the coming wrath"* (*1Th 1:9-10*). A living God, an anticipated Son, and coming from a real place—called heaven. Although His coming will mean condemnation for many (see *2Th 1:8-10*), He will rescue the believers from the coming wrath. It will be a time of exultation for those who have served Jesus faithfully (*1Th 2:19*), for God has called them *"into his kingdom and glory"* (*1Th 2:12*).

IGNORANT ABOUT THOSE
WHO FALL ASLEEP
1 THESSALONIANS 4:13-17

Because Jesus died and rose again, there is assurance that believers will live again as well. As Paul said, *"So we believe that God will bring with Jesus those who have fallen asleep in him"* (*1Th 4:14*). Significantly, although Paul said such persons have *"fallen asleep,"* he also said that God will *"bring them with Jesus."* This indicates that they have been with Jesus, a confirmation of the idea that the dead go immediately to their reward (see *Php 1:21-23*).

Then Paul gave specific details about the 2nd Coming (*1Th 4:16-17*). The Lord will come down from heaven with His own *"loud command,"* with *"the voice of the archangel"* (see *Mt 24:30*), and with *"the trumpet call of God"* (see *Mt 24:31; 1Cor 15:52*). (Part of Paul's concern in describing this noisy, conspicuous event was that some thought it was already over and they had missed it. See *2Th 2:2*). Next, significant for the misunderstanding of the Thessalonians, *"the dead in Christ will rise first"* (see *1Cor 15:52*). As discussed previously, this apparently refers to the resurrection of the physical body (see notes on *Php 1:21-23*). It seems that the saints returning with Jesus (*1Th 4:14*) will be in some sense reunited with their resurrected bodies (*v. 17*) as they join those still living to welcome the Lord. It is only then, after the noisy

2nd Coming and the resurrection of bodies, that those who are still alive will play their part. They will *"be caught up together with them in the clouds to meet the Lord in the air."*

> The idea of a "rapture" is drawn from **1 Thessalonians 4:17**. The word for "caught up" in the Latin version is *rapta*. In the sense of the Latin translation, at least, it is biblical to say that Christians will be "raptured" at Christ's return. It should be noted, however, that there is nothing in this passage to indicate a "secret" rapture. At the noisy 2nd Coming, when all the graves are opened, all the Christians will rise to meet the Lord in the air. There is nothing very secret about any of that.

Now . . . about Times and Dates
1 Thessalonians 5:1-6

Some of the believers in Thessalonica, like their counterparts in every generation of Christians since then, wanted to figure out when the 2nd Coming would take place. Paul, however, provided no clues to satisfy their curiosity *"about times and dates"* (**1Th 5:1**). They knew very well, since he had taught them himself, that *"the day of the Lord will come like a thief in the night"* (**v. 2**, see **Mt 24:43-44; 2Pet 3:10**).

Christians need to know that the Lord *is* coming, but not *when* He is coming. As long as they live in the light, they will not be caught unprepared (**1Th 5:4**). Paul's message for them was the same as that of Jesus Himself: always be ready! (See **Mt 24:42,44; 25:13**.)

Spirit, Soul, and Body
at the Coming of Our Lord
1 Thessalonians 5:23

In a closing benediction, Paul prayed that God might sanctify the Thessalonians completely (**1Th 5:23**). Specifically, he expressed his desire for each believer that the *"whole spirit, soul and body be kept blameless at the coming of our Lord Jesus Christ."* This is a good reminder that God has always considered mankind as a complete package: spirit, soul, and body. God will glorify, not eliminate, the body as part of the heavenly existence.

HEAVEN IN 2 THESSALONIANS

CONCERNING THE COMING
OF OUR LORD
2 THESSALONIANS 2:1-8

Certain false teachers had alarmed the young church in Thessalonica, claiming that Paul had said *"the day of the Lord had already come"* (*2Th 2:2*). So Paul set out to put the record straight. *"That day will not come,"* he said, *"until the rebellion occurs and the man of lawlessness is revealed"* (*v. 3*). Paul's purpose was not to provide information by which the time of the 2nd Coming could be predicted (see *1Th 5:1*). His point was that they could tell that it had not happened yet.

As with the interpretation of all prophecy (see *2Pet 1:20*, NASB), what Paul meant by this cannot be known for certain. The *"man of lawlessness"* may have been a historical figure in the 1st or 2nd century, or perhaps someone yet to come. For Paul's readers then, the point was that it had not happened yet. For Paul's readers today, the point is that we cannot use a private interpretation of this unknown person to figure out how soon the 2nd coming will be.

HEAVEN IN 1 TIMOTHY

THE KING ETERNAL, IMMORTAL,
INVISIBLE, THE ONLY GOD
1 TIMOTHY 1:17

Paul's *first letter to Timothy* includes this well-known statement of praise to God: *"Now to the King eternal, immortal, invisible, the only God, be honor and glory for ever and ever"* (*1Tm 1:17*). The Greek word translated "invisible" also means "unseen," and likely that should be our understanding here (see also *Col 1:15; Heb 11:27*). As noted in the Beatitudes, people will see God (*Mt 5:8*) when He dwells among us in heaven (*Rev 22:4*). A further note will be added at *1 Timothy 6:16*.

TAKE HOLD OF ETERNAL LIFE
1 TIMOTHY 6:12

Paul exhorted Timothy to *"fight the good fight of the faith"* and thereby to *"take hold of the eternal life to which you were called"* (*1Tm 6:12*). This life comes from God, *"who gives life to everything"* (*v. 13*).

Since God *"alone is immortal"* (**v. 16**), it is a gift of grace that God chooses to share life with His creatures. Men are not automatically immortal just because they have been born; every moment of life comes from God.

Timothy was also to exhort others to do what was necessary to lay hold on life. The rich, for instance, were to be generous and willing to share. By doing so they would *"lay up treasure for themselves as a firm foundation for the coming age, so that they may take hold of the life that is truly life"* (**1Tm 6:19**).

Who Lives in Unapproachable Light
1 Timothy 6:16

Near the close of his letter Paul made another statement of praise to God, saying that He *"lives in unapproachable light"* and that He is someone *"whom no one has seen or can see"* (**1Tm 6:16**). The brilliant majesty of God is so great that mortal man cannot bear to look at Him or approach Him. When Moses saw even the trailing remnant of God's glory, his face took on a supernatural glow (**Ex 34:29**). He was not allowed to see more than this, because God said, *"No one may see me and live"* (**Ex 33:18-23**).

It will be different in heaven. Even though God will still be the source of brilliant light (**Rev 21:23**), it will not make God unapproachable. God's light will be a gift, not a terror, for the saints. Since men could not approach God on His level, He will come to dwell among us on our level (**Rev 21:3**). Since He was previously unseen/unseeable, in heaven He will allow the saints to look at His face (**Mt 5:8; Rev 22:4**).

HEAVEN IN 2 TIMOTHY

What I Have Entrusted
to Him for That Day
2 Timothy 1:12

Paul wrote a final letter to Timothy during his second imprisonment, not long before his death. Now, at the end of his life, he had heaven very much in view. Although Nero would put him to death, he knew that Jesus *"has destroyed death and has brought life and immortality to light through the gospel"* (**2Tm 1:10**). He had complete confidence in his Lord, who *"is able to guard what I have entrusted to him for that day"* (**v. 12**). Paul had few treasures on earth, but his very life was safe in the hand of Jesus (see *Col 3:3; Jn 10:28*). He had firm confidence that he and all the saints *"will also live with Him"* and *"will also reign with Him"* (*2Tm 2:11-12*).

IN VIEW OF HIS APPEARING
AND HIS KINGDOM
2 TIMOTHY 4:1

Paul's famous charge to Timothy to *"preach the word"* (*2Tm 4:2*) was preceded by an acknowledgment that Jesus Christ *"will judge the living and the dead"* and that *"his appearing and his kingdom"* were in view (*2Tm 4:1*). In this same line of thought, a final comment near the end of the chapter expresses Paul's assurance that, *"The Lord will rescue me from every evil attack and will bring me safely to his heavenly kingdom"* (*v. 18*).

When all is said and done, the only thing that really matters is entrance into that kingdom. Christ will decide who is in and who is out; His word will be final. If someone should ask Him on that great Day, *"Lord, do you at this time restore the kingdom to Israel?"* (see *Acts 1:6*), His answer would be a joyful, *"Yes."*

I HAVE FOUGHT THE GOOD FIGHT,
I HAVE FINISHED THE RACE
2 TIMOTHY 4:7-8

Paul knew the end was near. The time of his "departure" (as a ship sails away, *Php 1:23*) was at hand. He had been released from an earlier imprisonment, but that would not happen again. So as he faced the certain fact of impending death, he took an inventory of his life. *"I have fought the good fight,"* he said, *"I have finished the race, I have kept the faith"* (*2Tm 4:7*). Whatever the regrets for what might have been different in his life, he had no regrets for everything he had done for Jesus. Whatever his failings, he had always hung on to Christ. For this, the Lord would award him *"the crown of righteousness,"* the victory wreath for the person who can stand before God covered with the righteousness of Christ. This crown is not given to just a few heroes as great as Paul, but *"to all who have longed for his appearing"* (*v. 8*). Every saint every day should think longingly of the 2nd Coming and heaven.

HEAVEN IN TITUS

Eternal Life . . . Promised
before the Beginning of Time
Titus 1:2

Paul wrote a brief letter to Titus, a coworker he had left with the new church on the island of Crete (*Tts 1:5*). He spoke of *"the hope of eternal life, which God, who does not lie, promised before the beginning of time"* (*v. 2*). From the beginning, therefore, even before mankind was created, God had a plan to redeem the race that would fall and to give them eternal life in heaven (see *Rev 13:8*).

The Glorious Appearing
Titus 2:13

With this hope of eternal life in mind, Paul added in the next chapter, *"While we wait for the blessed hope—the glorious appearing of our great God and Savior, Jesus Christ"* (*Tts 2:13*). Without reluctance Paul could speak of Jesus Christ as God (see also *Rom 9:5*). Just as God became man in the person of Jesus of Nazareth, so God shall come again to man in the person of Jesus our Savior.

Heirs Having the Hope
of Eternal Life
Titus 3:7

When Christ appeared the first time, He saved us by His mercy (*Tts 3:4*). We have hope in the Day of Judgment because we will not be "justified" (or found innocent and acquitted of all charges) by our own goodness, but by His grace (*v. 7a*). Because of this we are *"heirs having the hope of eternal life"* (*v. 7b*). This recurring theme of Paul (see *Gal 3:29*) reminds us that faith in Christ joins all believers in the family of Abraham—the true Israel—and that as heirs with Abraham we shall have eternal life.

CONCLUSION

Paul was vitally concerned about the reality of heaven. He repeatedly referred to eternal life as a "reward" for faithful service, given by God's grace to the fellow-heirs of Abraham. More than other NT writers, Paul gave details about the 2nd Coming and the nature of the resurrection body. Concerning the present state of the dead, Paul made some statements that support "soul-sleeping," but more statements that support going immediately into a conscious existence with Jesus. Paul spoke often of the coming wrath on the Day of Judgment, but saw it as a necessary part of purging and purifying all creation.

WHAT DO YOU SAY?

1. What does it say about God that He wants to share His glory with us?

2. Will we know everything when we get to heaven? Why or why not?

3. What does the expression *"heavenly realms"* mean in **Ephesians**?

4. What evidence in Scripture supports the idea that the dead will "sleep" until the 2nd Coming?

5. Can you make sense of the view that we all reach life beyond the grave simultaneously?

6. What Scriptures support the idea that we go immediately to Jesus when we die?

7. In what ways do you think our bodies in heaven will be more glorious?

8. How were the believers in Thessalonica mixed up about heaven?

9. Is God invisible?

10. Has it been God's plan all along to share heaven with us?

CHAPTER THIRTEEN

HEAVEN IN THE GENERAL EPISTLES

The general epistles—Hebrews through Jude—were written to the church at large, rather than to specific localities. That is why they are called the "general," or sometimes the "catholic," epistles. Like the rest of Scripture, they have much to say about heaven.

HEAVEN IN THE BOOK OF HEBREWS

IN THESE LAST DAYS HE HAS SPOKEN BY HIS SON
HEBREWS 1:1–4

In earlier times God spoke through dreams and visions, through a burning bush and a talking donkey, through high priests and prophets. Then, at the climax of the ages (*Heb 1:2; 9:27*), God spoke through His Son. The Son is the heir of the universe, because He is the one through whom God made the universe (*v. 2*) and He is the one who sustains the universe (*v. 3*). He gave His life to redeem the universe and then sat down—with the job finished—*"at the right hand of the Majesty in heaven"* (*v. 3*).

This becomes the theme of Hebrews: Jesus is the builder of the house (*Heb 1:10;*

3:3) who gave His blood as the perfect sacrifice (*9:13*) and is then invited to sit victoriously at God's right hand (*1:13*, see *Ps 110:1*). Throughout Hebrews, the focus is on Jesus as the great High Priest who is our mediator in heaven.

Your Throne, O God, Will Last for Ever
Hebrews 1:8

The Son at the Father's right hand is far greater than the angels. In fact, He shares the throne of the heavenly kingdom, the same restored kingdom that has featured so prominently throughout our study. *"Your throne, O God,"* the writer quotes, *"will last for ever and ever, and righteousness will be the scepter of your kingdom"* (**Heb 1:8**, see *Ps 102:25*). The throne of David, long awaiting its everlasting King, finds its fulfillment in Jesus. He is the Messiah, the one whom God has anointed *"with the oil of joy"* (*1:9*). Though the present heavens and earth will perish (**v. 11**), the messianic King will remain the same; His years will never end (**v. 13**).

This is one of several places in Scripture where Jesus is directly called God. (See, for instance, *Jn 1:1,18; 20:28; Rom 9:5; Tts 2:13; 2Pet 1:1*.) God the Son will sit with God the Father on the eternal throne. The everlasting kingdom will be heaven.

Angels Are Ministering Spirits
Hebrews 1:14; 2:5

Angels will live with us in heaven. But even as powerful and majestic as they are, God has subordinated them to serve mankind. *"Are not all angels ministering spirits,"* the writer says, *"sent to serve those who will inherit salvation?"* (**Heb 1:14**). Angels have been useful in delivering God's law to mankind (***Heb 2:2***; see ***Acts 7:53; Gal 3:19***), but they were the messengers, not the recipients, of God's message. Even more, as the writer explains, *"It is not to angels that he has subjected the world to come"* (***Heb 2:5***), but to Jesus as the representative of the human race (***vv. 6-9***). Man was created to rule (***Gen 1:26***) and is destined to rule (***Rev 22:5***), and Jesus has paved the way to make this possible. Finally, angels are less privileged than men in that they have no share in God's plan for salvation. It is not the angels that Jesus helps by His sacrifice, but Abraham's descendants (***Heb 2:16***).

BRINGING MANY SONS TO GLORY
HEBREWS 2:10-15

Jesus, the author of our salvation, suffered death so that He might *"taste of death for everyone"* (***Heb 2:9***). By doing this, Jesus was *"bringing many sons to glory"* (***v. 10***). The contrast between men and angels comes into even sharper focus. Men were created in the image of God, are saved by the Son of God, and are destined to reign with God. Angels are servants for men, will be judged by men, and were created to worship, not to reign.

Jesus redeems the fallen race of man and will bring them to "glory." It is the Father's pleasure to share His glory with us (see ***Rom 8:30***); it is the Son's pleasure to call us "brothers" (***Heb 2:12***). He has freed us from the fear of death (***v. 15***), and when He comes we will appear with Him in glory (***Col 3:4***)

A SABBATH-REST
FOR THE PEOPLE OF GOD
HEBREWS 4:6-11

When God finished the creation of the universe, He rested. This "rest" becomes an important synonym for heaven in ***Hebrews 3:7–4:11***. It is the intent of the writer of Hebrews to show that this great "Sabbath-rest" is open and available to the people of God (***Heb 4:9***). First, he shows that neither Moses nor Joshua really delivered the children of Israel into their final rest. God swore in a divine oath concerning the generation that came out of Egypt, *"They shall never enter my rest"* (***Heb 3:11***; see ***Ps 95:7***). But even though the next generation did enter the land of Canaan, God was still talking about entering that rest hundreds of years later in the time of David (***Heb 4:8***). God set a certain day for entering that rest, calling it "Today." As the Holy Spirit said through David, *"Today, if you hear his voice, do not harden your hearts as you did in the rebellion"* (**Heb 3:7-8; 4:7**). As long as it is still "Today," therefore, the promise of entering that rest remains. To sum up the line of argument:

God finished creation and made a day of rest.

Moses and Israel failed to enter that rest because of rebellion.

David still speaks of "Today" for entering that rest.

A Sabbath-rest remains for the people of God.

Rest is a key component of heaven, where the saints will *"rest from their labor"* (**Rev 14:13**). But the "rest" of heaven, like the original Sabbath of God, will not be enforced idleness. God has always been active, working in His universe (**Jn 5:17**). In the Sabbath-rest of heaven, the saints will "serve" God (**Rev 22:3**) and will "reign" with Him forever (**Rev 22:5**). Therefore, *"Let us make every effort to enter that rest, so that no one will fall by following their example of disobedience"* (**Heb 4:11**; see **6:12**).

The Eyes of Him to Whom We Must Give Account
Hebrews 4:13

Israel did not fool God in their rebellion in the wilderness. Neither can we hide from His all-seeing eyes. Everything is "uncovered" (literally, "naked") and "laid bare" (literally, "with neck exposed" in a fatally vulnerable position) in the sight of the Judge of the universe (**Heb 4:13**). The blessing of the promised rest in the preceding verses is balanced by the warning of the relentless judgment in this verse.

That is why we need Jesus as our High Priest in heaven (**Heb 4:14-16**). He knows all about out weakness, since He has been tempted as a man, Himself. But He also knows victory over temptation and has provided salvation from condemnation. He alone *"has gone through the heavens"* (**v. 14**) to finish the work of atonement in our behalf.

This Hope as an Anchor for the Soul
Hebrews 6:19-20

God cannot lie. This makes His oath and His promise to Abraham doubly sure (**Heb 6:18**). Therefore we, as children of Abraham by faith, have a hope that is *"an anchor for the soul, firm and secure"* (*v. 19*). This hope *"enters the inner sanctuary"* into the presence of God, just as Jesus Himself entered (*vv. 19-20*).

So God in heaven is not impossibly removed from us. Our hope is a lifeline that connects us to heaven. Our Savior is a High Priest who speaks for us there. In this sense, then, heaven is not a mirage in the distant future; it is real for us in the present time. We cannot go there yet, but our hope and our High Priest link us with that reality.

A SANCTUARY THAT IS A COPY AND SHADOW OF WHAT IS IN HEAVEN
HEBREWS 8:1-5

The Tabernacle in the wilderness was inferior. In spite of its careful construction ("everything according to the pattern"), it was only *"a copy and a shadow of what is in heaven"* (*Heb 8:5*). Christ, our great High Priest, has entered the greater tabernacle—the true sanctuary in heaven—and there He sits at the right hand of God (*vv. 1-2*). The contrast of the man-made tent in the wilderness and the God-made sanctuary in heaven is the contrast between the old covenant and the new.

CHRIST WENT THROUGH THE MORE PERFECT TABERNACLE
HEBREWS 9:11-15

The true tabernacle is *"not man-made, that is to say, not a part of this creation"* (*Heb 9:11*). Jesus entered this true sanctuary, the Most Holy Place in heaven. Just as the high priests on earth took blood into that chamber on earth every year on the Day of Atonement, Jesus entered the more perfect tabernacle in heaven to present His blood once and for all (*v. 12*, see also *Heb 9:24* and *Lev 16:3-17*). By doing this, Jesus became the *"mediator of a new covenant, that those who are called may receive the promised eternal inheritance"* (*v. 15*). Once again it can be seen that the ancient words and rituals of the OT were put in place by God as part of His unchanging plan.

TO DIE ONCE, AND AFTER THAT TO FACE JUDGMENT
HEBREWS 9:27-28

Every man must die. The only exception is for the generation still living when Christ returns. (As to an exception such as Enoch, see *Heb*

11:5.) So death is the destiny of all men, and after that comes judgment (*Heb 9:27*). This Scripture truth refutes any idea of reincarnation or a second time around. A man lives on earth once, dies, and then stands at the crossroad to heaven or hell.

Does this mean a separate Judgment Day for each man at his death, or do all men die and then wait for this Judgment? As discussed at *Philippians 1:23*, it is possible to conceive of a timeless Judgment Day, where men die at what seem to be different times on earth, yet enter eternity simultaneously in the eyes of God. It seems more likely, however, that each person faces the issue of reward or punishment *immediately* upon death. All the individual judgments would then be made formal and official in the proclamation of God on Judgment Day.

Then the end comes. After generations have lived and died and faced their judgment, Christ will come. In His first coming He dealt once and for all with sin, and in the second coming He will return *"to bring salvation to those who are waiting for him"* (*Heb 9:28*). Everything promised and prophesied will finally come to pass. Although it has seemed a long wait, *"In just a very little while, 'He who is coming will come and will not delay'"* (*Heb 10:37*; see *Hab 2:3*).

By One Sacrifice He Has Made Us Perfect Forever
Hebrews 10:12-19

Unlike the priests who stand at their duty, Jesus has sat down—because He is finished (*Heb 10:11-12*). With their endlessly repeated sacrifices, they never actually accomplished the cleansing men needed (see *v. 4*). By a single sacrifice He *"has made perfect forever those who are being made holy"* (*v. 14*). There will never be a day in heaven when someone needs to regain God's favor, because Jesus has made every believer *"perfect forever."* This points to an existence in heaven where we are no longer tempted by sin or harassed by the Tempter.

Because of the finality of Jesus' sacrifice, *"we have confidence to enter the Most Holy Place by the blood of Jesus"* (*v. 19*). Even now we have access to the God of heaven in prayer (see *Heb 4:14-16*), because the Son of heaven has opened the way.

Enoch Did Not Experience Death
Hebrews 11:5

Enoch, the father of Methuselah, *"walked with God,"* and *"then he was no more, because God took him away"* (*Gen 5:22-24*). Hebrews adds that he was *"commended as one who pleased God"* (*Heb 11:5*; see *Gen 5:22* LXX). So Enoch provides an interesting exception to the otherwise inescapable truth that all men must die (see *Heb 9:27*). Even more interesting is the fact that Enoch shows that going to be in the presence of God was a possibility even in the earliest points in human history. Surely this conclusion to his life was recorded in the book of man's beginning to create a hunger for heaven in all who followed.

They Were Looking Forward
to the City
Hebrews 11:8-19

Abraham was called by God to leave his homeland and go to a place God would show him. He obeyed and went, *"even though he did not know where he was going"* (*Heb 11:8*). Abraham never owned as much as a single acre of the Promised Land. By faith he could see beyond this life, *"looking forward to a city with foundations, whose architect and builder is God"* (*v. 10*). (Similarly, we and all readers of Hebrews are *"looking for the city that is to come,"* *Heb 13:14*.) He and his descendants kept looking to the future, even though for the present they were living in tents as nomads. They knew they were *"aliens and strangers on earth"* (*11:13*) and were *"longing for a better country—a heavenly one"* (*v. 16*).

The faith of Abraham was so unshakable that he even obeyed the demand of God that he sacrifice his son Isaac. And why not? God had promised that through Isaac his descendants would continue, so God would not leave Isaac dead. Thus, *"Abraham reasoned that God could raise the dead"* (*v. 19*) and was ready to obey Him completely. When faith in heaven is totally secure, obeying every command of God is reasonable.

They Were Looking Ahead to
Their Reward
Hebrews 11:26-40

And yet. The patriarchs had never seen a resurrection, and they had been given very little information about heaven. They only knew that God lived in heaven and they wanted to be there with Him. So Moses was not afraid of all the power of Egypt, *"because he was looking ahead to his reward"* (**Heb 11:26**). God's people endured persecution, fire, sword, and death, *"so that they might gain a better resurrection"* (**v. 35**). Even with the scant revelation they had been given about the afterlife, they put all their faith in God.

But still. The summary of the heroes of faith ends with a surprise: even though they were commended for their faith, *"none of them received what had been promised"* (**v. 39**). God's perfect plan was that *"only together with us would they be made perfect"* (**v. 40**). Only through the sacrifice of Christ could they—or anyone—be given their final and complete reward. Some scholars have taken this to mean that these heroes of faith were somehow "put on hold" for centuries until they could be forgiven by the blood of Jesus. It seems more likely, however, that, just like Enoch in his life, at their death they went to be with God. Since the blood of Jesus covered the sins of the earlier covenant (**Heb 9:15**) and since He was *"slain from the creation of the world"* (**Rev 13:8**), the timeless sacrifice of Christ brought them immediately to their reward.

THE GREAT CLOUD OF WITNESSES
HEBREWS 12:1-2

The heroes of faith constitute *"a great cloud of witnesses"* (**Heb 12:1**). They have witnessed the trials of life; they have witnessed the faithfulness of God. They "surround" the current readers of the book of Hebrews, giving their silent testimony to the goodness of God. By their patient endurance they are faithful examples of how the race should be run and that the race can be won.

But do these "witnesses" also witness the lives of those on earth? On the negative side, it is silly to imagine that the saints in heaven would rather spend their time watching earth than watching and serving God. Furthermore, the perfect happiness of paradise is scarcely compatible with constant gazing at this earthly veil of tears. On the positive side, however, it is reasonable to believe that certain victories on earth are known in heaven. There is rejoicing in heaven, for instance, over every sinner that repents (see *Lk 15:7*). It is also worth noting that the "witnesses" of *Hebrews 12* have not merely preceded us in the great race; they "surround" us. It is hard to escape the imagery of a crowd of supporters cheering us on as we run to the finish line and victory. Like Stephen who saw his Lord at the right hand of God (*Acts 7:56*), by faith we too can *"fix our eyes on Jesus"* who endured the cross and now sits *"at the right hand of the throne of God"* (*Heb 12:2*).

YOU HAVE COME TO MOUNT ZION
HEBREWS 12:22-28

Like weary marathon runners nearing the finish line, the longsuffering readers of the first century were approaching their reward. *"You have come to Mount Zion,"* the writer assures them, *"to the heavenly Jerusalem, the city of the living God"* (*Heb 12:22*). There the angels gather *"in joyful assembly"*; there are the firstborn saints *"whose names are written in heaven"* (*v. 23*). Most of all, they have come to *"God, the judge of all men,"* to *"the spirits of righteous men made perfect,"* and to *"Jesus the mediator of a new covenant"* (*vv. 23-24*). The city, the angels, the rejoicing, the fellow saints, the Father and the Son—what a beautiful picture of heaven!

Special note should be made of the *"righteous men made perfect"* (*v. 23*). This is a clue to the question about whether we can sin once we get to heaven. Since *"He who began a good work in us"* will bring us to completion (perfection) at the day of Christ (*Phil 1:6*), we can expect to be numbered among these *"righteous men made perfect."* In addition, there will be no tempter (*Rev 20:10*) or temptation in heaven. With perfected saints and with no temptation, there will never be an occasion for anyone to leave heaven and cross the great fixed chasm (*Lk 16:26*) that no one can cross anyway!

I WILL SHAKE THE EARTH
AND THE HEAVENS
HEBREWS 12:26-28

God has promised, *"Once more I will shake not only the earth but also the heavens"* (*Heb 12:26*; see *Hag 2:6*). As the writer of Hebrews explains, this indicates the removal of created things, so that what cannot be shaken will remain. This language fits well with Peter's description of the heavens and the elements being destroyed by fire (*2Pet 3:10*) and John's description of *"a new heaven and a new earth, for the first heaven and the first earth had passed away"* (*Rev 21:1*). The starry skies above and the worn-out earth below will be "shaken," purged by "fire," and replaced.

Christians, however, are already in the process of *"receiving a kingdom that cannot be shaken"* (*v. 28*). This is the kingdom over which Jesus will have everlasting rule. Therefore, the original readers of Hebrews should not give up and return to the old faith of Judaism; the modern readers of Hebrews should not give up either. We can be thankful, *"and so worship God acceptably with reverence and awe"* (*v. 28*).

HEAVEN IN JAMES

HE WILL RECEIVE THE CROWN OF LIFE
JAMES 1:12-17

The call to perseverance in **Hebrews** continues in the book of **James**. He also looked to heaven as the final reward for those who remain faithful. *"Blessed is the man who perseveres under trial,"* James said, *"because when he has stood the test, he will receive the crown of life"* (*Jas 1:12*). This "crown" is not the king's diadem, but the wreath awarded to the winner in an athletic contest. It is the crown that Paul anticipated (*1Cor 9:25; 1Th 2:19; 2Tm 4:8*) and that John wrote about (*Rev 2:10; 3:11; 4:4*). The *"crown of life"* is not a special category of reward to be given to a certain few. God has promised it to all the saints, *"to those who love him"* (*Jas 1:12*). Like every good and perfect gift, this will come *"down from the Father of the heavenly lights"* (*v. 17*). Once again, heaven is seen as a place of "lights."

THE WISDOM THAT COMES
FROM HEAVEN
JAMES 3:17

Heaven is a place of wisdom. It is not like the so-called wisdom of earth, born of envy and selfish ambition. James speaks of a wisdom that *"comes from heaven,"* God's wisdom that He makes available to us through Christ. Since this is the wisdom of heaven, it can be reasonably assumed that this wisdom therefore accurately describes the nature of heaven. We can expect heaven and its inhabitants to be *"peace-loving, considerate, submissive, full of mercy and good fruit, impartial and sincere"* (*Jas 3:17*). Peacemaking people who exercise this kind of wisdom can expect to reap *"a harvest of righteousness"* (*v. 18*).

Be Patient until the Lord's Coming
James 5:7-9

James knew that his readers faced *"trials of many kinds"* (*Jas 1:1*), but promised them that they would be rewarded if they persevered (*Jas 1:12*). In his closing chapter he revisited this theme, urging his people, *"Be patient, then, brothers, until the Lord's coming"* (*Jas 5:7*). Were they eager for their harvest and reward? They should be patient and stand firm, *"because the Lord's coming is near"* (*v. 8*). Were they grumbling and turning against each other? They should be aware that they will be judged, and that, *"The Judge is standing at the door!"* (*v. 9*).

The coming of the Lord is both a promise of reward and a warning of judgment. In every generation from the very beginning of the Christian era, faithful believers have realized how suddenly the Lord could come. "Perhaps Today" has been their watchword. Only if they ignore their Master's business and become abusive of His people do they need to worry.

HEAVEN IN PETER'S EPISTLES

An Inheritance That Can Never Perish, Spoil, or Fade
1 Peter 1:3-4

Peter also wrote to Christians who faced trials and persecution. They lived as strangers and aliens, scattered throughout various provinces of Asia Minor, but they were *"God's elect"* (*1Pet 1:1*). They had been given a "new birth" (see *Jn 3:3,5*) that brought with it a *"living hope"* (*1 Pet 1:3*). Because God had raised Jesus from the dead, they could expect to be raised themselves. With their resurrection would come *"an inheritance that can never perish, spoil or fade—kept in heaven for you"* (*v. 4*). In choosing to follow Christ they had chosen wisely. They were giving up the life they could not keep anyway, in exchange for the life in heaven they would never lose.

When Jesus Christ Is Revealed
1 Peter 1:7-13

When Jesus returns in glory, He will share that glory with the saints. The faith that has been refined by the fire of persecution will *"result in praise, glory and honor when Jesus Christ is revealed"* (*1Pet*

1:7). Peter assured his readers that this is the *"grace to be given **you** when Jesus Christ is revealed"* (*v. 13*).

Jesus Himself set the pattern: suffering followed by glory (*v. 11*). The prophets of old pointed to what would happen to the Christ, but did not really understand how it would all work out. Even the angels longed to *"look into these things"* (*v. 12*). He suffered, and then He was glorified. Faithful Christians can take courage in the promise that God has the same plan for them (see also *1Pet 5:1,4*).

JESUS CHRIST, WHO HAS
GONE INTO HEAVEN
1 PETER 3:22

Peter returned to the subject of suffering in chapter three. Christians should accept persecution without repaying evil for evil, in order that they may *"inherit a blessing"* (*1Pet 3:9*). The climax of this section speaks of *"Jesus Christ, who has gone into heaven and is at God's right hand—with angels, authorities and powers in submission to him"* (*v. 22*).

When the world around them was falling apart, the Christians of the first century were to take heart in the fact that Jesus reigns in heaven. When the local authorities and courts turned against them, they were to remember that Jesus sits at the right hand of the ultimate authority. Angels, authorities, powers—the spiritual hosts of heaven and hell (see *Eph 1:21; 6:12*)—bow in total subjection to Him. And when the ordeal on earth is finally over for God's children, they will join Jesus in heaven where *"they will reign for ever and ever"* (*Rev 22:5*).

THE END OF ALL THINGS IS NEAR
1 PETER 4:7

Although former friends were heaping abuse on the people who had become followers of Christ (*1Pet 4:3-4*), a better future lay ahead. They need not be concerned when men judge them, for the only judgment that matters will come from God (*v. 6*). And it would not be long before the books would be squared, because *"the end of all things is near"* (*v. 7*). Whether that end came at the 2nd Coming or at their own deaths did not matter. Their sufferings would be turned into glory.

So the persecuted Christians were told, *"Rejoice that you participated in the sufferings of Christ, so that you may be overjoyed when his glory* is revealed" (*v. 13*). If they had suffered insult or injury it was no matter of concern, *"for the Spirit of glory and of God rests upon you"* (*v. 14*). The ordeals of earth pale into insignificance in comparison to the glories of heaven.

AS ONE WHO WILL SHARE IN THE
GLORY TO BE REVEALED
1 PETER 5:1-10

Peter's final appeal was as one who was *"a witness of Christ's sufferings and one who also will share in the glory to be revealed"* (*1Pet 5:1*). Even though Peter had so often been a disappointment to his Master, he still knew that grace would permit him to share in Christ's glory in heaven. And not only so, he also promised his readers that this glory awaited them as well. *"When the Chief Shepherd appears,"* he wrote, *"you will receive the crown of glory that will never fade away"* (*v. 4*).

It has always been God's plan to share His glory with mankind, created in His image. As Peter exclaimed in a cry of benediction, *"And the God of all grace, who called you to his eternal glory in Christ, after you have suffered a little while, will himself restore you and make you strong, firm and steadfast"* (*v. 10*). These, then, are Peter's final promises to cheer the suffering saints: they will share in the glory to be revealed, receive the crown of glory, and go to God to live in His eternal glory in Christ.

A RICH WELCOME INTO THE ETERNAL
KINGDOM OF OUR LORD
2 PETER 1:10-15

Peter's second epistle was written near the end of his life, with his own martyrdom on the horizon. He knew that *"the tent of this body"* would soon be put aside (*2Pet 1:13-14*). He wrote to combat false teachers, urging his readers, *"that after my departure you will always be able to remember these things"* (*2Pet 1:15*). Even though Peter faced death, he was not afraid. He knew that he and all faithful Christians *"will receive a rich welcome into the eternal kingdom of our Lord and Savior Jesus Christ"* (*v. 10*). The thought of this *"rich welcome"* should set the tone for every Christian's approach to death. Whether we die in violent martyrdom or in peaceful sleep, we will be escorted by the angels to the welcoming arms of our Lord in heaven.

"WHERE IS THE PROMISE
OF HIS COMING?"
2 PETER 3:4-9

At least thirty-five years had passed since Jesus had ascended into heaven, and He still had not returned. Peter knew that in the days to come this would cause scoffers to sneer and say, *"Where is this 'coming' he promised?"* (*2Pet 3:4*). Such scoffers were deliberately ignoring the fact that God had destroyed the world once before (*v. 6*) and would do so again (*v. 7*). The first destruction was by water; the second would be by fire.

What seemed to be a delay, even a hesitation, was simply the way God's timetable worked. *"With the Lord,"* Peter reminded them, *"a day is like a thousand years, and a thousand years are like a day"* (*v. 8*). God is rather indifferent to what we call time! The apparent slowness on God's part is actually a matter of His grace. God does not want anyone to perish, but everyone to come to repentance (*v. 9*) and eternal life. Therefore, generations of Christians have not seen the 2nd Coming in their own lifetime. Whether at His coming or at their dying it was—and is—still true: *"The end of all things is near"* (*1Pet 4:7*).

THE ELEMENTS WILL BE
DESTROYED BY FIRE
2 PETER 3:10-13

When the Lord does return, it will be a sudden surprise. He will come unannounced, like a thief in the night (*2Pet 3:10*). Unannounced, but not unnoticed! With a loud roar the heavens (the sky and distant space) will disappear. *"The elements will be destroyed by fire,"* Peter said, *"and earth will be laid bare."* One should not think, however, that the earth will disappear. When the elements are *"destroyed"* by fire, just as when Noah's earth was *"destroyed"* by water (*v. 6*), they will be purged from all their former wickedness. This is how the earth is not said to *"disappear,"* but to *"be laid bare."*

The elements of earth will *"melt in the heat"* (*v. 12*), in preparation for an extreme makeover. The millennia of man's exploitation will dissolve away—the toxic wastes, the radioactive sites, the swelling landfills—all gone. With the entire universe cleansed and released from its fallen state (see *Rom 8:21*), Peter could say, *"We are looking forward to a new heaven* and *a new earth*, the home of righteousness" (*v. 13*). The ancient promise will at last come true (*Isa 65:17; 66:22; Rev 21:1*).

HEAVEN IN JOHN'S EPISTLES

THE WORLD AND ITS DESIRES PASS AWAY
1 JOHN 2:15-17

John outlived his fellow apostles. Near the end of the first century he wrote in his first epistle, *"The world and its desires pass away, but the man who does the will of God lives forever"* (*1Jn 2:17*). For this reason John did not allow himself to get too attached to the present world—especially in its fallen, sinful state. *"If anyone loves the world,"* he wrote, *"the love of the Father is not in him"* (*v. 15*).

John was clearly the kind of man who "can't feel at home in this world anymore." The world was not his home; it did not deserve his primary love. His heart was set on heaven; his aim was to live there forever. He knew that *"this is what he promised us—even eternal life"* (*1Jn 2:25*).

THE ANTICHRIST IS COMING
1 JOHN 2:18

The Antichrist is coming! The Antichrist is coming! Such could have been the cry of the Christians in the first century. In fact, as John said, *"Even now many antichrists have come"* (*1Jn 2:18*). It becomes immediately apparent that John did not use the word "antichrist" in the way it is commonly used today. For John, an "antichrist" was a false teacher who had gone out from the Christian community (*v. 19*) to deny that Jesus is the Christ (*v. 22*) and that He had come in the flesh (*2Jn 1:7*). No one except John used the term "antichrist" in Scripture, so what he meant by the word should be final. It is incorrect, therefore, to use "antichrist" in reference to the Man of Lawlessness (*2Th 2:3*) or the beast whose number is 666 (*Rev 13:11-18*).

WE SHALL BE LIKE HIM
1 JOHN 3:2

From the evil error of the antichrists, John turned to the lavish love of the Father. What a thought—that we should be called children of God (*1Jn 3:1*)! And that is not all; we shall be more. John could not give details about what we shall become, because the Lord has not yet made it known. But at least this much is true: *"When he appears, we shall be like him, for we shall see him as he is"* (*v. 3*).

This verse nicely combines several earlier passages. Jesus is coming again (*Acts 1:11*), and at His coming the saints will be brought to perfection (*Php 1:6*). Their bodies will be instantly changed into what is incorruptible and immortal (*1Cor 15:53*), transformed to be His own glorious body (*Php 3:21*). All this will happen when we *"see him as he is."*

Confidence on the Day of Judgment
1 John 4:17-18

The coming of Jesus will also mark the Day of Judgment. He will come to bring salvation to some (*Heb 9:28*), but flaming vengeance to others (*2Th 1:7-9*). The murderer, for instance, should fear this day, since *"no murderer has eternal life in him"* (*1Jn 3:15*). But we who have the love of God in our hearts need not fear. When God's love is made complete, we *"will have confidence on the day of judgment"* (*1Jn 4:17*). When love is perfected, it *"drives out fear"* (*v. 18*). That is why John could look forward to the return of Jesus with eager anticipation.

God Has Given Us Eternal Life
1 John 5:11-13

Believers in Christ have overcome the world (*1Jn 5:4*). We are victors in this world; we are more than conquerors in the world to come. We already have this victory because God *"has given us eternal life"* (*v. 11*). To reinforce this point John said it again: *"I write these things to you who believe in the name of the Son of God so that you may know that you have eternal life"* (*v. 13*).

Eternal life is more than a limitless future; it is a whole new present. Eternal life is life in Christ. It begins now and flows unchecked into eternity. He lives His life in us and through us (*Gal 2:20*), providing a foretaste of the power and purity of heaven. Eternal life is not just a future promise; it is a present reality.

The Deceiver and the Antichrist
2 John 1:7-8

John wrote his second epistle to warn believers not to be deceived by false teachers. *"Many deceivers,"* he warned, *"do not acknowledge*

Jesus Christ as coming in the flesh. Any such person is the deceiver and the antichrist" (*2Jn 1:7*). As noted in the comments on *1 John 2:18*, these "antichrists" were people who had gone out from the church to spread false doctrine about Christ. For the sake of biblical accuracy, teaching of the end times should avoid the use of the term "antichrist."

HEAVEN IN THE BOOK OF JUDE

ANGELS BOUND WITH EVERLASTING CHAINS
JUDE 1:6

Jude, the brother of the Lord, also wrote against men who *"deny Jesus Christ our only Sovereign and Lord"* (*Jude 1:4*). They face certain destruction from the same God who destroyed the people who came out of Egypt and did not believe (*v. 5*) and who has kept rebellious angels *"bound with everlasting chains for judgment on the great Day"* (*v. 6*). The future doom of unbelievers and angels sets the dark background against which what Jude says about heaven will shine all the more brightly.

TO PRESENT YOU BEFORE HIS GLORIOUS PRESENCE
JUDE 1:21-24

Although unbelieving scoffers will perish, Jude expected his *"dear friends"* in God's family to survive. He encouraged them to strengthen their faith and to keep in God's love as they *"wait for the mercy of our Lord Jesus Christ to bring you eternal life"* (*Jude 1:21*). He concluded with a beautiful doxology about the God *"who is able to keep you from falling and to present you before his glorious presence without fault and with great joy"* (*v. 24*).

At least four truths come to light in these words. First, eternal life is a gift of mercy, not of merit. Second, God is at work to keep His children from falling—we are not on our own. Third, God will enable us to be "without fault" as we join Him in His glory. Fourth, heaven will be a place of great and indescribable joy.

CONCLUSION

Hebrews presents Jesus as the eternal High Priest, the all-sufficient sacrifice, the One who brings many sons to glory. The book shows heaven as the ideal city/country sought by the heroes of faith, a place of joyous celebration. Peter's epistles show the saints called to eternal glory and the physical creation destined for a purging fire. John's epistles contrast eternal life for those in fellowship with God versus certain judgment for the antichrists. In a time of growing persecution and hardship, all the general epistles call for faithful endurance in view of the promise of heaven.

WHAT DO YOU SAY?

1. According to *Hebrews 1*, who made the universe?

2. Why is heaven called *"a Sabbath rest"* in *Hebrews 4*?

3. Is there a perfect tabernacle in heaven? Why is there no need for a temple or tabernacle in the final form of heaven (*Rev 21:22*)?

4. What did the ancient heroes of faith know about heaven? What were they looking for?

5. What should we think about the great cloud of "witnesses" who surround us as we run the race to heaven (*Hebrews 12*)?

6. Peter expected to *"share in the glory"* when he went to heaven (*1Pet 5:1*). How will we ourselves share in God's glory?

7. What does it mean that *"the elements will be destroyed by fire"* in *2 Peter 3:10*?

8. Why is God currently confining some of the angels in chains in darkness?

9. What is the overall teaching about heaven in the General Epistles?

CHAPTER FOURTEEN

HEAVEN IN JOHN'S REVELATION

O n a rocky, volcanic island thirty-five miles southwest of Asia Minor, the Apostle John endured a lonely exile. The church was coming under increased opposition from the Roman government, especially since the cities of Asia Minor embraced the cult of the emperor so enthusiastically. On this insignificant island John received an unparalleled revelation from the Lord. The bold scope of this revelation would strengthen his generation to stand firm in their faith, and would do the same for every generation of Christians since then. In the epic battle of evil versus good, good wins! In the final showdown between Babylon and Jerusalem—the tale of two cities—it is the New Jerusalem coming down out of heaven that victoriously awaits the saints.

The interpretation of the prophetic details in *Revelation* is notoriously difficult. However, that is not a good enough reason to ignore the book (*Rev 1:3*). And fortunately for our purposes, the timetable of historical

231

events preceding Judgment Day is not important. Our purpose in studying Revelation will be threefold: We will acknowledge the glimpses of heaven throughout the book as the throne room of God; we will notice the frequent fulfillment of OT prophecies; we will celebrate the final picture of heaven—our victory and reward.

THE REVELATION OF WHAT
MUST SOON TAKE PLACE
REVELATION 1:1

This is the revelation of Jesus Christ to John, *"the disciple whom He loved"* (see **Jn 13:23; 21:20**). It came with good news about *"what must soon take place"* (**Rev 1:1**). In the original Greek the emphasis is more on the "must" than on the "soon." The dramatic scenes are not just wishful thinking or probable projections; they are certainties decreed by a sovereign God. How "soon" these things would happen depended partly on what "soon" meant to the One with whom a thousand years is as a day. Some of the events were likely on the near horizon (**Rev 1:3**), while many awaited the final Judgment (**Rev 20:11**). Either way, the saints could take heart that in the end they would emerge victorious.

A KINGDOM AND PRIESTS
TO SERVE GOD
REVELATION 1:6

Jesus is *"the ruler of the kings of the earth"*—including Nero and Domitian. He loves His people and has forgiven their sins by shedding His blood. Amazingly, Jesus has not just forgiven sinners for their failures; He has promoted them! He makes those who believe in Him to be *"a kingdom and priests to serve his God and Father"* (**Rev 1:6**). As part of the kingdom, the saints will fulfill the original plan of God that man would "rule" (**Gen 1:26; Rev 22:5**). As priests, they will have immediate access to God and will do the bidding of God. With such a future in view, why should the saints worry about what Rome might try to do?

LOOK, HE IS COMING!
REVELATION 1:7

"Look," John said, *"he is coming"* (**Rev 1:7**). Could his readers see in their mind's eye what John could see in the revelation? Soon—in the blink of the eye of eternity—Jesus would be coming in the clouds,

and *"every eye will see him."* Those who pierced Him (**Ps 22:16; Isa 53:5; Zec 12:10**) will see Him return in triumph and will mourn. The opening vista of the revelation is a preview of the last. From beginning to end the book of Revelation is a cry of victory, based on Jesus' returning to give heaven to His people.

SOMEONE "LIKE A SON OF MAN" REVELATION 1:10-18

John was *"in the Spirit"* on the Lord's Day when he heard a loud voice behind him. When he turned around to see who was speaking, he saw *"someone 'like a son of man'"* (**Rev 1:10**). Dressed in the robe of a high priest, with a golden sash around his chest (see **Ex 28:4; 29:5**), the speaker was Jesus Himself. This vision of His appearance was in some ways similar to what John had earlier seen at the Transfiguration (see **Mt 17:1-2**). His head and hair were gleaming white and His eyes were like blazing fire (**Rev 1:14**). His feet were like glowing bronze; His voice was like the roar of rushing water (**v. 15**). Out of His mouth came a two-edged sword; His face had the brilliance of the sun (**v. 16**).

It is difficult to know which of the descriptions are to be taken more or less literally and which are primarily figurative. The brilliant light, at least, seems to be a literal manifestation of His glory. The purity of whiteness seems a bit more figurative, although there is no compelling reason why it could not be literal as well. The sword in His mouth and the stars in His hand (**v. 16**), however, seem to be more symbolic than literal. His word, as in **Hebrews 4:12**, is a double-edged sword that pierces to the heart of the matter. Holding the stars is a statement of His control over the universe. Likewise, standing on bronze feet and speaking with a powerful voice portray His power. What Roman emperor—or any ruler yet to come—could ever match the majesty of this King?

More significant than the details of His appearance is the fact that Jesus stands in such a position of power and authority in heaven. He is *"the First and the Last"* (**v. 17**), the beginning and the end of all life. Although He is the ever-living one, He died (**v. 18**). Then He rose again to live for ever and ever. Holder of the keys of death and Hades, He determines the eternal fate of all mankind. He who speaks to John is Jesus, and that is why this book is called *"The revelation of Jesus Christ"* (**Rev 1:1**).

TO HIM WHO OVERCOMES
REVELATION 2:7,11,17,26;
3:5,12,21

The first order of business for John was to take letters of dictation for seven churches in the province of Asia. Each church had its own history and its own words of rebuke or commendation from the Lord. The one phrase that all seven letters had in common was a promise *"to him who overcomes."* These early Christians were obviously facing hard times, whether by official government persecution or by local prejudice. They needed a word of encouragement, a promise that the struggle would be worth it.

He who overcomes:

1. Will eat from the tree of life in paradise *(2:7)*
2. Will not be hurt by the second death *(2:11)*
3. Will eat hidden manna and have a white stone with a new name on it *(2:17)*
4. Will have authority over nations and will get the morning star *(2:26,28)*
5. Will be dressed in white and have his name in the book of life *(3:5)*
6. Will be a pillar in God's temple with the Lord's new name written on him *(3:12)*
7. Will sit with Jesus on His throne *(3:21)*

The promises made to these seven churches apply to all believers. *"To the one who overcomes"* is a general category, one to which every Christian should aspire. The first promise is a reminder of man's first home. The tree of life that was taken away in the Garden of Eden will be restored in the paradise of God (**Rev 2:7**; see **Lk 23:43; Rev 22:2**). When people eat from this tree, they live forever (**Gen 3:22**). The second promise is immunity against the second death (**Rev 2:11**), the lake of fire into which the wicked will be cast (**Rev 20:14-15**). The one who overcomes does not fear the second death, because he has been given *"the crown of life"* (**Rev 2:10**). The third promise is twofold: the hidden manna and the white stone (**Rev 2:17**). The manna, recalling God's bread from heaven that sustained Israel in their exodus from Egypt (**Ex 16:31**), is food that will sustain God's new Israel in heaven. The white stone is permission to enter and to belong to God's people (whereas a black stone was used in ancient culture to "blackball" someone as not acceptable). The fourth promise is also twofold: authority over nations and the morning star (**Rev 2:26**). The authority to rule over nations was to be an important part of the Messiah's restored kingdom (**Ps 2:7-9**), and Jesus will gladly share this ruling power (see also **Rev 3:21**). The meaning of the "morning star" is not entirely clear. It may be symbolic of the victory of light over darkness, or it may be a reference to Jesus Himself as the source of light and life for the believer (**Rev 22:16**). The fifth promise is twofold: to be dressed in white and to have one's name in the book of life (**Rev 3:4-5**). Even though all our own acts of attempted righteousness are like filthy rags (**Isa 64:6**), in heaven we will be given white robes of righteousness (**Rev 6:11**). To have our names in the book of life is to have written assurance that we belong in heaven (see **Ex 32:32**). The believer is promised that Jesus Himself will *"acknowledge his name before my Father and his angels"* (**Rev 3:5**). The sixth promise is twofold: to be a pillar in God's temple and to have the Lord's new name (**Rev 3:12**). Just as James, Peter, and John himself were "pillars" in the early church (**Gal 2:9**), the faithful saints will be pillars—significant servant/leaders—in the sanctuary of God in heaven. They will have the name of God, the name of God's city, and the Lord's "new name" written on them. This marks them as permanent residents of heaven. The seventh and final promise is the right to sit with Jesus on His throne (**Rev 3:21**). Just as Jesus Himself overcame all obstacles and then went to sit with the Father on His throne, He will invite *"him who overcomes"* to reign with Him in heaven (see **Rev 22:5**).

THERE BEFORE ME WAS A THRONE IN HEAVEN
REVELATION 4:2-11

John saw a grand scene in the throne room of heaven, with the "living creatures" and elders assembled in the presence of God. John clearly lacked the words to do justice to the magnificent vista, saying *"had the appearance of," "resembling," "what looked like,"* and *"was like."* For this reason we should not stress the exact details of this vision to an extreme. Likewise, while we might hazard a guess as to the symbolism of each detail, it should not be overlooked that the Scripture text just gives an overall picture for us to appreciate.

John carefully avoided any attempt to describe the One who sat on the throne. But around and above Him were the majestic brilliance of

> ## John carefully avoided any attempt to describe the One who sat on the throne.

precious stones and the aura of an emerald rainbow (*Rev 4:3*). Twenty-four elders sat on twenty-four thrones, sharing God's reign (*v. 4*). Flashes of lightning and peals of thunder added to the impact. Seven lamps, signifying the seven spirits (or the sevenfold Spirit) of God were also there (*v. 5*). In front of the throne was a sea of glass, clear as crystal (*v. 6*).

Four living creatures—like a lion, an ox, a man, an eagle—circled the throne (see *Eze 1:10*). As in Isaiah's vision, each living creature had six wings and never stopped saying, *"Holy, holy, holy is the Lord God Almighty, who was and is, and is to come"* (*Rev 4:8; Isa 6:2-3*). Both the creatures (*4:9*) and the elders (*v. 10*) worshiped God *"who lives for ever and ever."* They honored God as creator and sustainer of all things, totally worthy of receiving their glory and honor (*v. 11*).

Majestic as this scene is, it seems wrong to assume that this picture of heaven is frozen, and that no one ever moves. The city has gates that are always open; the tree of life and the river of the water of life flow outside. Why should we think that the saints will always be assembled in this one position in this one room? (It should be noted that besides the twenty-four elders, the rest of the saints are not even mentioned in this chapter. The saints will gladly gather around the throne of God in grand worship in **chapter five**, but there is no indication that all the rest of heaven is off-limits to them.)

WORTHY IS THE LAMB
REVELATION 5:6-10

Then John noticed a scroll in God's right hand, sealed not once, but seven times. It seemed that there was no one in heaven or on earth or under the earth—absolutely no one anywhere—who was worthy to open the scroll. At that point, one of the elders spoke to John, *"Do not weep! See, the Lion of the tribe of Judah, the Root of David has triumphed. He is able to open the scroll and its seven seals"* (**Rev 5:5**). The *"Root of David"* was none other than Jesus, David's long awaited Greater Son, who was to rule over the restored kingdom forever.

Then John saw Him, and He was not a Lion, but a Lamb (**Rev 5:6**). This is the first of twenty-eight times throughout *Revelation* that John will refer to Jesus as the "Lamb." Does this mean that Jesus will always look like a lamb, and not like a man, in heaven? For sev-

> **David's long awaited Greater Son will rule over the restored kingdom forever.**

eral reasons, the answer is no. First, John the Baptist (**Jn 1:29**) and Peter (**1Pet 1:19**) both call Jesus a lamb with reference to His significance, not His appearance. Second, the Apostle John has already described Jesus as looking like a man (**Rev 1:13**) and will do so again (**Rev 14:14**). Third, the language of *Revelation* must sometimes be taken as figurative or symbolic, rather than as literal. The verse in question (**Rev 5:6**) is the only place where the Lamb has any animal-like description. Here, the *"seven horns"* and *"seven eyes"* have clear symbolic value. Jesus is all-powerful and all-seeing, completely filled with God's Spirit, *"the seven spirits of God."* He is called the Lamb in recognition of His sacrifice, not in recognition of His appearance.

The four living creatures and the twenty-four elders fell down to worship the Lamb. Each had a bowl of incense, stated to be symbolic of the prayers of the saints; each one also had a harp (**v. 8**). Together they sang the song of the Lamb. He has not only saved men by His blood; He has *"made them to be a kingdom and priests to serve our God, and they will reign on the earth"* (**vv. 9-10**). Twin themes are raised here: the fact of a restored kingdom and the fact that those in the kingdom will serve God as His priest/kings. In the light of *Revelation 21 and 22*, this should be seen as the new heaven and new earth, where the saints will reign forever (see **Rev 21:1; 22:5**).

IN A LOUD VOICE THEY SANG
REVELATION 5:11-14

The majestic simplicity of this scene is most impressive. In contrast to the multiple layers of aristocracy that filled the courts of royalty in Europe in centuries past, the only "dignitaries" that surround God and the Lamb are the four living creatures and the twenty-four elders. As they sang to the Lamb, they were joined by the local populace—myriads of angels. Thousands upon thousands, *"ten thousand times ten thousand,"* the angels added their voices to the swelling chorus (*Rev 5:11*). It should not be overlooked that the praise of these angels is voluntary and sincere, in contrast to other angels who rebelled against God and were punished.

Then *"every creature in heaven and on earth and under the earth and on the sea"* made the chorus even more grand (*v. 13*). All creation joined the song, for the Lamb is worthy of their praise. What John saw was a dramatic fulfillment of the final verse of the Psalms: *"Let everything that has breath praise the LORD"* (*Ps 150:6*). Since we as humans can enjoy the devotion and affection of certain animals, how much more should God and Jesus receive the heartfelt appreciation of all creatures!

"HOW LONG, SOVEREIGN LORD?" REVELATION 6:9-17

One by one the seven seals of the scroll were opened. With the opening of the fifth seal, John saw *"under the altar the souls of those who had been slain because of the word of God and the testimony they had maintained"* (*Rev 6:9*). These early martyrs, perhaps from the bloody era of Nero, gathered at the altar before the throne of God. (For the location and purpose of this altar, see *Rev 8:3*.) Mingled with the prayers of the saints, rising like incense before the face of the Lord, was the plea of the martyrs. *"How long, Sovereign Lord, holy and true,"* they cried, *"until you judge the inhabitants of the earth and avenge our blood?"* (*v. 10*). Each one was given a white robe (signifying the purity that comes from being washed in the blood of the Lamb, *Rev 7:9,13-14; 19:13; 22:14*). Then they were told to wait (*6:11*). Only later would the end come, when the kings of the earth would cry out to the mountains, *"Fall on us and hide us from the face of him who sits on the throne and from the wrath of the Lamb!"* (*v. 16*).

Four observations may be made from this text: 1) Martyrs for the faith (if not all faithful saints) are already in the presence of God while other men continue to live on the earth. 2) They have opportunity to speak to God. 3) They have a sense of time (in protesting *"How long?"* and in being told to wait *"a little while longer"*). 4) They wait patiently, and then suddenly it is time for judgment. When that final day of wrath comes, the enemies of God will suffer a humiliating defeat.

THE NUMBER OF THOSE WHO WERE SEALED: 144,000
REVELATION 7:3-8

Much (far too much!) has been made of the 144,000 who have elite status and protection in *Revelation 7*. They are made up of 12,000 from each of the twelve tribes of Israel, and are marked with a seal on their foreheads to preserve them from harm (*Rev 7:3-4*). Without attempting to judge the theories that put the 144,000 into various points of history, past or present, we will make two major observations from the text. First, whoever these people are, they are on earth and not in heaven. They live during a time when others on earth are suffering harm. Their place and time of abode is clearly not the eternal existence. (The cult that puts the 144,000 in heaven and all the other saints on earth has it exactly backwards!) Second, the number is obviously symbolic. To have an exact 12,000 from each tribe is highly unlikely. Whether the 144,000 are all Jewish or are the combined Jew/Gentile church, the picture is that of God protecting His people at some point in human history. It is in the following verses that we find information about heaven.

A GREAT MULTITUDE THAT NO ONE COULD COUNT
REVELATION 7:9-17

| The number of the saints in glory is not limited to 144,000.

Another scene opened before John's astonished eyes. There was *"a great multitude that no one could count . . . standing before the throne and in front of the Lamb"* (*Rev 7:9*). John proceeded to make so many statements about this scene that we will need to list them separately:

1. This countless "multitude" in heaven shows that the number of the saints in glory is not limited to 144,000 (*v. 9*). Neither is that

number limited to the paltry few that some sectarian groups imagine. As Jonathan Swift wrote in satire:

> We are the chosen few
> > All others will be damned
> There is no room for you
> > We can't have heaven crammed.

2. The people come from *"every nation, tribe, people and language"* (*v. 9*). God and the Lamb are too great to be like the tribal gods worshiped by a handful of people. As Creator of all mankind, the Father and Son deserve to be worshiped by everyone. Does this verse imply that every single people-group will be evangelized before the end comes? Some would say so, referring to **Matthew 24:14**. Others would say that God will save some people from every people-group even if they have not yet heard (a position called "inclusivism"). Still others would say that "every" should not be forced beyond reason, citing parallels such as **Revelation 11:9** and **13:7**. Perhaps, then, it means people from all over the earth heard the gospel (see **Col 1:23**) and will come and worship.

3. They wore white robes (*v. 9*). These robes symbolize righteousness (**Rev 3:4**) and have been washed in the blood of the Lamb (**Rev 7:14**). Those dressed in white have access to the tree of life and the right to enter the City (**Rev 22:14**).

4. They hold palm branches in their hands (*v. 9*). The palm branch in John's day was a symbol of Jewish nationalism (see **Jn 12:13**, where the people went out to welcome the arrival of their Messiah). In heaven the true Israel of God will celebrate the restored kingdom.

5. They cried out in worship of God (*v. 10*). One part of the activity of heaven will be to shout aloud the wonderful truth, *"Salvation belongs to our God!"*

6. They joined the angels, the elders, and the four living creatures in worship (*v. 11-12*). These all (including the multitude?) fell on their faces before God in total adoration.

7. They were identified as those who came *"out of the great tribulation"* (*v. 14*). While this could limit this group to only the martyrs of a special tribulation at the time of the 2nd Coming, it seems more likely that *"the great tribulation"* is the earthly struggle that all saints must come through. Since the multitude in white robes was so large that *"no one could count"* its size (*v. 9*), it seems better to understand the group as including the saints of all ages.

8. They were before the throne of God, where they were to *"serve him day and night in his temple"* (**v. 15**). This text is a beautiful composite of prophetic statements by Isaiah (see **Isa 4:5-6; 49:10; 25:8; 65:19**). It is perhaps also the primary basis for the statement of Augustine that the only activity of heaven will be "to stand, to see, to love, to praise" (*City of God* 22:30). This same poetic passage, however, also soon says that the Lamb *"will lead them to springs of living water"* (**v. 17**). We conclude, therefore, that we will serve God forever and enjoy His presence with us forever, but we will not spend eternity in a single, prolonged praise service.

9. The saints in heaven will not hunger or thirst (**v. 16**). This does not mean that we will have no appetite; it means that we will not go hungry for lack of food, or go thirsty for lack of water. Our faithful Shepherd will see to it that we do not go without (**v. 17**; see also **Ps 23:2**). For people of the Middle East who lived in a dry climate, the promise of the *"springs of living water"* and the *"river of the water of life"* (**Rev 22:1**) was good news, indeed. Not to be overlooked is the beautiful irony that the Shepherd of the saints is a Lamb.

10. God will wipe away every tear. As in the original context of this promise from **Isaiah 25:8**, the picture is that of people coming out of tragic hardship (see **Rev 7:14**). God comes to them, wipes away their tears, and erases the cause of their sorrow. The sequence of events in **Revelation** appears to be as follows: battered, sorrowing saints go to heaven; God wipes away their tears (**Rev 7:17**); after that, there will be no more mourning or crying (**Rev 21:4**).

SILENCE IN HEAVEN FOR HALF AN HOUR
REVELATION 8:1-4

There is a dramatic pause before John saw what was to happen next. For John, at least, there was a sense of the passing of time in heaven. This cautions us against assuming that time will not exist in heaven. (This misconception arose partly because of a misunderstanding of **Revelation 10:6**, which the KJV translated, *"There should be time no longer."* The correct understanding, as the NIV makes clear, is that when the Lord's trumpet is ready to sound, *"There will be no more delay."*)

After this half hour of silence, John saw an angel present incense to God. This incense was *"the prayers of all the saints, on the golden altar before the throne"* (*8:3*). This is the same altar mentioned earlier, where the martyrs voiced their own pleas to God (*Rev 6:9*). It cannot be said with certainty if the praying saints are the ones already in heaven, or the ones still on earth, or both. Their prayers rise before God, who readily accepts them as sweet incense.

GO AND MEASURE
THE TEMPLE
REVELATION 11:1

Several times John referred to the temple that he saw in heaven (*Rev 11:1,19; 15:5,8; 16:7*). This seems to be an echo of Ezekiel's extended prophecy about the New Temple and the measuring rod with which it is to be measured (*Eze 40:3–47:12*). The temple includes the altar in heaven where prayers ascend from earth; it is the tabernacle where sins on earth are atoned (see *Heb 9:11-12*). As long as life on the fallen earth continues, God's temple in heaven will be needed.

Then the time comes when life on earth is brought to an end, when *"the kingdom of the world has become the kingdom of our Lord and of his Christ, and he will reign for ever and ever"* (*Rev 11:15*). This is the time when the final wrath of God is poured out, the *"time for judging the dead"* (*v. 18*). God's temple is opened, with accompanying *"flashes of lightning, rumblings, peals of thunder, an earthquake and a great hailstorm"* (*v. 19*).

But the temple that John saw in heaven is only temporary. After life on earth has concluded, the temple in heaven will no longer be needed. At the conclusion of his vision, John saw a new heaven and a new earth, and the new Jerusalem in which God will dwell with His people (*Rev 21:1-3*). As John inspected the eternal city that we call heaven, he *"did not see a temple in the city, because the Lord God Almighty and the Lamb are its temple"* (*Rev 21:22*).

> **After life on earth has concluded, the temple in heaven will no longer be needed.**

THERE WAS WAR IN HEAVEN
REVELATION 12:7-10

Figuring out the chronology of *Revelation* is notoriously difficult. Did all the events happen in the time of the Roman empire? Are the events strung across all the centuries from the cross to the 2nd coming? Will all the events happen at some future time? Or are the events a repeating picture of the Christian era, seen as many as seven times?

When John said, *"There was war in heaven"* (**Rev 12:7**), was this the primeval battle before creation, the spiritual battle won at the cross, or some epic struggle at the end of time? It would seem that the conclusion of this battle, when Satan and his angels were *"hurled to the earth"* had already happened before the words of Jesus, *"I saw Satan fall like lightning from heaven"* (**Lk 10:18**).

Whatever the time frame, several things are certain. First, the site of the contest was/is/will be heaven itself. How wrong for the holy home of God to be the battleground! Second, Michael and his angels fight on God's side. Third, Satan loses. The triumphant cry of the loud voice in heaven is, *"The accuser of our brothers, who accuses them before our God day and night, has been hurled down"* (**Rev 12:10**). Whenever—and however—this ever happened, it will not happen ever again.

THE LAMB SLAIN FROM THE CREATION OF THE WORLD REVELATION 13:8

With Satan, the *"great dragon"* and *"ancient serpent,"* hurled to the earth (**Rev 12:9,13**), great struggles ensue. He succeeds in forcing all the inhabitants of earth to worship him—all the inhabitants, that is, except those whose names are written in the book of life belonging to the Lamb.

Then a most significant thing is said about the Lamb. He is called *"the Lamb that was slain from the creation of the earth"* (**Rev 13:8**). This statement reveals the intention of heaven from the beginning: Jesus Christ would die as the sacrifice for the sins of the world. No picture of heaven would be complete without this awareness of the eternal plan. From the moment that Father and Son brought the universe into existence, they were in agreement about what would have to be done. The Son would leave heaven for an earthly incarnation, and after His death and resurrection, He would return to heaven in glory.

THE LAMB AND HIS 144,000 REVELATION 14:1-7

As John continued to watch, the scene shifted from the terrible Beast to the beautiful Lamb. With Him on Mount Zion stood the

144,000 who had His name—not the name of the Beast—on their foreheads (*Rev 14:1*). In an earlier vision the 144,000 represented the faithful tribes of Israel on earth (see *Rev 7:4-8*). Now the 144,000 are those who have resisted the Beast and have remained faithful to the Lamb. They have been rescued from the earth, and now they raise their voices in worship of the Lamb (*Rev 14:3*). With the sound of harpists playing their harps in the background, the 144,000 sing a song that no one else could learn to sing. It is not that the song is so difficult, but that it is a secret song that is reserved only for God's people. These are the people who are undefiled; these are the people who follow the Lamb wherever He goes.

Just as it was in *chapter 7*, the mention of the 144,000 is immediately followed by a reference to *"every nation, tribe, language and people"* (*Rev 14:6*). The gospel message is to be proclaimed to them so that they can all worship their Creator. There is to be no arbitrary number limiting the number of saints in heaven!

THE TORMENT
AND THE BLESSING
REVELATION 14:9-17

Next, John heard voices describing the extreme fates that await the lost and the saved. Anyone who accepted the mark of the Beast *"will drink of the wine of God's fury, which has been poured full strength into the cup of his wrath"* (*Rev 14:9-10*). Such a person will be *"tormented with burning sulfur in the presence of the holy angels and of the Lamb"* (*v. 10*). (This passage led some early Fathers to teach that one of the joys of heaven would be watching condemned people burn in agony. There is no mention here, however, of the saints watching . . . or enjoying.) The smoke of their burning torment *"rises for ever and ever,"* and they have no rest or respite night or day (*v. 11*).

But how different it will be for the saved! *"Blessed are the dead who die in the Lord from now on,"* said the heavenly voice (*Rev 14:13*; note that this is the same Greek word for "blessed" as is found in the Beatitudes.) Then the voice of the Spirit continued, *"They will rest from their labor, for their deeds will follow them."* The monetary benefits of earthly work cannot be taken to heaven, but the satisfaction of having worked for the Kingdom will go with us to glory.

Another picture of the contrast of the lost and the saved followed. One *"like a son of man"* sat on a cloud, with a gold crown on His head and a sharp sickle in His hand (*Rev 14:14*; see also *Rev 1:13*). The crown was the *stephanos* wreath of victory; the sickle was the sharp "pruning hook" of the vine dresser. Now the time of reaping had come. He who had triumphed over the Beast would gather the clusters of grapes from the earth and throw them into the winepress of God's wrath (*14:19*). These clusters represented the people who followed the Beast, and they were trampled like grapes in a winepress.

THE SONG OF VICTORY
REVELATION 15:2-8

The scene of joyous victory over the forces of the Beast is repeated. As before (*Rev 14:2*), there are singers and harps (*Rev 15:2*). They stand beside (or upon, since the Greek preposition is *epi*) a sea that has the appearance of glass mixed with fire. It is an appropriately majestic site for the worship of God. They sing a song that is a combination of the song of Moses (*Ex 15:1-18*, a song sung every Sabbath in the ancient synagogue), and the song of the Lamb (*Rev 5:9-10*). It is the song of a conquering King, a song of worship by the nations.

The scene includes another look at the temple, *"the tabernacle of the Testimony"* in heaven. As noted in *Revelation 11:1*, this temple exists in heaven during the intermediate state when life on earth still continues. It is necessary as the place where sin is atoned (see *Heb 9:1-14*) and the purity and glory of God are to some extent withheld from the people (*Rev 15:8*). In the final heaven of eternity, there is no temple because *"the Lord God Almighty and the Lamb are its temple"* (*Rev 21:22*). No longer will access to the glorious presence of God be restricted.

> **In the final heaven, the Lord God and the Lamb are the temple.**

THE WEDDING SUPPER
OF THE LAMB
REVELATION 19:1-9

Yet once more the great victory of the Lamb over the Beast must be shown. John heard *"the roar of a great multitude in heaven"* (*Rev 19:1*) shouting in the way that a crowd cheers its winning team. God has won the victory over the scarlet Beast, who has been in league with a harlot whose name is: "BABYLON THE GREAT" (*Rev 17:5*).

God has *"condemned the great prostitute"* and *"the smoke of her torment goes up for ever and ever"* (**Rev 19:2-3**). Then, if possible, the cheering crowd got even louder. John heard the voice of a great multitude *"like the roar of rushing waters"* combined with *"loud peals of thunder"* (**v. 6**). These were the two loudest kinds of noise known in John's world.

In their excitement the crowd repeatedly cried, *"Hallelujah!"* (**vv. 1,3,4,6**). The reason for their exuberance was that, *"The wedding of the Lamb has come"* (**v. 7**). Interestingly, this beginning of everlasting heaven is described as a feast, a *"wedding supper"* (**v. 9**). With the evils of the world left behind, there will still be food to enjoy in heaven.

"Hallelujah" (also written "Alleluia") is a Hebrew word that means, "Praise the Lord!" The "jah" or "yah" syllable at the end is an abbreviated form of the name of God, "Yahweh" or "Jehovah." "Hallelujah" is found 24 times in the **Psalms** (see, for instance, **Pss 111-117** and **145-150**), and four times in **Revelation (19:1,3,4,6)**. It was used by the Jews as a call to worship in the Temple and later in the synagogues.

This final victory over evil ushers in the dawn of a new relationship between God and man. God the Son will embrace the church as His bride (see also **Eph 5:25-32**). She will wear *"fine linen, bright and clean,"* which John explained to be symbolic of the righteous acts of the saints (**19:8**). Only those who are dressed in this garment will be welcome at this banquet, just as in the parable of Jesus (see **Mt 22:11-13**). This is why the angel told John to write, *"Blessed are those who are invited to the wedding supper of the Lamb!"* (**v. 9**).

THE THOUSAND YEARS
REVELATION 20:1-10

John saw an angel seize the dragon, tie him up, and throw him into the Abyss for a thousand years (**Rev 20:2**). Life on earth continued during this thousand years, but so did life in heaven. John saw people seated on thrones, *"the souls of those who had been beheaded because of their testimony for Jesus,"* and these people *"came to life and* reigned with Christ a thousand years" (*v. 4*; see also **Rev 6:9-11**). These are people over whom the second death—eternal death in the lake of fire (*20:14*)—has no power. As befits the purpose of mankind's creation in the beginning, these saints reign with their Maker.

An alternative view of this passage holds that the saints and Christ reign for a thousand years on the present earth, not in heaven. *Revelation 5:10* and *11:15* are cited in support of this position, although we have argued in both passages that the scene is the new earth.

When does this happen? And does Jesus return before or after this 1,000 year period? This passage, the only one in Scripture that mentions the 1,000 year reign, has become the focus of much controversy. It is beyond the scope of this book on heaven to enter the millennial fray and attempt to establish or rebut every argument. For the sake of clarity, however, the following summary of the major positions may be made:

Sequence of Millennial Events		
Premillennial	Amillennial	Postmillennial
2nd Coming	1st Coming (Birth)	1st Coming (Birth)
Defeat of Satan	Defeat of Satan at cross	Defeat of Satan at cross
Resurrection of saints	Life after death for saints as each one dies	Life after death for saints as each one dies
Literal 1,000 years	Symbolic 1,000 years (as entire church era)	Literal (?) 1,000 years (era of increasing perfection)
Release of Satan	Release of Satan 2nd Coming	Release of Satan (?)\ 2nd Coming
Judgment Day	Judgment Day	Judgment Day
New heaven & earth	New heaven & earth	New heaven & earth

Frankly, it must be admitted that nowhere in **Revelation 20** does the text say whether the 2nd Coming is before (premillennial) or after (postmillennial) the 1,000 years, or whether the 1,000 years is a literal time period at all (amillennial). Furthermore, all attempts to construct an elaborate calendar of events are about as futile as the attempt to calculate the exact date when Christ will return. In the end, one's views on the millennium have little to do with what he thinks of life after Judgment Day, anyway, since all three views converge on the new heaven and earth after that Day.

THE GREAT WHITE THRONE
REVELATION 20:11-15

After the 1,000 years and the defeat of Satan, John saw a great white throne on Judgment Day (*Rev 20:11*). Good and bad, great and small—all the dead were resurrected from the sea, the grave, and Hades to stand before the Judge of all the earth. Books were opened, and all the dead were judged by their deeds that were recorded in these books (*v. 13*). Since *"all have sinned and fall short of the glory of God"* (*Rom 3:23*), the future of all humanity was not bright.

But there was another book to be opened, the Lamb's book of life (*v. 12*; see also *Rev 21:27* and notes on *Ex 32:32*). Anyone whose name was found written in this book was exempt from the terrible fate awaiting all the rest. All the sinners, along with death and Hades itself, were to be thrown into a lake of fire (*20:14-15*; see also *Rev 19:20* and *21:8*). This place of eternal fire, prepared for the devil and his angels (*Mt 25:41*), was to be the destiny of all those who chose to follow him rather than to follow God. The lake of fire was called *"the second death,"* because it is a place of spiritual death that follows the earlier physical death. The second death is a dying that never ends, where the torment continues day and night forever (*Rev 20:10*).

A NEW HEAVEN
AND A NEW EARTH
REVELATION 21:1-7

In the final two chapters of Revelation we have the finest and most detailed picture of what heaven will ultimately look like. These two chapters are a fitting climax to the entire saga of salvation history, the epic story of paradise lost and regained. There are many echoes of the original Garden of Eden found in these two chapters; there are many allusions to the promises of the ancient prophets (esp. *Isaiah 60, 65* and *Ezekiel 40–48*). There is no doubt that human words were not adequate to describe all that John saw; he had to use such words and images as he had available in his attempt to describe what he saw. We should not be too hasty, however, in dismissing every description as merely figurative. And where we do conclude that the language is figurative, we should understand that the final reality will be more—not less—than what John declared. Until we see heaven with our own eyes, we cannot improve on this great scriptural finale.

Just as Isaiah predicted centuries earlier (*Isa 65:17; 66:22*), John saw *"a new heaven and a new earth"* (*Rev 21:1*). The first heaven and the first earth—the entire fallen, decaying universe—had passed away. The sea, the untamed deep that had swallowed up so many of their dead (*Rev 20:13*) and from which the Beast had arisen (*Rev 13:1*), was no more. (Even though the oceans as we have known them will cease to exist, new kinds of seas will be in heaven; see *Rev 4:6; 15:2*.) In the extreme makeover of the universe, everything will be improved.

Then John saw the crown jewel of the life to come, the Holy City, the New Jerusalem (*21:2*). The city was beautiful, radiant, and pure—looking just like a bride as she is presented to her husband (see *Eph 5:25-32; Rev 19:7-9*). The Holy City is both a place and a people, the city where the saints of ages past will join the saints still living and be the bride of Christ.

Since the time of David the city of Jerusalem had been the center of the kingdom; now it would be the home of heaven's King, as well. John heard a loud voice from the throne declaring, *"Now the dwelling of God is with men, and he will live with them"* (*v. 3*). The fellowship of God and man, broken by sin in the Garden, is finally restored. God the Son had once before lived briefly among His people; now in a grander, eternal way, God will live among His people forever.

> The Greek word for "dwelling" in *Rev 21:3* is *skene*. It is the word for the "tent" or "Tabernacle" in which the presence of God dwelt in the days of Moses (*Ex 25:9*). In the verb form, the same word tells how the Word became flesh and "dwelt" among us (*Jn 1:14*). Everything that was prefigured in the Tabernacle and in the incarnation will finally become a reality in heaven, where it will be said, "Now the dwelling of God is with men!"

All sorrows and heartaches will become things of the past, as God wipes every tear from their eyes. Never again will His people experience *"death or mourning or crying or pain"* (*v. 4*). The old order of things will be over (see *Isa 48:6*), because the One who sits on the throne promises, *"I am making everything new"* (*21:5*). The Greek word for "new" is *kainos*, indicating that things will not be "new" in the sense of fresh copies of what already existed, but in the sense of things that are completely new and different.

But the One who does all this is not new. He is the God of the beginning (*Genesis*) and of the finale (*Revelation*). He is *"the Alpha and the Omega, the Beginning and the End"* (*v. 6*). God the Father was called by the first and last letters of the Greek alphabet in *Revelation 1:8* and here in *Revelation 21:6*, but it will be Jesus the Son who wears this title in *Revelation 22:13*. To the believer who is faithful to the end, God promises to provide the *"water of life"* (*v. 6*), forever abundant and free. In fact, everything John could see in the New Jerusalem was promised as an inheritance to those who persevere and overcome (*v. 7*). Such is the promise for everyone who is a child of God (*v. 7b*; see *1Jn 3:1*).

THE NEW JERUSALEM
REVELATION 21:9-21

"Come," said the angel to John, *"I will show you the bride, the wife of the Lamb"* (*Rev 21:9*). What follows is John's detailed description of what he saw, couched in terms that were understandable to his readers. Heaven's capital city has walls, gates, jewels, gold. If John were to describe this city to a 21st-century audience, perhaps the way he would describe things would change. Or perhaps not. At any rate, we lose much if we rashly discard the whole picture as merely "spiritual" or entirely "figurative." Then we are left, as in fact many modern Christians are left, without a clue about what heaven will be.

> **We lose much if we rashly discard the whole picture as entirely "figurative."**

The glittering city shines with the glory of God (*v. 11*). Its brilliance is like a precious jewel, perfectly clear and flawless. Surrounding the city—like all ancient cities—is a great, high wall (*v. 12*), and this wall has twelve gates. The gates (which are never shut and locked, *v. 25*) show that the saints will have ready access to all the rest of the new heaven and the new earth. God's people will not be forever shut up in that single city.

But are the walls real? Are the gates necessary? While it is easy to dismiss walls and gates as a relic of first-century understanding, one significant fact must not be overlooked. The angel took a gold measuring rod and measured everything—the city, the gates, the walls. If the walls are irrelevant, why measure them? The city turns out to be a perfect cube, just as the Holy of Holies in the original Tabernacle was a cube. This giant city-cube measures 12,000 *stadia* in each direction (*v. 16*). Since each *stadion* is 605 English feet, this works out to be 1,375 miles. The city therefore contains a mind-boggling 2.6 billion cubic miles of space. The walls measure 144 cubits (about 200 feet), and John did not specify whether this was how thick or how high. The twelve foundations of the walls, named for the twelve apostles (*v. 14*), are each adorned with its own kind of jewels (*vv. 19-20*). Each great gate is made of a single giant pearl; each great street is made of pure gold (*v. 21*). It should be noted that the gold is *not* transparent, but is as pure as transparent glass is pure. Thus, the most precious treasures presently known to man become the mere bricks and pavement of heaven!

WHAT IS NOT IN THE CITY
REVELATION 21:22-27

John also described the New Jerusalem by what it did not contain. Unlike the scenes of the intermediate heaven (*Rev 7:15; 11:1-2,19; 14:17; 15:5-8; 16:17*), in this picture there is no temple (*Rev 21:22*). In ages past the Temple was the dwelling place of God, restricted from His people, but now that God lives with mankind *"the Lord God Almighty and the Lamb are its temple"* (*v. 22*).

John next presented a rapid list of additional things that are not to be seen in heaven. The city also has no sun or moon, for all the light the city needed is provided by the glory of God and of the Lamb (*v. 23*). There are no closed gates in the heavenly city (*v. 25*), which means that the saints have easy access in and out of heaven's capital city. There is nothing impure allowed in the city (*v. 27*), which means that no shameful or deceitful people will be permitted inside. Only those whose names are written in the Lamb's book of life have the right to live in heaven.

THE WATER OF LIFE AND
THE TREE OF LIFE
REVELATION 22:1-5

The final chapter of John's revelation once more echoes the sights and sounds of Eden. A great river flows in the New Jerusalem, just as a river flowed in Eden (*Gen 2:10*) and in the restored Jerusalem of prophecy (*Ps 46:4; Eze 47:5-9; Joel 3:18; Zec 14:8*). This river has crystal clear water, which issues from the very throne of God Himself (*Rev 22:1*). It flows down the middle of the great street of the city, with the tree of life planted on each side of the river (*v. 2*). Once forbidden to mankind (*Gen 3:22-24*), now the tree will provide an unending supply of life-sustaining fruit. The water from the river and the fruit from the tree are additional indications that the saints will have bodies (and appetites) in heaven.

The leaves of the tree of life are said to be *"for the healing of the nations"* (*22:2*). This can be understood in several different ways. First, such healing may be a one-time healing for the wounded and broken bodies of saints when they first arrive. Second, such healing may be for the painless wounds and scrapes that the saints may get (as they try out their rock-climbing skills in Zion?). Third, the healing may be understood as a preventative healing that keeps all the saints healthy all the time.

A highlight of this passage in John's revelation is the statement: *"No longer will there be any curse"* (*v. 3*). The original curse of the fallen world is removed! The pains, the thorns, the sweat of tiring toil, the inexorable dying and return to the dust—all the penalties of Eden are over (*Gen 3:16-19*). The relentless decay and hopeless frustration of all creation, likewise—over! (See *Rom 8:20-22*.) All the tragedies and heartaches of living in a fallen world will no longer plague God's people.

Freed from the curse of the fallen world, God's people will gladly serve Him (*v. 3*). Finally, just as Jesus promised, they will see God's face (*v. 4*; see *Mt 5:8*). Never again will they live in darkness, for God will always be present and His glory will provide their light. And they—the saints—*"will reign for ever and ever"* (*v. 5*). Just as God has always intended for the people He created (see *Gen 1:26*), their destiny is to rule. Where once Adam and Eve ruled over the fish, the birds, and the land animals, the saints in heaven will also reign once more. We can only speculate about what animals might fill the parks and forests of heaven (see *Isa 11:6-8*) and about the way men will be over even the angels (see *1Cor 6:3*). God may very well have an endless supply of new creatures over which mankind will rule. But this much is certain: we have been made in the image of God . . . to rule.

Where once Adam and Eve ruled, the saints in heaven will also reign once more.

I AM COMING SOON!
REVELATION 22:12-17,20

At the close of his revelation John hears the voice of Jesus once more. *"Behold,"* He says, *"I am coming soon"* (**Rev 22:12**). What welcome words to the exile on Patmos and to the persecuted believers of his generation! In their case, the rescue came for them individually as they died. Ultimately, in the Father's own appointed time, Jesus will come for all the saints. He will richly reward His people, taking note of what each of them has done (**v. 12**). He has a threefold title: *"the Alpha and the Omega, the First and the Last, the Beginning and the End"* (**v. 13**). Such a title has been used for the Father (**Rev 1:8; 21:6**), but it is equally appropriate for the Son (see also **Rev 1:17**). Everything in all creation begins and ends with Him.

When Jesus comes to bring salvation to those who are faithfully waiting for Him (see **Heb 9:28**), there will be a dramatic division of the human race. Those who have washed their robes in the blood of the Lamb (**Rev 22:14**; see also **7:14**) will have the right to the tree of life in the New Jerusalem. All others will be denied access. They are called *"the dogs, those who practice magic arts, the sexually immoral, the murderers, the idolaters and everyone who loves and practices falsehood"* (**v. 15**). They will not lurk forever just outside the gates of the Holy City, however, because Scripture has already stated that they will be cast into the lake of fire (**Rev 20:15**). One of the great blessings of heaven is that we will no longer live in a world infested with such people.

Then Jesus states that He has another threefold title: *"the Root and the Offspring of David, the bright Morning Star."* **Isaiah 11:1** had prophesied that *"a shoot"* would come *"from the stump of Jesse"* (David's father), but Jesus is both the original Root and the final messianic Branch that comes from David (see **Rev 5:5**). In Him the kingdom is eternally restored, and He will reign forever. As the rising Morning Star, Jesus is the truth that arises in our hearts (**2Pet 1:19; Rev 2:28**) and the One who has risen from the dead to crush the works of darkness forever. In vain Satan once claimed to be the Morning Star (**Isa 14:12**), but the rightful claimant is Jesus.

The Spirit, largely absent in the pages of **Revelation**, joins the bridal community in an urgent plea to the human race. *"Come!"* they say (**22:17**). Whoever is spiritually thirsty, whoever truly wishes to have peace with God, may take the water of life as a free gift. As the story of Scripture began with man's wrong choice, now it draws to a close with this invitation to make the right choice.

It is an urgent decision. In one way or another, Jesus is coming soon. For most, He is only a heartbeat away; only one final breath separates them from eternity. For all, He is only a lightning flash and a trumpet blast away; at any moment the curtain may fall on this present stage of life. All those who are hungry for heaven should keep Jesus' closing words always before them: *"Yes, I am coming soon"* (**v. 20**).

CONCLUSION

The study of the Book of *Revelation* is difficult, but rewarding. While it was first written for the benefit of the early church struggling to withstand the Roman Empire, it has a message of hope for every generation. There are pictures of Jesus to instill courage: the Warrior on a white horse, the Lamb that was slain and rose again, the Son of God who sits on the throne of the restored kingdom. There are pictures of heaven as the restored paradise of God: the throne room with God and the Lamb and the angels, the praise of an innumerable multitude of saints, the intermediate heaven that awaits judgment against the enemies, the wedding feast of the Lamb, the final heaven of perfect happiness (with real gold, real jewels, real measurements, real food and water). There are the promises that God will keep: Satan will fall; the wicked will be cast into the lake of fire; the saints will overcome and have the right to the tree of life; the saints will serve God as priests and kings—who reign forever; Jesus is coming soon.

WHAT DO YOU SAY?

1. What should we look for when we read the Book of Revelation?

2. What will God give to *"him who overcomes"*?

3. What is the picture of heaven in **chapter four**?

4. What do we know about singing in heaven?

5. Does "Babylon the Great" exist today? In what form?

6. Describe the wedding supper of the Lamb.

7. How large is the new Jerusalem? Is that all there is in heaven?

8. What will *not* be in heaven?

9. Which of the descriptions of the new Jerusalem do you honestly find the hardest to imagine?

10. Of all John's descriptions of heaven, which is your favorite?

Part 2

Hell

CHAPTER FIFTEEN

HELL AND
THE NATURE OF GOD

We speak of hell by necessity, not by choice. We describe its horrors without gloating or gladness. Most of all, we shall speak of hell only after affirming the fundamental goodness and fairness of God.

A proper understanding of the reality of hell begins with a brief study of the nature of God. God is Creator: the world and all creatures are His. He has authority as Author to do with the world as He sees fit. In addition to this, however, it must be stressed that God is also loving. While He could snuff out all life with a mere word, He has made provisions to save men from this peril. Even so, God is also holy and just. A holy God cannot tolerate wickedness; a just God cannot condone it. When men persist in wickedness, something has to be done. It must even be acknowledged that when God looks down on man's sinfulness, He is angry. The wrath of God is rightly poured out on those who choose to follow the devil and live in moral darkness. Finally, it must not be forgotten that God is almighty. He is perfectly capable of carrying out His decrees of condemnation.

GOD IS CREATOR

"In the beginning, God" (*Gen 1:1*). The story of hell must begin here, with God as the author of all things. He made the earth and if He chooses to destroy it with a purging fire (*2Pet 3:12*) in order to release it from its bondage to decay (*Rom 8:21*), it is His right. He created mankind in His own image (*Gen 1:26*), and if men refuse to reflect that image, God has every right to address that rebellion.

I. God Is Creator
II. God Is Loving
III. God Is Holy
IV. God Is Just
V. God Is Angry
VI. God Is Capable
VII. Conclusion

David understood clearly God's ownership, as he wrote, *"The earth is the LORD's, and everything in it, the world, and all who live in it"* (**Ps 24:1**). He also wrote, *"He is to be feared above all gods. For all the gods of the nations are idols, but the LORD made the heavens"* (**1Chr 16:25-26; Ps 96:4-5**). It is not necessary to quote every Scripture in defense of this basic truth, but one might also remember Paul's famous words on the Areopagus (Mars Hill): *"The God who made the world and everything in it is the Lord of heaven and earth. . . . For in him we live and move and have our being"* (**Acts 17:24,28**).

GOD IS LOVING

God showed His love for mankind from the very beginning. He designed a garden of delights for Adam, with *"trees that were pleasing to the eye and good for food"* (**Gen 2:9**). Since it was not good for Adam to be alone, God designed a suitable helper and partner for him (**Gen 2:18-25**). Most of all, God offered His fellowship to Adam and Eve (**Gen 3:9**). God's essential love oozes from every line of the Creation account.

God openly announced His gracious love to His chosen people, Israel. He will punish *"to the third and fourth generation of those who hate me,"* but will show *"love to a thousand generations of those who love me and keep my commandments"* (**Ex 20:5-6**). His unfailing love was called *hesed*, the covenant love of the loyal God. (See "HEAVEN: THE ASSURANCE OF *HESED*" in chapter 6.) In the NT the Apostle John wrote it most succinctly, ***"God is love"*** (**1Jn 4:8**).

God does not want men to be lost. He *"wants all men to be saved and come to a knowledge of the truth"* (**1Tm 2:4**). He does not want *"anyone to perish, but everyone to come to repentance"* (**2Pet 3:9**). While the nature of God will be seen to include judgment and wrath, the overwhelming abundance of His love must not be forgotten. Even the eternal punishments of hell must be understood as necessary to the proper expression of God's love. How could He love the righteous if He gave their reward to the wicked?

GOD IS HOLY

As Moses led the children of Israel out of Egypt, he reintroduced them to their God. Together they sang this song: *"Who among the gods is like you, O LORD? Who is like you—majestic in holiness, awesome in glory, working wonders?"* (**Ex 15:11**). By means of the laws of the covenant, Israel was taught to respect and to emulate the sacred holiness of their God. After a lengthy chapter on clean and unclean foods, God said, *"Do not make yourselves unclean by means of them or be made unclean by them. I am the LORD your God; consecrate yourselves and be holy, because I am holy"* (**Lev 11:43-44**). They were to understand that holiness and purity went hand in hand.

If men were to enter the presence of God, they could not be unholy or unclean. David wrote, *"You are not a God who takes pleasure in evil; with you the wicked cannot dwell. The arrogant cannot stand in your presence; you hate all who do wrong"* (**Ps 5:4-5**). *"LORD,"* David also wrote, *"who may dwell in your sanctuary? Who may live on your holy hill? He whose walk is blameless and who does what is righteous"* (**Ps 15:1-2**). Similarly in another psalm David wrote, *"Who may ascend the hill of the LORD? Who may stand in his holy place? He who has clean hands and a pure heart, who does not lift up his soul to an idol or swear by what is false"* (**Ps 24:3-4**). It was clear in Scripture: unholy men could not enjoy the presence of a holy God.

Isaiah felt the awe and terror of facing God unworthily. In his vision he saw the LORD and heard the seraphs calling out, *"Holy, holy, holy is the LORD Almighty; the wholly earth is full of his glory"* (**Isa 6:3**). Then he thought of his own unworthiness and said, *"Woe to me! I am ruined! For I am a man of unclean lips, and I live among a people of unclean lips, and my eyes have seen the King, the LORD Almighty* (**Isa 6:5**). He could only survive in God's presence when his guilt was taken away and his sin was atoned for (**Isa 6:7**).

A holy God requires holy people. In the NT the demand of **Leviticus** was repeated by the Apostle Peter. *"But just as he who called you is holy,"* Peter wrote, *"so be holy in all you do; for it is written, 'Be holy, because I am holy'"* (**1Pet 1:15-16**). *"Without holiness,"* wrote the author of Hebrews, *"no one will see the Lord"* (**Heb 12:14**).

GOD IS JUST

So the Creator wants to show His love to His creatures, but He cannot embrace them in their unholiness. Furthermore, God cannot simply ignore man's unholy state, because God is completely just. *"His works are perfect,"* Moses said, *"and all his ways are just. A faithful God who does no wrong"* (**Deut 32:4**).

Israel learned, sometimes to her own hurt, that God always

administers justice. For instance, when the nation abandoned God under Rehoboam, God withdrew His protection from the nation. As the Jewish leaders humbled themselves in repentance, they had to admit, *"The LORD is just"* (**2Chr 12:5-6**). As one of the psalms of David phrased it, *"God is a righteous judge, a God who expresses his wrath every day"* (**Ps 7:11**). Again, *"The LORD reigns. . . . He will judge the peoples with equity. . . . He will judge the world in righteousness and the peoples in his truth"* (**Ps 96:10,13**).

The Judge of all the earth will do the right thing (see **Gen 18:25**). In the NT the truth remains: *"The eyes of the Lord are on the righteous and his ears are attentive to their prayer, but the face of the Lord is against those who do evil"* (**1Pet 3:12**). This shows that God continues to condemn the wicked, even as He rewards the righteous. But we should never think that God takes malicious delight in sending people to hell. Here is God's own statement: *"As surely as I live, declares the Sovereign LORD, I take no pleasure in the death of the wicked, but rather that they turn from their ways and live"* (**Eze 33:11**; see also **Eze 18:23,32**).

GOD IS ANGRY

Whenever there is wickedness, God is angry. This is an unpleasant, but unavoidable, truth about God's nature. To call this merely God's "displeasure" would be to fall far short of what the Bible really says. Throughout the OT there is a rising crescendo of warnings about God's wrath.

It begins quietly. When Adam and Eve sin, they receive specific curses, and they are evicted from the Garden of Eden (**Gen 3:16-24**). At no point in the Genesis narrative, however, is God's emotional state mentioned. In the days of Noah, when man's wickedness on the earth has become so great, the LORD is *"grieved"* that He has made mankind and His heart is *"filled with pain"* (**Gen 6:5-6**). Even in His declaration that He will wipe mankind from the face of the earth, however, there is no specific statement of His wrath.

It is later, as God establishes His covenant through Moses, there begin to be increasing statements that God is angry. When the people make a golden calf to worship, the LORD's anger burns and He is ready to destroy them (**Ex 32:10**). When the people complain about their hardships, His anger is aroused, and a fire is sent to consume some of the people (**Num 11:1**). When the people refuse to trust God to give them victory in Canaan, in God's wrath He sends them to wander and die in the desert over the next forty years (*Num 14:32-35; Ps 95:10-11*).

Then the next generation comes of age and is willing to cross into the Promised Land. Moses gives this stern warning against anyone who turns away from God: *"His wrath and zeal will burn against that man"* (*Deu 29:20*). And when people see the land laid waste and wonder how God could let it happen, the answer will be: *"It is because this people abandoned the covenant of the LORD, the God of their fathers"* (*v. 25*). *"In furious anger and in great wrath"* the LORD will uproot Israel from their land.

But when Israel does finally settle in Canaan, they repeatedly dishonor God and fail to keep His covenant. In response, God is increasingly disgusted with the people. He warns that a time of punishment is coming, when His *"anger will burn against this place and will not be quenched"* (*2Kgs 22:17*). God threatens to reject Judah, Jerusalem, and the Temple itself (*2Kgs 23:27*). Throughout the Psalms, the Proverbs, and especially in the Prophets, the anger and wrath of God are repeatedly announced. Ezekiel alone repeats warnings of God's wrath thirty-four times with statements such as, *"I will gather you in my anger and my wrath and put you inside the city and melt you . . . and I will blow on you with my fiery wrath . . . and you will know that I the LORD have poured out my wrath upon you"* (*Eze 22:20-22*).

Apparently God's people did not think He would do it. Perhaps the warnings had been repeated so many times that their ears no longer heard and their minds no longer reacted. But they should have taken note of a timeless truth: *"Because of such things God's wrath comes on those who are disobedient"* (*Eph 5:6*).

A survey of the uses of the word "wrath" in connection with God reveals an interesting fact. The wrath of God is mentioned 136 times in the OT and 35 times in the NT (NASB). This means that, on average, God's wrath is mentioned once every 10 pages in the OT and once every 11 pages in the NT. When the study is extended to include the words "anger" and "angry," however, the proportion changes dramatically. God's "anger" is mentioned 198 times in the OT and He is said to be "angry" 44 times (contrasted with only 2 times for each word in the NT). It is still incorrect, however, to think that the old God of wrath has been replaced by a God of love. In fact, God has always had wrath for the wicked and love for the righteous.

It may be objected that anger and wrath are not appropriate responses and that they are not a true representation of God's nature. After all, Christians are told not to be angry with a brother (*Mt 5:22*) and to *"get rid of all bitterness, rage and anger"* (*Eph 5:31*). If *man's* anger does not produce the righteousness God desires (*Jas 1:20*), how can *God's* anger accomplish it? Thus, many people have concluded, in the end God will not be angry after all.

Such arguments overlook the fact that God is not a man. He is the Creator and the Judge, and it is His solemn duty to punish the wicked. *"It is mine to avenge,"* says the LORD, *"I will repay"* (*Deu 32:35*; see also *Rom 12:19* and *Heb 10:30*). While wrath and vengeance are too hot to handle for humans, they are appropriate for God. In the same Deuteronomy passage God further states,

> I lift my hand to heaven and declare:
> As surely as I live forever,
> when I sharpen my flashing sword
> and my hand grasps it in judgment,
> I will take vengeance on my adversaries
> and repay those who hate me. (*Deu 32:40-41*)

GOD IS CAPABLE

It is clear that God is holy and just, and that the Judge of all the earth will do the right thing. It is also clear that God has a righteous anger against all wickedness. What is not clear—at least in the minds of some—is whether God is capable of carrying out the terrible threats of punishment He has made. The question is not whether God has the power to enforce the sentence of death, for He is almighty and can do whatever He chooses. The question is whether He can actually go through with it. Does God "have the stomach" to destroy the wicked?

The serpent was the first to question whether God really meant what He said about punishment (*Gen 3:1-4*). Adam and Eve found out, to their sorrow, that God was not bluffing. Expelled from paradise, they came under the curse of a fallen world—a world in which everything decays and everybody dies.

Adam and Eve found that God was not bluffing.

The next confirmation that God is capable of bringing wrath upon the wicked came with the Flood. God *"saw how great man's wickedness on the earth had become,* and that every inclination of the thoughts of his heart was only evil all the time" (*Gen 6:5*). So He determined to wipe mankind from the face of the earth. He did spare Noah, *"a righteous man, blameless among the people of his time"* (*Gen 6:9*), even using him as *"a preacher of righteousness"* to his generation (*2Pet 2:5*). Except for Noah and his family, however, the entire population of the planet perished.

Still early in the chapters of *Genesis*, Abraham also had a firsthand glimpse of the wrath of God. The cities of Sodom and Gomorrah had sin so grievous that the LORD decided to destroy them (*Gen 18:20-33*). Abraham pled with God to spare them, even if only ten righteous people could be found there. But the righteous ten were not to be found, so *"the LORD rained down burning sulfur"* on the cities and they were completely destroyed (*Gen 19:23-29*).

Later, when Moses was about to bring the children of Israel out of slavery in Egypt, God showed once more that He is able to deliver His sentence of death. Because the Pharaoh repeatedly ignored the warning of the plagues, God finally pronounced impending doom on every firstborn male in the land. He said nothing of a "death angel" or other intermediary; it would be God himself who would strike down the firstborn (*Ex 11:4; 12:12,29*).

Adam, Noah, Abraham, Moses—all the great patriarchs witnessed the fierce wrath of God. The Apostle Peter used their stories as proof that God is able to carry out punishment:

> If he did not spare the ancient world when he brought the flood on its ungodly people . . . if he condemned the cities of Sodom and Gomorrah by burning them to ashes . . . then the Lord knows how to rescue godly men from trials and to hold the unrighteous for the day of judgment. (*2Pet 2:4-9*)

One final incident from Israel's history will complete the picture of the God who is able to punish. In the days of Jeremiah the LORD—just as He had warned—brought the armies of Nebuchadnezzar to destroy Jerusalem and carry the people into captivity. In distress for his people Jeremiah prayed to God for deliverance. *"Ah, Sovereign LORD,"* he prayed, *"you have made the heavens and the earth by your great power and outstretched arm. Nothing is too hard for you"* (*Jer 32:18*). Surely the God who delivered His people out of Egypt would now deliver them from the hand of the Babylonians! But God turned Jeremiah's words against him. *"I am the LORD, the God of all mankind.*

Is anything too hard for me? Therefore, this is what the LORD *says . . ."* and God proceeded to declare how He would turn the city over to her enemies (*Jer 32:27-28*). The Babylonians would attack the city, destroy the Temple, and enslave the people— while God watched and did not intervene. It would not be easy for God to see His people and His Temple destroyed, but just as He proclaimed, nothing is too difficult for Him.

> **It is not easy for God to see His people destroyed, but nothing is too difficult for Him.**

CONCLUSION

God has revealed His nature through His Word. He does not need to fit any human definition of what a god must be; He is who He is. For the purposes of this study on hell, God's revealed nature answers many objections in advance:

1. *He has no right to send people to hell.* But the Creator has the authority of the Author. It is His world; we are His creatures.

2. *Hell is not an expression of love.* It is true that God is gracious and loving. But the love of God coexists with the justice and wrath of God. If we leave out parts of His revealed nature, we produce a distorted and false picture of God.

3. *It is OK if people are not perfect.* But God exists in perfect holiness, and if men are not holy, they cannot live with Him. It is understandable that flawed men should be ready to ignore each other's flaws, but God cannot.

4. *It is not fair to send anyone to hell.* But it is the very nature of what is fair and just that is the point. God's own nature requires that He do what is right. His justice is our doom!

5. *Surely God will overlook our failures.* But in fact, God is angry with our failures. They are not mere imperfections; they are treasonous rebellion against the laws of the Almighty. We cannot suppose that God is casual about sin—He is angry!

6. *A loving God simply cannot send His own children to hell.* It is true that God takes no pleasure in the death of the wicked, but He has no lack of determination to carry out their sentence of condemnation. God is not restrained by our hesitation; neither is He controlled by our definitions of what He can and cannot do.

It is true that the scripture texts of this chapter do not directly address the issue of eternal punishment in hell. They do show, however, that the nature of God is fully consistent with the concept of drastic punishment. God's nature is not only consistent with the concept of punishment; in fact, the holiness and justice of His nature require it. As Moses warned the children of Israel before they crossed into the Promised Land, *"The LORD your God is a consuming fire, a jealous God"* (**Deu 4:24**).

WHAT DO YOU SAY?

1. Why is it important to consider the nature of God in this study about hell?

2. God is Creator. How does that teach us anything about hell?

3. God is Love. How does that teach us anything about hell?

4. God is Holy. How does that teach us anything about hell?

5. God is Just. How does that teach us anything about hell?

6. God is sometimes Angry. How does that teach us anything about hell?

7. Because God is Almighty, He is capable. How does that teach us anything about hell?

8. How can anger and vengeance be right for God, but wrong for man?

9. Is there any other aspect of God's nature that should be included in this study?

CHAPTER SIXTEEN

PREVIEWS OF HELL IN THE OLD TESTAMENT

In the previous chapter it was established that God can and must punish evil. Scattered throughout the OT there are numerous previews of what lies beyond the grave—especially for the wicked. While none of these previews gives a complete description of what hell will be like, together they present a sobering picture of the grim reality. First we will consider the places: *sheol,* the "pit," and the Valley of Ben Hinnom. Then we will investigate other terms that preview hell: fire, destruction, and death.

SHEOL

Sheol is the Hebrew word for the place of the dead. It was first used in Scripture when Jacob thought his son Joseph had been killed by a ferocious animal. He said, *"In mourning will I go down to the **grave** to my son"* (***Gen 37:35***). Later, fearing the death of his son Benjamin, he said, *"You will bring my gray head down to the **grave** in sorrow"* (***Gen 42:38***). This use of *sheol* as the grave, without any discrimination between the righteous and the wicked, shows its usual function in Scripture.

As the ultimate place of the dead, *sheol* was understood to be a dead-end destination. Job voiced this well when he said, *"He who goes down to the **grave** does not return. He will never come to his house again; his place will know him no more"* (***Job 7:9***). Understandably, references to *sheol* are usually cast in a negative light. Since God is the author of life, any final defeat by death could not be a good thing. Death is the *"last enemy,"* as Paul would say later (***1Cor 15:26***). Job further described

269

> *Sheol* is used 65 or 66 times in the OT. (A difference in reading the Hebrew vowel pointing at **Isaiah 7:11** creates the discrepancy in statistical totals.) A comparison of versions shows how *sheol* has been translated:
>
> KJV: "hell" 31×, "grave" 31×, "pit" 3×.
> NASB: "sheol" 66×
> NIV: "grave" 55×, "death" 6×, "depths" 2×, "depths
>   of the grave" 2×, "realm of death" 1×

death as going *"to the place of no return, to the land of gloom and deep shadow, to the land of deepest night, of deep shadow and disorder, where even the light is like darkness"* (**Job 10:21**).

Psalm 88
The Psalmist Ponders *Sheol*

*For my soul is full of trouble
    and my life draws near the grave **(sheol)**.
I am counted among those who go down to the pit;
    I am like a man without strength.
I am set apart with the dead,
    like the slain who lie in the grave,
whom you remember no more,
    who are cut off from your care.
You have put me in the lowest pit,
    in the darkest depths.
Your wrath lies heavily upon me;
    you have overwhelmed me with all your waves.
You have taken from me my closest friends
    and have made me repulsive to them.
I am confined and cannot escape;
    my eyes are dim with grief.
I call to you, O LORD, every day;
    I spread out my hands to you.
Do you show your wonders to the dead?
    Do those who are dead rise up and praise you?
Is your love declared in the grave,
    your faithfulness in Destruction **(Abaddon)**?*

> *Are your wonders known in the place of darkness,*
> *or your righteous deeds in the land of oblivion?*
> **(Ps 88:3-12)**

Sometimes the descent into *sheol* was the penalty for wickedness. During Korah's rebellion in the wilderness, Moses warned those who were opposing God's will that they would *"go down alive into the* **grave"** (**Num 16:30**). Likewise, in the **Psalms** the wicked *"return to the* **grave"** (**Ps 9:17**). David said, *"Let death take my enemies by surprise; let them go down alive to the* **grave"** (**Ps 55:15**). Wisdom warns those who are tempted to go the house of Folly, *"Little do they know that the dead are there, that her guests are in the depths of the* **grave"** (**Prov 9:18**). Yet even these references still primarily portray *sheol* as simply the place of the dead.

All men—whether good or evil—were helpless to avoid the descent into *sheol*. But *sheol* was not stronger than God. Several passages show, even in that early point of revelation about future life, that righteous men could escape *sheol*. David said, *"You will not abandon me to the* **grave**, *nor will you let your Holy One see decay"* (**Ps 16:10**). He did not then know that these words would have special application to the Messiah and His resurrection, as Peter explained in his sermon at Pentecost (**Acts 2:27**). David also recognized in **Psalm 139:8** that God is stronger than *sheol*: *"If I go up to the heavens, you are there; if I make my bed in the depths* **(sheol)**, *you are there."* He gladly praised the LORD as the one *"who redeems your life from the pit* **(sheol)** *and crowns you with love and compassion"* (**Ps 103:4**). Centuries later the prophet Hosea proclaimed God's triumph over death and *sheol* in these words:

> *I will ransom them from the power of the grave* **(sheol)**;
> *I will redeem them from death.*
> *Where, O death, are your plagues?*
> *Where, O grave* **(sheol)**, *is your destruction?*
> **(Hos 13:14; see 1Cor 15:55)**

In a similar vein, Jonah said, *"In my distress I called to the LORD, and he answered me. From the depths of the grave* **(sheol)** *I called for help, and you listened to my cry"* (**Jonah 2:2**). So while *sheol* was the inevitable destiny of darkness and death, there was still hope in a greater destiny with God.

THE PIT

The OT often speaks of "the pit," a figure that combines the images of a trap, a grave, and a place of decay and corruption. As examples of the trap usage, the evil man may dig a hole as a snare, but will fall into "the pit" he has made (*Prov 26:27; 28:10; Ps 7:15*), and the nations *"have fallen into the pit they have dug; their feet are caught in the net they have hidden"* (*Ps 9:15*).

More often, the image of the grave and destruction are in mind with "the pit." Elihu exhorted Job to repent and turn back to God, who would redeem his soul from *"going down into the pit"* and *"turn back his soul from the pit, that the light of life may shine on him"* (*Job 33:28,30*). David and the other psalmists spoke often of "the pit" in the same sense. David knew that without God as his Rock, he would *"be like those who have gone down to the pit"* (*Ps 28:1*). In another psalm he cried to the LORD for rescue, saying, *"What gain is there in my destruction, in my going down into the pit?"* (*Ps 30:9*). The sons of Korah sang similar words, calling on God to relent and rescue them from *"the lowest pit, in the darkest depths"* (*Ps 88:6*). Evil men, however, could expect no escape from the pit. David declared, *"But you, O God, will bring down the wicked into the pit of corruption"* (*Ps 55:23*).

The prophets continued this use of "the pit" as an image of final destruction. Isaiah thanked God that He had kept him *"from the pit of destruction"* (*Isa 38:17*; literally, "from the pit of wasting away"; an alternative translation is "the pit of nothingness" as in the NASB). Ezekiel wrote vividly of the pit when he said,

> I will make you dwell in the earth below, as in ancient ruins, with those who go down to the pit, and you will not return or take your place in the land of the living. I will bring you to a horrible end and you will be no more (*Eze 26:20-21*).

The image of this dreadful pit, coupled with the image of *sheol*, prepared the way for understanding the Abyss (*Rev 20:3*).

THE VALLEY OF BEN HINNOM

In addition to the somewhat figurative images of *sheol* and the pit, there was an all-too-real location in Israel that was a vivid preview of hell. First mentioned when Israel took over the Promised Land, the Valley of Ben Hinnom ran alongside the southern slope of the Jebusite city that would later become Jerusalem (*Josh 15:8; 18:16*).

Later, in the days of the Divided Kingdom, this valley was the site where Ahaz sacrificed some of his sons in the fire to a pagan god (*2Chr 28:3*). His grandson Manasseh also sacrificed his sons in this valley, along with practicing sorcery, divination and witchcraft (*2Chr 33:6*). Then Manasseh's grandson Josiah tried to put an end to this abomination. He desecrated the Valley of Ben Hinnom (at a specific part called Topheth) *"so no one could use it to sacrifice his son or daughter in the fire to Molech"* (*2Kgs 23:10*). Midway through the reign of Josiah, Jeremiah used what had become a site of destruction as an object lesson: *"So beware, the days are coming, declares the LORD, when people will no longer call this place Topheth or the Valley of Ben Hinnom but the Valley of Slaughter"* (*Jer 19:6*).

For the rest of OT history this valley continued to be associated with idolatry and human sacrifice. As Jeremiah later declared to Judah as the word of the LORD, *"They built high places for Baal in the Valley of Ben Hinnom to sacrifice their sons and daughters to Molech, though I never commanded, nor did it enter my mind, that they should do such a detestable thing"* (*Jer 32:35*). By the time of Jesus this valley was an unclean place, a place for the constant burning of refuse. They called it Gehenna.

> The Hebrew words *ge hinnom* literally mean "valley of Hinnom." The Greek word *geenna* abbreviates the Hebrew words; in English we spell it "Gehenna." The word *geenna*, translated "hell," is used twelve times in the NT: eleven times by Jesus and once by James.

FIRE

Throughout the OT fire is often associated with condemnation by God. When the sin of Sodom and Gomorrah became so grievous that their punishment could not be delayed, God sent angels to destroy the cities (*Gen 18:20; 19:13*). As Lot and his family fled to safety, the LORD rained down burning sulfur to punish the wicked cities (*Gen 19:15,24*). The next day Abraham looked in the direction of Sodom and Gomorrah and saw *"dense smoke rising from the land, like smoke from a furnace"* (*Gen 19:28*).

God often used fire as a means of punishment. Nadab and Abihu died when *"fire came out from the presence of the LORD and consumed* them" (*Lev 10:2*). The 250 men who joined Korah's rebellion were likewise consumed when *"fire came out from the LORD"* (*Num 16:35*). God's great men repeatedly warned His people that He was a God who punished with fire. Moses said, *"Be careful not to forget the covenant. . . . For the LORD your God is a consuming fire, a jealous God"* (*Deu 4:23-24*). David warned, *"On the wicked he will rain fiery coals and burning sulfur"* (*Ps 11:6*).

The God of Fire in the Psalms

"Consuming fire came from his mouth" (*Ps 18:8*)

"In his wrath . . . his fire will consume them" (*Ps 21:9*)

"He burns the shields with fire" (*Ps 46:9*)

"Our God comes . . . a fire devours before him" (*Ps 50:3*)

"As wax melts before the fire, may the wicked perish before God" (*Ps 68:2*)

"He was very angry; his fire broke out against Jacob" (*Ps 78:21*)

"He was very angry with his inheritance. Fire consumed their young men" (*Ps 78:62-63*)

"Will you be angry forever? How long will your jealousy burn like fire?" (*Ps 79:5*)

"How long will your wrath burn like fire?" (*Ps 89:46*)

"Fire goes before him and consumes his foes on every side" (*Ps 97:3*)

"Fire blazed among their followers; a flame consumed the wicked" (*Ps 106:18*)

"May they be thrown into the fire, into miry pits, never to rise" (*Ps 140:10*).

Combining fire with the image of Topheth (the Valley of Hinnom), Isaiah warned of coming punishment:

> Topheth has long been prepared;
>   it has been made ready for the king.
> Its fire pit has been made deep and wide,
>   with an abundance of fire and wood;
> the breath of the LORD,
>   like a stream of burning sulfur sets it ablaze. (*Isa 30:33*)

Isaiah also warned those who chose to walk in spiritual darkness to set their torches ablaze, saying this fire is what they would receive from God's hand and then they would *"lie down in torment"* (**Isa 50:11**). In the last chapter of the OT, there is this final warning: *"Surely the day is coming; it will burn like a furnace. All the arrogant and every evildoer will be stubble, and that day that is coming will set them on fire"* (**Mal 4:1**). When John the Baptist came as the fulfillment of **Malachi 4:5** (the prophet Elijah) his message was a continuation of **Malachi 4:1** (the chaff will be burnt in the fire; **Mt 3:12** and **Lk 3:17**).

DESTRUCTION AND DEATH

God will destroy the wicked. This truth is seen throughout the pages of the OT. Usually this destruction comes in the form of physical death, but this is a preview of hell—the second death. When God brings destruction and death on the wicked, it is seen as a necessary consequence of His holy wrath and their evil sinfulness.

Moses pronounced God's words of doom on an unfaithful generation: *"For a fire has been kindled by my wrath, one that burns to the realm of death [**sheol**] below. It will devour the earth and its harvests and set afire the foundations of the mountains"* (**Deu 32:22**). David warned his people not to fret or be envious of evil men, because, *"Like the grass they will soon wither, like green plants they will soon die away"* (**Ps 37:1-2**). The righteous *"will inherit the land and dwell in it forever,"* but all sinners *"will be destroyed"* and the future of the wicked *"will be cut off"* (**Ps 37:29,38**). Those who do not know God and do His will are destined to dwell *"in the silence of death"* (**Ps 94:18**).

The prophets projected this kind of destruction and death onto the canvas of the ages. Isaiah looked into the future and spoke these words of the LORD against His enemies: *"For the moth will eat them up like a garment; the worm will devour them like wool. But my righteousness will last forever"* (**Isa 51:8**). Isaiah's final picture of the age to come—the time of *"the new heavens and the new earth"*—pronounces final doom on the wicked: *"And they will go out and look upon the dead bodies of those who rebelled against me; their worm will not die, nor will their fire be quenched, and they will be loathsome to all mankind"* (**Isa 66:24**; see **Mk 9:48**). Daniel added this statement of judgment as a preview of the end times: *"Multitudes who sleep in the dust of the earth will awake: some to everlasting life, others to shame and everlasting contempt"* (**Dan 12:2**).

> Daniel's prophecy that the dead will rise to either everlasting life or everlasting contempt is the first and only clear declaration of the double resurrection in the entire OT.

In the hundreds of times throughout the OT that God punishes the wicked, His condemnation is neither capricious nor misguided: *"The soul who sins is the one who will die"* (**Eze 18:4,20**). No matter how powerful or how privileged, the wicked will be destroyed. This was God's pronouncement of doom on ancient Tyre:

> I will bring you down with those who go down to the pit, to the people of long ago. I will make you dwell in the earth below, as in ancient ruins, with those who go down to the pit, and you will not return or take your place in the land of the living. I will bring you to a horrible end and you will be no more. (**Eze 26:20-21**)

Even in the midst of God's righteous destruction of evil men, however, one last fact must not be forgotten. God takes *"no pleasure in the death of the wicked,"* but would rather see them *"turn from their ways and live"* (**Eze 33:11**).

CONCLUSION

Sheol and "the pit" are frequent images of death in the OT. They portray a dark, shadowy land of dreary inactivity. They are often, but not always, a punishment for the wicked. The Valley of Ben Hinnom came into history as the site where children were sacrificed to Molech, and became the place of burning refuse we meet in the NT as *Gehenna*. The prophets waxed eloquent in their description of how God would condemn the wicked. Their punishment will be like corpses whose worm does not die and whose fire cannot be quenched, but the punishment will be just.

WHAT DO YOU SAY?

1. Are there many clear statements about hell in the OT? Why is that so?

2. What does the OT mean by *sheol*? How did men like Job and David picture *sheol*?

3. How is "the pit" of the OT like "the Abyss" into which the devil is cast in *Revelation 20:3*?

4. Where was the Valley of Ben Hinnom? What happened there? What was it like in Jesus' day?

5. How is God *"a consuming fire"*?

6. How do the many references to punishment by fire tie in to the teaching about hell in the NT?

7. What did *Ezekiel 26:20* mean by saying that Tyre would be destroyed and made to dwell *"in the earth below"*? Is that where hell is located?

CHAPTER SEVENTEEN

HELL IN THE
TEACHINGS OF JESUS

Jesus is our primary authority on hell. The Old Testament laid the groundwork of God's judgment in fire and destruction, but most of what we know about hell comes from the lips of Jesus Himself. He spoke frequently and vividly on the horrors of hell.

Liberal scholars, however, long ago dismissed hell as an unacceptable concept. How could a God of love send anyone to hell? Since such scholars did not view the Bible as the actual word of God, anyway, it was not difficult for them to reject Christendom's historic teaching about eternal, fiery punishment. In recent years there has been a growing tendency among evangelical scholars, as well, to reject the traditional view of hell. While still clinging to Scripture as authoritative and divine, they maintain that Jesus has been misunderstood. With many pulpits today either softening or ignoring the unpopular doctrine of hell, it is necessary that we examine the issue afresh. What *did* Jesus say about hell?

HELL: A PLACE OF FIRE
MATTHEW 5:22

Jesus called hell a place of fire. In the opening chapter of the Sermon on the Mount, He warned anyone who called his brother "fool" that he was *"in danger of the fire of hell"* (**Mt 5:22**). The Greek word for "hell" in the original language of this Gospel was *geenna*. An extended discussion of this term in the previous chapter, "Previews of Hell in the Old Testament," identified Gehenna as the burning waste dump outside Jerusalem. This site was a useful illustration for Jesus in explaining the nature of hell: it had a fire that kept on burning all the time.

It has been argued by some that the burning trash pit was only a figure, and should not be taken too literally. However, it should be noted that fire was the only thing about Gehenna that Jesus mentioned. Moreover, Jesus repeatedly stressed fire as a part of the final destruction of the wicked. Near the end of the Sermon on the Mount, for instance, Jesus said that false prophets were like bad trees, known by the bad fruit they produced. *"Every tree that does not bear good fruit,"* He said, *"is cut down and thrown into the fire"* (**Mt 7:19**). He also warned that anyone who does not remain in Him *"is like a branch that is thrown away and withers; such branches are picked up, thrown into the fire and burned"* (**Jn 15:6**). Several more passages that mention "fire" will be examined in the pages that follow. If Jesus did not want His followers to associate fire with the final judgment, why did He mention it so often?

HELL: AN ETERNAL FIRE TO BE AVOIDED AT ALL COSTS
MATTHEW 5:29-30; 18:8-9

Jesus warned His followers to take any drastic steps necessary to avoid hell. Even if it were something as precious as a man's right eye that was causing him to sin, he should gouge it out and throw it away. *"It is better for you to lose one part of your body,"* Jesus said, *"than for your whole body to be thrown into hell"* (**Mt 5:29**). Then He emphasized His teaching by saying the same thing about one's right hand (**v. 30**). Later in His ministry He said it again: *"If your hand or foot causes you to sin, cut it off and throw it away. It is better for you to enter life maimed or crippled than to have two hands or two feet and be thrown into eternal fire"* (**Mt 18:8-9**). Hell is not only fire; it is *eternal* fire. Why would Jesus repeatedly use such language if hell were not a place of fire, or if its punishments were only temporary?

HELL: THE OUTER DARKNESS, WEEPING, GNASHING OF TEETH
MATTHEW 8:12; 13:40-42,49-50; 22:13; 25:30; LUKE 13:28

In six passages on five separate occasions Jesus described the future punishment of the wicked as *"weeping and gnashing of teeth,"* usually in a place called the *"outer darkness."* None of these passages uses the term "hell" (*geenna*), but all six are clear references to the final execution of judgment on sinners.

"There Will Be Weeping and Gnashing of Teeth . . ."

1. When men like the believing centurion join Abraham at the feast in the kingdom of heaven, but the unfaithful sons of kingdom are thrown *"outside"* **(Mt 8:12)**.
2. When angels gather the weeds (people who do evil) and throw them into the *"fiery furnace"* **(Mt 13:40-42)**.
3. When angels separate the bad fish (the wicked) and throw them into the *"fiery furnace"* **(Mt 13:49-50)**.
4. When an improperly dressed man at the wedding banquet for the king's son is tied hand and foot and thrown *"outside into the darkness"* **(Mt 22:13)**.
5. When the worthless servant who buried his talent is thrown *"outside, into the darkness"* **(Mt 25:30)**.
6. When evildoers, who have not chosen to enter the narrow door, are *"thrown out"* and do not get to take a seat at the feast in the kingdom of God **(Luke 13:28)**.

There will be *"weeping and gnashing of teeth"* for several reasons. First, men will weep and gnash their teeth in tragic disappointment when they find out they have been excluded from what they had assumed would be their reward (**Mt 8:12; 22:13; 25:30; Lk 13:28**). Second, men will weep and gnash their teeth in pain in their place of punishment, a *"fiery furnace"* of extreme torment (**Mt 13:42,50**). Third, the gnashing of teeth in all six passages may well indicate frustration and rage against God, whom they have made their enemy.

The "darkness" of those who are thrown outside proves to be a problem for some interpreters. Since these passages are clearly referring to the *"fiery furnace"* as the fire of hell, how could it be dark? Does not fire necessarily produce light? Actually, the answer is no. Not every kind of combustion produces visible light. Perhaps more significantly, a man who is blinded lives in darkness even when others can see a light. (With the modern physics of dark energy, dark matter and black holes that swallow up all light, it seems quaintly old-fashioned to insist that fire must produce light!) Whatever the case, it is certainly not beyond the power of God to combine fire and darkness, and that is exactly what Jesus said the final punishment would be. In striking contrast, the saints in heaven will live in perpetual light, provided by God and the Lamb Themselves.

HELL: A PLACE FOR BOTH
BODY AND SOUL
MATTHEW 10:28; LUKE 12:5

In two very similar passages (but spoken on separate occasions), Jesus encouraged His disciples not to be afraid of those who kill the body but cannot kill the soul. *"Rather,"* He said, *"be afraid of the One who can destroy both soul and body in hell"* (*Mt 10:28; Lk 12:5*). The One who has such power is God. (It is not the devil, for he himself is victim—not the enforcer—of the punishments of hell.) Because the power to destroy in hell includes *both* soul and body, it must be concluded that hell is a real place where real bodies perish. If hell were only a spiritual anguish that dealt only with the inner soul of man, why did Jesus say otherwise?

HELL: A PLACE FOR
THE CONDEMNED
MATTHEW 23:33

Another of the specific uses of "hell" (*geenna*) by Jesus came in His denunciation of the teachers of the law and Pharisees. *"You snakes! You brood of vipers!"* He said. *"How will you escape being condemned to hell?"* (*Mt 23:33*). This text underscores an obvious truth: hell is the place for people who have been condemned by God. It is likely, therefore, that we should understand this same punishment in many other texts where the "judgment" or "condemnation" of God falls upon men.

HELL: TO BE CUT OFF
FROM GOD
MATTHEW 25:41-46

One of the most vivid pictures of Judgment Day is Jesus' parable of the sheep and the goats (*Mt 25:31-46*). The Son of Man returns in all His glory and takes His place as the great Shepherd. As surely as a shepherd can tell the difference between a sheep and a goat, Jesus will divide humanity into those who will receive an inheritance and those who will be cursed. To those on His left, those who disregarded Jesus and their fellow man, Jesus will say, *"Depart from me, you who are cursed, into the eternal fire prepared for the devil and his angels"* (*v. 41*). A few verses later Jesus also says of this group, *"Then they will go away to eternal punishment, but the righteous to eternal life"* (*v. 46*).

There are at least six facts about hell to be derived from these verses. (1) The judgment will be unerring. The Shepherd can easily tell the difference between one group and the other. (2) The goats are told, *"Depart from me,"* indicating that at least part of the punishment of hell is separation from the Lord. (3) The goats are called *"you who are cursed."* To be "cursed" is to come under the declaration of God's wrath and judgment. (4) The condemned are sent into *"the eternal fire."* This is consistent with all the other passages where God's punishment involves fire (see *Mt 5:22*, etc.). (5) This eternal fire was *"prepared for the devil and his angels."* There are, then, *two* "prepared" places in eternity. Heaven is prepared for those who follow Jesus (*Jn 14:2*), and hell is prepared for the devil and his angels. It seems fair to say that God never wanted people in hell; that doom was prepared for the devil. But if people insist on following the devil instead of following Jesus, they will follow him to his final destiny. (6) In the closing verse Jesus said the lost will *"go away to eternal punishment."* A growing number of evangelical scholars are deciding that the punishment of hell is not going to last forever. (See chapter 19, "Alternative Views of Hell.") It must not be overlooked, however, that Jesus applied the word "eternal" to both the fire (*v. 41*) and the punishment (*v. 46*). Why would Jesus have used these descriptions if He were really trying to say that hell was *not* eternal? In fact, the "eternal" punishment will last just as long as the "eternal" life (*v. 46*).

> **Eternal punishment will last just as long as eternal life.**

HELL: THE UNDYING WORM, THE UNQUENCHABLE FIRE
MARK 9:43-48

The everlasting nature of hell is also underscored in the warning of Jesus in *Mark 9:43-48*. He urged His followers to take every drastic step (such as losing a hand, a foot, or an eye) to avoid being cast into hell. Hell, Jesus said, is a place where *"their worm does not die, and the fire is not quenched"* (**v. 48**; see **Isa 66:24**). The worm is the maggot that infests and devours a corpse; the fire is the consuming flame that devours trash and refuse. (It is often noted that Gehenna, the garbage dump of Jerusalem, would have had both worms and fire.)

These words of Jesus echo the earlier warning of John the Baptist. As John called the nation to repentance, He said God was going to clear His threshing floor. God would put the wheat into the barn, but He would burn the chaff *"with unquenchable fire"* (**Mt 3:12**). But would not the fire eventually consume the chaff? If it did, then the fire would go out. In spite of this, Jesus and John both spoke of unquenchable fire. Perhaps we should remember that we have already seen in the burning bush of Moses that God can keep a fire going as long as He wants (**Ex 3:2**).

HELL: DEGREES OF PUNISHMENT
MARK 12:40 LUKE 12:47-48

From the human point of view, it seems logical and necessary that there should be degrees of punishment in hell. (Why should a sweet little old lady and a murderous dictator get the same penalty?) In the OT, for instance, there were provisions for greater or lesser penalties for wrongdoing based on degrees of culpability (for example, **Lev 5:17-19; Num 15:22-31**). Two of Jesus' statements seem to support this concept. When He condemned the teachers of the law for hypocrisy and for devouring widows' houses, He said, *"Such men will be punished most severely"* (**Mk 12:40**). This implies that some will be punished worse than others. On another occasion Jesus explained that the servant who knows his master's will and fails to do it *"will be beaten with many blows,"* while the servant who fails to act because he does not know *"will be beaten with few blows"* (**Lk 12:47-48**). This implies that some will be punished less than others. In addition, His statement that it will be *"more bearable"* in judgment for Tyre and Sidon than for Capernaum may indicate either degrees of penalty or, perhaps, a greater harshness in the judging process (**Mt 11:21-24**).

Various writers through the ages have developed fanciful ideas about eternal punishment, such as Dante's nine circles of hell in *The*

Inferno. But how can hell be divided into degrees of torment? Are some parts a bit cooler? Do some people stay conscious longer? All such speculation goes well beyond what the Bible says. We must accept the intriguing statements of Jesus and be content.

HELL: THE RICH MAN AND LAZARUS
LUKE 16:23-26

Jesus told a famous story about a rich man and a beggar named Lazarus. Was this "only" a parable? Should we avoid making too much of the fine points? Luke used the word "parable" eighteen times in his Gospel, but he did not call this story a parable. In addition, no "parable" in Scripture ever names an individual as an actual person. It seems best, therefore, to take this account as an actual event about which Jesus knew the details.

When the rich man died, he went to a place in *Hades* where people are punished, because he had lived in luxury and had left poor Lazarus to starve (*Lk 16:19-20*). The details of Jesus' story provide much information about what lies immedi-

> The rich man of **Luke 16** is sometimes called Dives, because the Latin word for "rich" is *dives* (pronounced "DEE-wess"). Unlike Lazarus, in Jesus' story the rich man is unnamed.

ately beyond death. (1) Immediately upon death people go to either a place of reward or a place of punishment (*vv. 22-23*). (2) *Hades* includes a place of fire. The rich man was *"in torment"* (*v. 23*) and *"in agony in this fire"* (*v. 24*). (3) Part of the rich man's anguish was that he could see Lazarus and Abraham on the other side (*v. 23*). (4) Both the rich man and Lazarus had bodies. The rich man wanted Lazarus to dip *"his finger"* in water and cool *"my tongue"* (*v. 24*). (5) A *"great chasm has been fixed"* to prevent anyone from crossing from one place to the other (*v. 26*). (6) While the rich man was already in *Hades* and Lazarus was already with Abraham, there were brothers living back on earth (*v. 28*). (7) A person *"in torment"* has no desire to have his family come to join him (*v. 28*). (8) Lazarus, on the other hand, as one favored by God, was escorted by angels to be comforted with Abraham (who was already living with God) (*v. 22*; see *Ex 3:6*; *Mt 22:32*).

Hades: The Place of the Dead

Hades is the Greek equivalent of the Hebrew *sheol*. Both refer to the grave and the realm of the dead, and both are sometimes used in a negative sense. The word *Hades* is only used ten times in the NT, where the NIV translates it "hell" only once. In every instance *Hades* could just as well be translated "the place of the dead."

"You [Capernaum] will go down to **the depths**" **(Mt 11:23)**

"I will build my church and the gates of **Hades** will not overcome it" **(Mt 16:18)**

"You [Capernaum] will go down to **the depths**" **(Lk 10:15)**

"In **hell**, where he [the rich man] was in torment" **(Lk 16:23)**

"You will not abandon me [the Messiah] to **the grave**" **(Acts 2:27)**

"He [the Messiah] was not abandoned to **the grave**" **(Acts 2:31)**

"I [Jesus] hold the keys of death and **Hades**" **(Rev 1:18)**

"Its rider [on a pale horse] was named Death, and **Hades** followed close behind him" **(Rev 6:8)**

"Death and **Hades** gave up the dead that were in them" **(Rev 20:13)**

"Death and **Hades** were thrown into the lake of fire" **(Rev 20:14)**

HELL: ALLUSIONS IN JOHN'S GOSPEL

When Jesus first appeared in Jerusalem as an adult, He cleansed the temple (*Jn 2:15-17*). Like His Father, Jesus had a passion to eliminate evil. He came to bring eternal life to all who put their faith in Him, but those who stubbornly rejected Him would be condemned and perish (*Jn 3:16-18*). The conclusion of John's third chapter puts it bluntly: "*Whoever believes in the Son has eternal life, but whoever rejects the Son will not see life, for God's wrath remains on him*" (*Jn 3:36*).

Jesus said judgment was coming on the world, and He would be the Judge. "*The Father,*" He said, "*has entrusted all judgment to the Son*" (*Jn 5:22,27,30*). Echoing the words of *Daniel 12:2*, Jesus said that all those in their graves would hear His voice and come out, and then "*those who have done good will rise to live, and those who have done evil will rise to be condemned*" (*Jn 5:29*). In His final public discourse in this Gospel, Jesus repeated the warning of judgment: "*There is a judge for the one who rejects me and does not accept my words; that very word which I spoke will condemn him at the last day"* (*Jn 12:48*). Judgment Day was coming and wicked people, along with the devil they served, would be condemned (*Jn 12:31; 16:11*).

Nowhere in the Gospel of John did Jesus speak more plainly about hell than when He spoke of the Vine and the Branches. The vine was a symbol of Israel in the OT, usually in the context of disappointing results (see *Ps 80:8-16; Isa 5:1-7*). Now Jesus is the Vine—He will not disappoint!—and the people are the branches. Every branch that does not bear fruit is cut off (*Jn 15:2*). Additionally, any branch that chooses not to remain in Jesus will wither. *"Such branches,"* Jesus said, *"are picked up, thrown into the fire and burned"* (*Jn 15:6*). The imagery of the fire of hell is clear.

Finally, the crucifixion of Jesus indicates the horror of hell. Throughout His ministry Jesus urged people to come to Him for life. At the end, He went to the cross to secure this life for them. The agony and alienation Jesus endured at Calvary demonstrate the awful penalty of sin and how much He was willing to endure to save us from it.

WHAT DO YOU SAY?

1. Is there a modern tendency among Christians to pick and choose which biblical teachings they accept? How does that affect modern concepts of hell?

2. Is it necessary to prove that hell is reasonable?

3. What was Gehenna? How did it figure in the teachings of Jesus?

4. What terms did Jesus use that support the idea of an endless hell?

5. In some modern descriptions of hell, how did the lake of fire become a lack of fire?

6. How many different images (fire, darkness, etc.) did Jesus use to describe hell?

7. What can we learn from the story of the rich man and Lazarus?

8. Is Hades the same thing as hell?

9. What do we learn about hell from the Vine and the Branches?

CHAPTER EIGHTEEN

HELL IN APOSTOLIC TEACHING

The Apostles taught what Jesus taught. They did not hesitate to proclaim *"the whole will of God"* (**Acts 20:27**), and this included many warnings about hell. At the same time, it can be observed from the sermons of the book of *Acts* that hell was not the primary theme of their preaching. Rarely did they warn their listeners that they would go to hell; more often the message was more positive: *"Believe on the Lord Jesus Christ and you will be saved"* (**Acts 16:31**).

As we consider what the apostolic writers did say about hell, it will be convenient to group the texts by the key words they emphasized. There will come a day of *"judgment,"* when the *"wrath"* of God will be poured out. The wicked will be *"excluded"* from God's presence. They will be eternally *"punished"* in the *"fire"* of hell with *"destruction"* and *"death."*

JUDGMENT

The first apostolic word on the judgment to come was spoken by Peter in his sermon following the healing of the crippled beggar at the gate called Beautiful. Peter warned his listeners that Jesus was the leader that Moses promised, saying, *"Anyone who does not listen to him will be completely cut off from among his people"* (**Acts 3:23**). Much later Paul also warned that a day was coming when God would separate the human race based on what they have done with Jesus. *"For he has set a day,"* Paul said to the men of Athens, *"when he will judge the world with justice by the man he has appointed"* (**Acts 17:31**).

Paul warned his readers in **Romans** that they could not escape God's judgment (**Rom 2:3**). The day of His righteous judgment is coming (**v. 6**), when God *"will give to each person according to what he has done"* (**v. 7**). Neither Jew nor Gentile could expect special treatment on judgment day, because God *"does not show favoritism"* (**v. 11**). All this *"will take place on the day when God will judge men's secrets through Jesus Christ, as my gospel declares"* (**v. 16**). It can be observed, therefore, that while judgment and hell were not the primary part of Paul's preaching, he did consider this warning an essential part of his gospel message.

The truth of coming judgment is echoed in numerous other places. *"Eternal judgment"* is part of *"the elementary teachings about Christ"* (**Heb 6:1-2**). Everyone must *"appear before the judgment seat of Christ, that each one may receive what is due him for the things done while in the body, whether good or bad"* (**2Cor 5:10**). Although some men may think they are free to plunge into dissipation, they *"will have to give account to him who is ready to judge the living and the dead"* (**1Pet 4:5**). Jude warned with an oddly emotional emphasis: *"The Lord is coming . . . to convict all the ungodly of all the ungodly acts they have done in the ungodly way"* (**Jude 15**). This much is certainly true: *"The Lord **will** judge his people"* (**Heb 10:30**).

WRATH AND FURY

Most of the human race is in rebellion against the Creator, and God is not amused. *"The wrath of God is being revealed from heaven,"* Paul wrote, *"against all the godlessness and wickedness of men who suppress the truth by their wickedness"* (**Rom 1:18**). Although God has given men time to repent, they *"are storing up wrath"* against themselves *"for the day of God's wrath, when his righteous judgment will be revealed"* (**Rom 2:5**). God will give eternal life to the righteous, but for those *"who reject the truth and follow evil, there will be wrath and anger"* (**Rom 2:8**).

Paul did not speak of the wrath of God carelessly or capriciously. On the day that God's wrath is finally poured out, it will be for good cause. When men have lived in sin and followed the ways of the prince of this world, in such disobedience they are *"by nature objects of wrath"* (**Eph 2:1-3**). Twice Paul warned that men should not underestimate this danger, saying, *"Let no one deceive you with empty* words, for because of such things God's wrath comes on those who are disobedient" (**Eph 5:6; Col 3:6**).

Paul had a special warning for his own countrymen. In their effort to keep the gospel from being preached to the Gentiles, they were heaping up their sins to the limit. Therefore, *"The wrath of God has come upon them at last"* (**2Th 2:16-17**). But all those who accepted Jesus—whether Jews or Gentiles—were not destined *"to suffer wrath, but to receive salvation"* (**2Th 5:9**).

One of the most fearsome descriptions of God's wrath is found in the **Revelation** of John. He heard an angel say in a loud voice:

> If anyone worships the beast and his image and receives his mark on the forehead or on the hand, he, too, will drink of the wine of God's fury, which has been poured full strength into the cup of his wrath. He will be tormented with burning sulfur in the presence of the holy angels and of the Lamb. And the smoke of their torment rises for ever and ever. (**Rev 14:9-11**)

It is, indeed, *"a dreadful thing to fall into the hands of the living God"* (**Heb 10:31**).

EXCLUSION

"Depart from me," the Lord will say to those who are cursed (**Mt 25:41**). This exclusion from the presence of God is in itself perhaps the worst punishment of hell. Cut off from the Creator, cut off from eternal love, cut off from the community of the saints, the condemned will suffer in the isolation of the outer darkness (see **Mt 8:12; 13:40-42,49-50; 22:13; 25:30; Lk 13:28**). They will be *"shut out from the presence of the Lord and from the majesty of his power"* (**2Th 1:9**).

God had made it clear early in the OT that exclusion would be part of the penalty of unrighteousness. The writer of Hebrews recalled God's statement about the faithless Israelites in the wilderness, *"I declared on oath in my anger, 'They shall never enter my rest'"* (**Heb 3:11; Ps 95:11**). It is also clear at the end of the NT that the wicked will be excluded. *"Nothing impure will ever enter it,"* wrote John, *"nor will anyone who does what is shameful or deceitful"* (**Rev 21:27**). Again he wrote, *"Outside are the dogs, those who practice magic arts, the sexually immoral, the murderers, the idolaters and everyone who loves and practices falsehood"* (**Rev 22:15**; see **21:8**). In view of the danger of being banished from God's presence, this exhortation is appropriate:

"Let us, therefore, make every effort to enter that rest, so that no one will fall by following their example of disobedience" (**Heb 4:11**).

PUNISHMENT

Hell is for punishment. The NT writers confirm the teaching of Jesus that the wicked will *"go away to eternal punishment"* (**Mt 25:46**). People who violated the old covenant received their *"just punishment"* (**Heb 2:2**), and there were scores of OT passages that detailed how "punish" and "punishment" should be carried out. The writer of Hebrews later asked, *"How much more severely do you think a man **deserves to be punished**"* who has rejected Jesus, disdained His blood, and treated the Holy Spirit with contempt? (**Heb 10:29**). Peter assured his readers that the Lord *"knows how . . . to hold the unrighteous for the day of judgment, while continuing their punishment"* (**2Pet 2:9**).

Peter spoke of a place called *Tartarus* (translated "hell" in the NIV). This is a "gloomy dungeon" where rebellious angels are held for final judgment **(2Pet 2:4)**. Jude said these angels are *"kept in darkness, bound with everlasting chains for judgment on the great Day" (**Jude 1:6**)*.

Jude said the wicked would suffer *"the punishment of eternal fire"* (**Jude 1:7**). So when Jesus comes, it will be to *"punish those who do not know God and do not obey the gospel. . . . They will be punished with everlasting destruction and shut out from the presence of the Lord"* (**2Th 1:8-9**). It is important to notice how the passages on punishment emphasize the concepts: *"go away to eternal punishment," "eternal fire,"* and *"everlasting destruction."*

FIRE

All the writers of the NT confirm what Jesus said about the fire of hell. Paul said that at the end of the age, Jesus will come from heaven *"in blazing fire with his powerful angels,"* to punish those who did not obey the gospel (**2Th 1:7-8**). The author of Hebrews wrote that like worthless land that produces thorns and thistles, the wicked will be cursed and burned (**Heb 6:8**) in a *"raging fire that will consume the enemies of God"* (**Heb 10:27**). *"Our God,"* he said, *"is a consuming fire"*

(*Heb 12:29*). James said the tongue is a fire that corrupts the whole person, setting the whole course of his life on fire, *"and is itself set on fire by hell"* (*Jas 3:6*; the only NT use of *geenna* outside the Gospels.) Peter reminded his readers that God condemned the cities of Sodom and Gomorrah *"by burning them to ashes"* and that this was *"an example of what is going to happen to the ungodly"* (*2Pet 2:6*). Jude referred to the same cities, saying they served *"as an example of those who suffer the punishment of eternal fire"* (*Jude 1:7*).

More than any other writer, John made numerous references to the fire of hell. He described the fate of whoever worshiped the beast: *"He will be tormented with burning sulfur"* and the smoke of that torment *"rises for ever and ever"* (*Rev 14:10-11*). Likewise, when Babylon has fallen, *"The smoke from her goes up for ever and ever"* (*Rev 19:3*). At the great Judgment scene in **chapter 20**, the devil is *"thrown into the lake of burning sulfur"* (*v. 10*), and anyone whose name is not found written in the book of life is *"thrown into the lake of fire"* (*v. 15*). Finally, John wrote,

> The cowardly, the unbelieving, the vile, the murderers, the sexually immoral, those who practice magic arts, the idolaters and all liars—their place will be in the fiery lake of burning sulfur. This is the second death. (*Rev 21:8*)

Is the fire of hell a fire that "consumes"? Yes and no. As seen in the paragraphs above, it is a fire that *"burns to ashes"* and *"consumes the enemies of God."* At the same time, it is called *"the punishment of eternal fire."* When we recall the burning bush of Moses that did not totally consume and then die out, we have a possible preview of the kind of fire that is eternal. (See the comments on "Hell: The Undying Worm, the Unquenchable Fire," **Mark 9:43-48**.)

DESTRUCTION

God will destroy the wicked. He destroyed Noah's world with a flood (*Gen 6:17*), and He destroyed Sodom and Gomorrah with fire (*Gen 19:14*). God will destroy the wicked because He is disgusted, because His holy sense of justice is provoked to wrath. Paul said that people who were the objects of His wrath are *"prepared for destruction"* (*Rom 9:22*). Such people include the *"enemies of the cross of Christ,"* of whom Paul said, *"Their destiny is destruction"* (*Php 3:19*). Such people include the false teachers of whom Peter said, *"Their con-*

demnation has long been hanging over them, and their destruction has not been sleeping" (**2Pet 2:3**). They may think they are getting away with their ungodly behavior, but while they are saying, *"Peace and safety,"* destruction will come on them suddenly (**1Th 5:3**).

God's destruction will be sudden, but it will not be capricious or unjust. People who have opposed God's will are going to get what they deserve. As Paul told the beleaguered believers in Thessalonica, *"God is just: He will pay back trouble to those who trouble you. . . . They will be punished with everlasting destruction"* (**2Th 1:6,9**). Likewise, people who have lived only for themselves will be condemned. *"The one who sows to please his sinful nature,"* Paul said, *"from that nature will reap destruction"* (**Gal 6:8**). In the meantime, the *"present heavens and earth are reserved for fire, being kept for the day of judgment and destruction of ungodly men"* (**2Pet 3:7**). It should be noted that it will be "ungodly men" who are doomed to destruction.

In the day of destruction there will be a clear division in humanity. In prospect of that day Paul spoke of *"those who are being saved and those who are perishing"* (**2Cor 2:15**). Similarly, when the Christians in Philippi stood fast in the face of their persecutors, this was *"a sign to them that they will be destroyed, but that you will be saved"* (**Php 1:28**). There may be some in the Christian community who *"shrink back and are destroyed,"* but the writer of Hebrews could rejoice that faithful Christians are *"of those who believe and are saved"* (**Heb 10:39**). God, after all, does not really want *"anyone to perish, but everyone to come to repentance"* (**2Pet 3:9**; see also **Jn 3:16**).

But what does it mean to "perish" or to "be destroyed"? Some argue that it is to cease to exist. The Greek word for "perish," however often means to be lost, ruined, or wrecked. Like the unquenchable fire, the *"everlasting destruction"* of the wicked will never end. (For an extended argument, see the section on "Hell as Prelude to Annihilation" in the next chapter, "Hell: Alternative Views.")

DEATH

People who are filled with wickedness *"deserve death"* (**Rom 1:29-32**). This death is more than just capital punishment, however, as one might first suppose. Paul showed the larger, eternal issue of death when he created this contrast: *"For the wages of sin is death, but the gift of God is eternal life in Christ Jesus our Lord"* (**Rom 6:23**). This is likely the same idea James had in mind when he wrote, *"Sin, when it is full-grown, gives birth to death"* (*Jas 1:15*). But if someone can turn a sinner from the error of his ways, he *"will save him* (literally, 'his soul') *from death"* (*Jas 5:20*). Likewise, when John wrote of *"a sin that leads to death"* (*1Jn 5:16-17*), he meant spiritual, eternal death, not just death of the physical body.

John speaks quite clearly about this death in his **Revelation**. He wrote to the church in Smyrna, *"He who overcomes will not be hurt at all by the second death"* (*Rev 2:11*). While this is the first explicit mention of the "second death" in Scripture, it is an obvious reference to what Paul, James, and John had in mind, as cited in the above paragraph. Near the end of **Revelation**, in the passage about judgment at the great white throne, John said the devil and the damned will be thrown into a lake of fire. *"The lake of fire,"* he said, *"is the second death"* (*Rev 20:14*). Again in the next chapter John asserted that cowards, unbelievers, murderers, etc. *"will be in the fiery lake of burning sulfur. . . . This is the second death"* (*Rev 21:8*).

But what is "death"? In the first death the body dies and the individual loses all contact with those living on earth. But Jesus' story of the Rich Man and Lazarus teaches us that both individuals went on living, although in a different place, and they both still had bodies (see *Lk 16:19-31*). From the perspective of others they were dead, but in the next world they were very much alive. The second death is somehow also a termination and a continuance. The condemned die, but their dying never ends. The same lake of fire that is called *"the second death"* is the place where they will suffer *"eternal punishment"* (*Mt 25:41*) in *"the punishment of eternal fire"* (*Jude 1:7*).

CONCLUSION

The apostolic preachers and writers did not make hell the main theme of their preaching. They preached the crucified Christ and the hope of eternal salvation in heaven. At the same time, when they did speak of hell they were completely in agreement with Jesus. They said there will come a day of *"judgment,"* when the *"wrath"* of God will be poured out. The wicked will be *"excluded"* from God's presence. They will be eternally *"punished"* in the *"fire"* of hell with *"destruction"* and *"death."*

WHAT DO YOU SAY?

1. Why do you think the apostolic preachers and writers did not talk about hell more often?

2. What will be the scenario for Judgment Day?

3. Is God more angry about sin than we are?

4. How will separation from God be such an awful punishment? (Especially since some people want nothing to do with God, anyway!)

5. Why must evil be punished (and not just eliminated)?

6. Does it really matter whether hell is literally a fire?

7. What does "destruction" mean?

8. Is it possible to be eternally dying, yet never finally dead?

CHAPTER NINETEEN
ALTERNATIVE VIEWS OF HELL

Not everyone agrees about hell. In fact, there has been a rising chorus of dissent in recent years against the classic scene of fire and endless torment. If this only came from people who do not believe the Bible, it would be easy to ignore. But the various views that will be considered in this chapter are held by people who do believe the Bible. They just understand it differently.

From what has been presented in the previous chapters on hell, it will be obvious that I do not believe that any of these alternative views accurately describe what the Bible says about hell. In an attempt to be fair, however, I will attempt to present an unbiased explanation of each view and the biblical evidence that may support it. Then I will present reasons for continuing to believe in a literal hell. There are, of course, other views that could also be included, but I have chosen three as representative of recent evangelical thought. For our purposes it is not important to identify *who* holds each view; rather, it will be useful to consider *what* the view is and what the Bible may say in support or in refutation of it.

HELL AS A PRELUDE TO HEAVEN

The most optimistic alternative view of hell is that it is a prelude to heaven. This is a form of universalism, the view that virtually everyone will end up in heaven. It is not that everyone just automatically goes

I. Hell as a Prelude to Heaven
II. Hell as a Metaphor
III. Hell as a Prelude to Annihilation
IV. Conclusion

to heaven, but that hell is a temporary and limited punishment that cleanses the wicked. Then they go to heaven. After all, how can God win the final victory if most of mankind, made in God's own image, perish in hell? There are two main lines of biblical evidence that are offered to support this view: (1) God's plan is ultimately to save all people; (2) God has a way to forgive people after they die.

First, there are many Scriptures that speak of God's plan for the reconciliation and salvation for all men. Speaking of His death on the cross, Jesus said, *"But I, when I am lifted up from the earth, will draw all men to myself"* (*Jn 12:32*). God worked through Christ and the cross *"to reconcile to himself all things, whether things on earth or things in heaven"* (*Col 1:20*). Paul further explained that *"just as the result of one trespass was condemnation for all men, so also the result of one act of righteousness was justification that brings life for all men"* (*Rom 5:18*). This is how we can expect that one day *"every knee"* will bow and *"every tongue"* will confess that Jesus Christ is Lord (*Php 2:10-11*). God will *"bring all things in heaven and on earth together under one head"* and that head will be Christ (*Eph 1:10*). In the great scene of the throne room in *Revelation*, the enormous multitude that praises God is made up of people from *"every nation, tribe, people and language"* (*Rev 7:9*). God is too great to be worshiped by only part of His creation; God's victory is too complete to let vast numbers of the unsaved perish in hell.

Second, even though a majority of mankind admittedly dies in unbelief, God has a plan to save them. This can be inferred from Jesus' statement that *"every sin and blasphemy will be forgiven men,"* but the unique sin of blasphemy against the Holy Spirit *"will not be forgiven, either in this age or in the age to come"* (*Mt 12:32*). This implies the availability of forgiveness beyond the grave for all the other kinds of sins. In addition, Paul wrote that on the Day of Judgment, *"The fire will test the quality of each man's work. . . . If it is burned up, he will suffer loss; he himself will be saved, but only as one escaping through the flames"* (*1Cor 3:13-15*). The flames of hell somehow burn away the dross and leave a person purified and ready for heaven.

What can be said in response to this view? As to the plan of God and Jesus to save "all men" and "all things," the passages are speaking only of salvation that is potentially offered to all men. Such verses must be read in the light of clear statements that people who believe will be saved, but people who do not believe will perish (*Jn 3:16-18*). Jesus Himself said that the majority of the human race would take the broad road that leads to destruction (*Mt 7:13*). He also said the unrighteous will *"go away to eternal punishment"* (*Mt 25:46*). The concluding—and conclusive—pictures of hell in **Revelation 20** and **21** show the devil and the unsaved being thrown into the lake of fire, where their torment is for ever and ever. There is certainly no mention of any possibility of rescue.

And what of the Scriptures that speak of forgiveness after death and salvation after the fire? Frankly, that line of evidence is very weak. (That view is essentially a belief in some kind of purgatory, which the Catholic Church struggles to support by a single passage in the Apocrypha, 2 Maccabees 12:41-46.) Jesus' point about blasphemy against the Spirit was simply that it will not be forgiven—not now, not ever. Nowhere does Jesus extend hope that a person can change his destiny after death. Paul's point about being saved *"as one escaping through the flames"* (*1Cor 3:15*) is about a man having his life's work burn up as meaningless, but the man himself is saved. Scripture never says that sins will be cleansed by any fire; sins are cleansed by the blood of Christ.

> **Sins are not cleansed by fire but by the blood of Christ.**

HELL AS A METAPHOR

Perhaps hell is a figure of speech. Maybe the whole idea of people roasting forever in God's fireplace should have been abandoned in the Dark Ages. Or maybe not. If the whole idea of hell on fire seems too hideous to accept or too ludicrous to believe, there still needs to be biblical evidence. The issue is not what someone decides is or is not acceptable; the real issue is what the Bible says.

First, it must be admitted that biblical language is sometimes figurative. David said the LORD was a *"rock"* (*Ps 18:2; 28:1*), but he obviously did not mean God was an idol made of stone. More specifically, some passages about fire are clearly figurative. The tongue is called *"a fire"* (*Jas 3:6*) and even God Himself is called *"a consuming fire"* (*Deu 4:24; Heb 12:29*). In the same way, therefore, the "fire" of hell could be a metaphor for some kind of intense spiritual suffering and anguish.

Second, if the language about hell is literal, it is self-contradictory. How can hell be both fire and darkness? How can fire and worms coexist? And how can the devil—a spirit without a body—burn in a literal fire? These difficulties seem to require that some, if not all, of the language about hell must be taken figuratively.

Third, a literal understanding is not actually necessary, anyway. The anguish of hell is sufficiently frightening without the fire and the maggots. With or without literal fire, hell is a terrible destiny. Proponents of this view often suggest that the figurative language about hell might well be symbolic of something even worse.

So what can be said to these lines of argument? First, normal interpretation requires that words are to be taken as literal unless there is a compelling reason that they must be figurative. Nearly all the uses of the word "fire" in Scripture are literal. The repeated emphasis of Jesus and others on *"fire," "fiery punishment,"* and *"the lake of fire"* shows that they really meant fire. Second, it has already been shown that fire does not necessarily produce light (see the section on "Hell: The Outer Darkness" in chapter 17). If God wants to prepare a dark fire that burns the devil, but not the worms, there is nothing to stop Him! Third, if the spiritual anguish is as bad as the literal fire, the original opposition to such a hideous hell is nullified. Either way, God executes His judgment in the unspeakable torment of millions. In the end, therefore, treating hell as a figure of speech solves nothing.

> **Treating hell as a figure of speech solves nothing.**

HELL AS A PRELUDE TO ANNIHILATION

The alternative view of hell that is getting the most attention in recent years is a form of delayed annihilationism. It is not the kind of annihilation that simply snuffs out the very existence of the sinner at death. That older view emphasized that evil men are *"like brute beasts . . . and like brute beasts they too will perish"* (*2Pet 2:12*). If hell were only quick extinction, however, many people would find it a welcome end: the final relief from a tiring life. Just as a person welcomes the unconsciousness of sleep at the end of the day, he could understandably welcome the eternal unconsciousness of annihilation. In the end, that kind of annihilationism is not much different from the view of most atheists: we live, we die, and that's it. Period.

A growing number of Evangelical scholars, especially in Britain, are adopting a variation on the idea of annihilation. They see hell as real, perhaps even with literal fire, which sinners must endure for a prescribed period of time. Perhaps the worse the sinner, the longer his time in the fire. At the end of each sinner's allotted time, however, he will cease to exist. The fire is not a prelude to heaven, as in the doctrine of purgatory; instead, it is a prelude to annihilation.

What are the arguments and the biblical evidence that support this view? First, one must accept the premise that man is not inherently immortal. It is not as though he has to go on living somewhere—if not forever in heaven, then forever in hell. God alone is immortal (*1Tm 6:16*), and men live only because He sustains them (*Acts 17:28*). Every man will live only as long as God chooses to give him life (see *Jn 5:21,26*). In the case of the wicked, God will *"destroy both soul and body in hell"* (*Mt 10:28*).

> Proponents of this view say it is more accurate to speak of "conditional" immortality. For this reason their view is sometimes called "conditionalism" or "conditional annihilationism."

Second, one must emphasize the fact that God is gracious. He shows love to a thousand generations, but limits punishment to the third or fourth generation (*Ex 20:5-6*). This could imply that the length of blessing for the righteous and the length of punishment for the wicked do not have to be the same. David was entirely right when he said,

> The LORD is compassionate and gracious,
>   slow to anger, abounding in love.
> He will not always accuse,
>   nor will he harbor his anger forever. (*Ps 103:8-9*)

God will not keep people alive forever just to prolong their suffering. Finally, mercifully, He will allow the wicked in hell to perish.

> At least some of the Jews in NT times believed in a limited time of punishment in hell. Rabbi Akiba, who died in 135 in the revolt of Bar Kokhba, is quoted in the Mishnah as saying, "The judgment of the unrighteous in Gehenna shall endure twelve months" (*Eduy.* 2. 10).

Third, one must emphasize several words about hell in such a way as to say that the wicked will cease to exist. For instance, Hell is called *"the second death"* (**Rev 20:14**), not the place of "always dying." Hell is the place where the wicked are *"destroyed,"* not merely damaged. Hell is the place where the wicked *"perish."* Why would these terms—death, destruction, perishing—mean that the wicked go on living, that they survive destruction, and that they do *not* perish? (For Scripture passages about "destruction," "death," or "perish" see the previous chapter.) Surely it is better if these words mean that God is able, finally, to bring closure to the awful chapter of mankind's sin and rebellion.

Fourth, one must minimize words such as *"eternal"* and *"forever."* The Greek word for "eternal" (*aionios*) can also mean "age-long," and the Greek phrase for "forever" (*eis ton aiona*) is literally "into the age." If both these words can somehow mean less than their commonly accepted meaning, then a shorter hell becomes possible.

What can be said about these arguments for "conditional annihilationism"? It must be admitted that this view holds certain attractions. It gets God off the hook; He is no eternal Sadist. It takes Scripture seriously and tries to find new ways to understand it rather than rejecting it outright. But the view is fatally flawed.

As to the first argument, I am willing to grant that men are mortal and that they live only because God keeps them alive. This fact itself is neutral to the argument. It does not prove in any way whether God will or will not keep the wicked alive for eternity.

As to the second argument, it is obviously true that God is gracious. It is also true for most of us that we cannot emotionally accept the idea of His keeping His enemies in agony forever. If He would finally close the curtain on the tragic scene, that act of mercy would seem commendable. This would free Christians from the unpleasant task of defending the reality of hell, and it makes God a nicer fellow.

But God is not man. His thoughts are not our thoughts and His ways are higher than our ways (**Isa 55:8-9**). He actually does quite a number of things that are right for Him, but are wrong for humans.

God is not man. His thoughts are not our thoughts.

He accepts worship, passes judgment on motives, kills thousands of people, etc. Just because it may strike us as wrong for God to punish people forever, that alone does not mean it really is wrong.

Right for God, but sinful for man:

1. He demands complete loyalty to Himself *(Ex 20:4-5)*
2. He refuses to admit that anyone could be greater *(Ex 20:3)*
3. He thinks He has all the answers *(Job 38–41)*
4. He decides to make all the rules the way He wants them *(Gen 2:17; Exodus 20)*
5. He demands that people worship Him *(Deu 6:13)*
6. He forbids anyone to speak against Him *(Ex 20:7)*
7. He gets angry enough to kill *(Gen 6:6-7; Ex 12:29)*
8. He claims the right to pass judgment on people *(Ps 7:11; 9:8-12)*
9. He claims the right to take vengeance *(Deu 32:35; Rom 12:19)*

As to the third argument, it is common for words of "destruction" and "death" to be used in Scripture in contexts where the victims do not cease to exist. The most common Greek word for "destroy" is *apollymi*, which is also translated "lose," "spoil," and "ruin." Rarely does the word mean to "cease to exist." The most common Greek word for "destruction" is *apoleia*, which is also translated "waste," as in the perfume that was poured out on Jesus *(Mt 26:8)*. A careful examination of the following passages will show that "destroy" and "destruction" usually mean to ruin something so thoroughly that it can no longer function as it was originally intended.

"Destroy" (*apollymi*) as in **Matthew 10:28; 18:14; Luke 17:27; John 3:16**
    Men who *drown* *(Mt 8:25)*
    Busted wineskins and *wasted* wine *(Mt 9:17)*
    A *lost* sheep *(Lk 15:4)*
    A *lost* coin *(Lk 15:9)*
    A *lost* (but now found) son *(Lk 15:24)*
    A hair that *falls out* from the head *(Lk 21:18; Acts 27:34)*
    Leftover bread that would be *wasted* *(Jn 6:12)*
    Gold that is *melted* (but refined!) in fire *(1Pet 1:7)*
"Perish" (*aphanizo*) as in **Acts 13:41; James 4:14**
    A face, when *disfigured* to show that one is fasting *(Mt 6:16)*
    A *moth-eaten* garment *(Mt 6:19)*
    Rusted metal *(Mt 6:19)*
"Destruction" (*apoleia*) as in **Romans 9:22; Philippians 3:19; 2 Peter 2:3**
    Desire for riches plunges men into *ruin*
"Destruction" (*phthora*) as in **Galatians 6:8**
    The ongoing *decay* of the present universe *(Rom 8:21)*

The examples shown above clearly warn us not to think automatically that the "destruction" of hell makes men cease to exist. They will be ruined, disfigured, decayed, rusted, melted, wasted, and lost from their Owner. But they will still exist.

As to the fourth argument, it is here that we come to the crux of the matter. How can we explain away the obvious intent of the words "eternal" and "forever"? Even if "eternal" is translated "age-long," how long *is* the age to come? The same word that describes *"eternal punishment"* also describes *"eternal life" (Mt 25:46)*. If hell is only temporary, then heaven is, too!

If we should suppose that Jesus and the NT writers knew that hell is, in fact, a temporary place, then why did they carefully avoid saying so? What conclusion, other than the obvious, can one draw from these Scriptures?

> *"Thrown into eternal fire" (Mt 18:8)*
>
> *"They (those on the left) went away into eternal punishment" (Mt 25:46)*
>
> *"The penalty of eternal destruction" (2Th 1:9)*
>
> *"The punishment of eternal fire" (Jude 1:7)*
>
> *"The blackest darkness has been reserved forever" (Jude 1:13)*
>
> *"The smoke of their torment rises for ever and ever" (Rev 14:11)*
>
> *"The smoke from her (Babylon) goes up for ever and ever" (Rev 19:3)*
>
> *"They (devil, beast, prophet; and by association also the wicked in the same lake of fire) will be tormented day and night for ever and ever" (Rev 20:10)*

CONCLUSION

Some take the overly optimistic view that hell is a prelude to heaven. In some way the fire and the suffering will cleanse and redeem, so that nearly everyone goes to heaven in the end. Others see all the statements about hell as metaphor, not to be taken literally. They assume we know only that hell will be bad—really bad. Still others believe that the wicked will suffer appropriately in hell and then finally will cease to exist.

All three of these alternative views about hell have something in common: they are attempts to lessen the horror of hell and thereby preserve the good name of God. But does God need to be defended? Shall He stand trial in any human court? In the end, God does not need our approval of what He has planned for eternity. In the end, we need His approval and the words, "Well done."

WHAT DO YOU SAY?

1. How should we deal with people who hold a view about hell that is different from our own? Have you ever felt embarrassed to defend your view of hell?

2. If you could pick the view you personally "liked" (apart from biblical evidence), which one would it be? Why?

3. What are some Scriptures that support the idea that most people will be saved? What are the Scriptures that say otherwise?

4. Would it matter if hell is a figure of speech for something else—perhaps something that we are unprepared to understand now?

5. What is "conditional immortality"?

6. Is there much difference between simple annihilation at death and ultimate annihilation after suffering for a while in hell?

7. Does it matter if we understand why God made hell the way He did?

Scripture Index

Subject Index

Subject Index